Crossing Boundaries, Redefining Faith

Crossing Boundaries, Redefining Faith

Interdisciplinary Perspectives on
the Emerging Church Movement

EDITED BY

Michael Clawson

AND

April Stace

FOREWORD BY

Josh Packard

☙PICKWICK *Publications* · Eugene, Oregon

CROSSING BOUNDARIES, REDEFINING FAITH
Interdisciplinary Perspectives on the Emerging Church Movement

Copyright © 2016 Wipf & Stock Publishers. All rights reserved. Except for brief quotations in critical publications or reviews, no part of this book may be reproduced in any manner without prior written permission from the publisher. Write: Permissions, Wipf and Stock Publishers, 199 W. 8th Ave., Suite 3, Eugene, OR 97401.

Pickwick Publications
An Imprint of Wipf and Stock Publishers
199 W. 8th Ave., Suite 3
Eugene, OR 97401

www.wipfandstock.com

PAPERBACK ISBN: 978-1-4982-1968-6
HARDCOVER ISBN: 978-1-4982-1970-9
EBOOK ISBN: 978-1-4982-1969-3

Cataloguing-in-Publication data:

Names: Clawson, Michael. | Stace, April.

Title: Crossing boundaries, redefining faith: interdisciplinary perspectives on the emerging church movement / edited by Michael Clawson and April Stace; foreword by Josh Packard.

Description: Eugene, OR: Pickwick Publications, 2016 | Includes bibliographical references and index.

Identifiers: ISBN 978-1-4982-1968-6 (paperback) | ISBN 978-1-4982-1970-9 (hardcover) | ISBN 978-1-4982-1969-3 (ebook)

Subjects: LSCH: Emerging church movement | Postmodernism—Religious aspects—Christianity | Church renewal | Christianity—21st century

Classification: BR121.3 C41 2016 (print) | BR115.P74 (ebook)

Manufactured in the U.S.A.   11/01/16

Dedicated to all who have concluded that American churches just need more cowbell . . .

a lot more cowbell.

Contents

List of Contributors | ix

Foreword | xi
 —*Josh Packard*

Introduction | 1
 —*Michael Clawson & April Stace*

Part 1: Defining Boundaries

1 A Brief History of the Emerging Church Movement in the United States | 17
 —*Michael Clawson*

2 Emerging Christianity through a Social Scientific Lens: The ECM as a Case of Religious Institutional Entrepreneurship | 45
 —*Gerardo Marti*

3 The Ancient-Future Time-Crystal: On the Temporality of Emerging Christianity | 71
 —*Jon Bialecki and James S. Bielo*

4 A Feminist Theological Analysis of the Leadership Structures of the Emerging Church | 92
 —*Xochitl Alvizo*

5 The Possibility of Conflict | 120
 —*Timothy K. Snyder*

CONTENTS

Part 2: Crossing Boundaries

6 From Boundaries to Borderlands: The Emerging Church's Imaginative Work of Fostering Relationships across Difference | 139
   —Lloyd Chia

7 "There Are Not Two Worlds": Transcending the "Modern" Categories of Sacred and Secular in the Emerging Church Movement | 164
   —Jason Wollschleger

8 The Kingdom of Heaven Is Within You: Emerging Churches and (Un)Secular Music | 179
   —April Stace

9 "Messy Vitality": The Diverse Musical Canon of a West-Coast Emerging Congregation | 192
   —Heather Josselyn-Cranson

10 Emergence in the Americas: Points of Convergence between Latin American and North American Emerging Church Networks | 215
   —Juan José Barreda Toscano and Dee Yaccino

Index | 237

Contributors

Xochitl Alvizo, Assistant Professor at California State University, Northridge.

Jon Bialecki, Honorary Fellow at the School of Social and Political Science at the University of Edinburgh.

James S. Bielo, Assistant Professor of Anthropology at Miami University (Oxford, Ohio).

Lloyd Chia, Assistant Professor of Sociology at Spring Arbor University.

Michael Clawson, Adjunct Instructor at Seminary of the Southwest and Austin Presbyterian Theological Seminary.

Heather Josselyn-Cranson, Sister Margaret William McCarthy Endowed Chair of Music at Regis College.

Gerardo Marti, L. Richardson King Associate Professor and Chair of Sociology at Davidson College.

Josh Packard, Assistant Professor of Sociology at the University of Northern Colorado.

Timothy K. Snyder, Adjunct Instructor of Theology and Spirituality at Wartburg Theological Seminary.

Juan José Barreda Toscano, PhD at Instituto Universitario ISEDET and Executive Director of Biblica Virtual.

April Stace, Adjunct Instructor at Hartford Seminary and The John Leland Center for Theological Studies.

Jason Wollschleger, Assistant Professor of Sociology at Whitworth University.

Dee Yaccino, PhD candidate at Trinity International University.

Foreword

THIS VOLUME IS THE pinnacle of academic understanding of the Emerging Church Movement; that much is obvious. Taking just a moment to scan through the contributions contained herein, we find that Wollschläger and Chia give us the best current framework for understanding the ECM both in terms of extant characteristics as well as a thick description of a given congregation. Stace and Josselyn-Cranson take us deep into the ways that ECM worship practices are reflective of a world where people increasingly blur traditional boundaries purposively, as a way of expressing and developing spirituality. Clawson provides a full and robust history of the ECM while identifying key moments and players, and Toscano-Barreda and Yaccino trace out some of the theological roots of the movement. Theorizing more broadly, Alvizo, Marti, and Bialecki and Bielo bring amazingly insightful essays that explore the social framework that helps to shape and give energy to the ECM, and Snyder helps us to think beyond the limits of the ECM to understand how people deal with diversity more generally. In short, there does not exist anywhere else a more fully rounded and deeply theorized work about the Emerging Church.

However, the greatest achievement of this anthology is not the full and complete description of the ECM, as important as that may be. What makes this collection truly important is that it manages to be rooted in the empirical reality of the movement while also looking beyond the boundaries of this relatively narrow expression of Christianity in the early 21st century. The ECM is important for scholars of religion and other fields not because of its size and scope, but because of what it tells us about the entirety of the religious landscape in this era. These selections point out very clearly that the ECM is part and parcel of a general move away from large, monolithic institutional expressions of cultural life.

Future generations of researchers will no doubt turn to the ECM, and to this volume, to learn how we can begin to look for the signs of shifting institutional structures in the new movements which wield influence beyond their size. Indeed, despite never coalescing into anything that has challenged mainstream evangelical Christianity, the ECM retains outsized importance, which many of these chapters demonstrate so well. Once obscure people associated with the ECM are now household names. For example, Rob Bell, Rachel Held-Evans, Brian McLaren, Tony Jones, David Crowder, and Nadia Bolz-Weber regularly find themselves at the top of bestseller lists (or hosting their own show on Oprah's network), and the late Phyllis Tickle emerged as one of the most important theologians of her generation because of her work about the Emerging Church. The data about the ECM in terms of size suggests that this simply should not be the case. A movement this small should not be producing such a high number of Christian "celebrities." This incongruence points to the fact that the ECM was the earliest gathering of people to tap into a coming anti-institutional movement that extends far beyond the borders of the movement itself.

A decade from now, it is quite possible that there will not be a single congregation who identifies as "emerging," and yet that will not have diminished the importance of the movement even slightly. The researchers in this volume understand what the religious marketplace has brought to bear. Namely, the ECM is important because of the conversation that it started, the ideas to which it gave birth, and the anti-institutional stance that it fostered. Whether congregations or people identify with the movement in the coming years hardly matters. The ECM ship, so to speak, has already left the harbor and the impulses that it both tapped into and developed are already appearing on the religious landscape in a number of ways.

Take, for example, my own recent work about religious Dones, people who claim a religious affiliation but have made an intentional decision to leave the institutional church (Packard and Hope, *Church Refugees*). During the course of over 100 interviews, the Emerging Church was barely acknowledged by my respondents as a part of their journey. And yet it is my firm belief that this work would not have been possible without the ECM. Much of the literature, ideas and conversation that sustain my respondents outside of the institutional church are linked back to the ECM. As a long-time scholar of the movement, I was even able to see these connections when my respondents were unaware of the history into which they were tapping.

That, in and of itself, speaks volumes about the "success" of the movement. Think about it this way, one would have been hard pressed to read *A Generous Orthodoxy* by Brian McLaren when it was first published in 2004 *without* knowing that it and he were connected to the Emerging Church. Now, however, Brian McLaren is not an "Emerging Church theologian and author." He is simply a theologian and author. My respondents frequently mentioned his book while simultaneously expressing no knowledge of or experience with the Emerging Church Movement. The movement has not fallen away because it lacked resonance and support. Instead, the ideas and people that shaped the movement have simply been extended beyond the confines of the ECM. The practices identified in the excellent ethnographic works about the ECM here and elsewhere have, to a large extent, been absorbed by congregations across the country.

The task for future researchers, then, is to identify the extent to which these ideas, practices, and people have been appropriated by larger religious institutions or whether they have given shape to new movements, new communities, and new ways of doing church that live entirely outside of the traditional institutions. The ECM was largely a response and reaction to overly institutionalized religious structures, but that battle is now over and the ECM has won. No, the traditional structures have not fallen away, but there are now legitimate alternatives in the religious landscape for people who reject those structures. What remains to be seen is whether the ideas and core values of the ECM can be generative as opposed to simply reactive. In short, can these ideas produce and sustain entirely new ways of doing church without a foe, real or imagined. I suspect they can, largely because I think the empirical evidence tells us that the history of the church in this country is one of innovation. Anti-institutionalism runs deep among religious people at this point in history, and new forms and structures will rise up to meet that need.

This task of assessing the long-term impact of the ECM inherently requires an interdisciplinary approach. Social scientists alone cannot assess the impact of changing rituals on people's belief systems. We need theologians and religious studies scholars for that task. Similarly, historians of religion, while correctly able to assess the role of this movement in historical context, are not in a position to comment on the social and organizational dynamics at work in the movement. That, again, is one of the core strengths of the volume you hold now. It provides a model for how an interdisciplinary approach to the ECM should be organized. As I remarked above, there is some overlap among the contributions, but only just enough to hold the volume together. Each piece can stand on its own, but they are better off when read collectively. It is exactly the kind of scholarship the ECM calls for.

Perhaps it is best to close with a brief look at how far this scholarship has come in such a short amount of time. When I began researching for my dissertation about the organizational dynamics of the Emerging Church in 2005, there was scarcely a single academic article printed. In less than a decade, scholars have produced numerous books, articles, and conference presentations. This swift production of research is rare in academia and speaks to both the impact and importance of the ECM as well as the foresight of the researchers working in the field. This volume stands as the culmination of much of that scholarship while helping to point a new way forward in research about the ECM.

—*Josh Packard, University of Northern Colorado*

Bibliography

McLaren, Brian. *A Generous Orthodoxy: Why I Am a Missional, Evangelical, Post/Protestant, Liberal/Conservative, Mystical/Poetic, Biblical, Charismatic/Contemplative, Fundamentalist/Calvinist, Anabaptist/Anglican, Methodist, Catholic, Green, Incarnational, Depressed-Yet-Hopeful, Emergent, Unfinished Christian*. Grand Rapids: Zondervan, 2004.

Packard, Josh, and Ashleigh Hope. *Church Refugees: Sociologists Reveal Why People Are Done with Church But Not Their Faith*. Loveland, CO: Group, 2015.

Introduction

Why This Book?

NEARLY ALL RELIGIOUS MOVEMENTS are multifaceted, often dealing with interrelated changes in beliefs, hermeneutics, personal or liturgical practices, institutional organizations, politics, and social dynamics. Most, however, tend to have their primary focus on one or two of these facets, while the rest follow, if at all, only as secondary considerations. The Charismatic Movement of the 1960s and 70s, for instance, was primarily concerned with introducing new spiritual practices while only occasionally impacting institutional structures, and with only a few relatively minor theological shifts necessary to accommodate them. The rise of the Christian Right in the 1970s and 80s, on the other hand, had to do almost exclusively with politics, with almost nothing explicit to say about ritual practices or church structures, and was built primarily on theologies already present among conservative evangelicals (among others). Similar points could be made about the theological/political orientation of the Social Gospel movement of the early twentieth century, or the Liturgical Renewal Movements of the nineteenth century. This is not to say that these movements did not also often produce or include change to other aspects as well, but typically these were not explicit goals but unintentional by-products of their primary emphases; not so with the Emerging Church Movement (ECM) as it arose in the United States during the 1990s and 2000s. From the beginning, but even more so as the movement evolved, participants in the ECM deliberately and self-consciously engaged in rethinking Christianity not just in one or two aspects, but across the board, in all of the areas mentioned and more. For instance, influential books in the movement have proposed a need to radically reimagine spiritual formation,[1] theology,[2] biblical hermeneutics,[3] institutional structures,[4] liturgical practices,[5] Christian political engagement,[6] ways of relating within Christian communities,[7] and the relationship of Christians to their history and traditions,[8] among many other issues. More to the point, few of these books deal with only one of those topics exclusively, and the Emerging churches and leaders influenced by these authors are typically engaged with this conversation on multiple levels as well. In short, the ECM is not simply a theological shift, a liturgical or methodological trend, a social movement, or an institutional restructuring. It is all of the above and more.

This is why the study of the ECM must be interdisciplinary, and why the volume you now hold in your hands exists. There is no lack of books analyzing the ECM from particular angles. Many of the earliest were ideologically driven, aimed at either attacking or defending the theology of the movement.[9] These were followed by a number of excellent book-length academic studies typically describing the ECM from a social-scientific perspective.[10] Each of these is based on top-notch scholarship and adds much to our understanding of this movement. However, each, by their very nature, describes the topic from a singular disciplinary perspective. In so doing, they ask the kinds of questions specific to their disciplines and bring only those particular set of analytic tools to bear. This is expected and appropriate of course. No single scholar can ever describe a movement comprehensively, and especially not one so multifaceted as the ECM. But that is precisely why we need a work that offers interdisciplinary perspectives. We must ask questions about history and theology alongside questions about social and cultural dynamics, institutional structures, and musical or liturgical practices—and let historians, theologians, anthropologists,

1. Pagitt, *Church Reimagined*.
2. McLaren, *Generous Orthodoxy* and *New Kind of Christianity*.
3. McKnight, *Blue Parakeet*.
4. Brewin, *Signs of Emergence*.
5. Kimball, *Emerging Church* and *Emerging Worship*.
6. Claiborne and Haw, *Jesus for President*.
7. Myers, *Search to Belong* and *Organic Community*.
8. Webber, *Ancient-Future Faith*.
9. Carson's *Becoming Conversant with the Emerging Church* is the most well-known of the former. Jones's *The New Christians* is an example of the latter.
10. See Bielo, *Emerging Evangelicals*; Gibbs and Bolger, *Emerging Churches*; Marti and Ganiel, *Deconstructed Church*; Packard, *The Emerging Church*.

sociologists, and ethnographers help us gain a more complex and nuanced understanding of the total phenomenon.

Defining the Emerging Church Movement

This multifaceted nature of the ECM leads to great fluidity when trying to identify its boundaries or even pin down a singular definition. The difficulty caused by this diversity becomes readily apparent as soon as one begins to visit various Emerging churches first hand, as many of the contributors to this volume have done in the course of their research. One non-denominational Emerging church in Austin, Texas, for instance, typically eschews corporate singing in their Sunday gatherings, but frequently incorporates other forms of artistic expression—painting, communal craft projects, and elaborate art installations, for example—even as they draw from Buddhist wisdom or Sufi poetry alongside Christian doctrine in their preaching. Another congregation in Denver, on the other hand, proudly embraces its Lutheran liturgical and doctrinal heritage, even while creatively experimenting with new ways to express that heritage as they reach out to the alternative subcultures in their city. At the same time, a small Emerging house church in the Chicago suburbs replaces traditional preaching with interactive discussions, and directs its primary efforts at missional engagement with its community rather than coordinating an elaborate Sunday worship event. In a similar vein but radically different context, a self-described "intentional community" of predominantly young, white evangelicals take monastic-like vows to live communally with and for the multi-racial poor in inner-city Philadelphia, inspiring dozens of similar such neo-monastic communities across the United States. Examples could be multiplied. Indeed, it is doubtful whether any two Emerging churches would look or feel very much the same. This multiplicity of expressions makes defining the ECM as a whole feel a great deal like attempting to nail the proverbial Jell-O to the wall.

Despite such wide diversity, for a collaborative volume such as this some kind of common definition is necessary, if for no other reason than to establish that we are all indeed attempting to analyze the same broad phenomenon. A working attempt at such a definition might describe the ECM as a social movement among Christians who share a sense of dissatisfaction with various aspects of late-twentieth century Christianity and are

INTRODUCTION

in conversation with one another to actively deconstruct these forms and experiment with new religious practices, communal structures, theologies, and political identities.[11] The fluidity of this description comes in the fact that Emerging Christians often differ on which specific aspects of modern Christianity they seek to deconstruct and which alternative directions they choose to pursue. Nevertheless, several frequently recurring traits can be observed among Emerging Christians and their communities. These include but are not limited to the following:

1. Decentralized, non-hierarchical, open-sourced organizational structures, along with a strong aversion to institutionalization;
2. An affinity for irregular, experimental, multi-sensory, and participatory worship experiences;
3. An "ancient/future" orientation that seeks to reclaim and reshape historic spiritual practices for contemporary use;
4. A constructive engagement with the surrounding culture that rejects sacred-secular dualism;
5. A belief that Christians should be missionally engaged in the world by serving those outside of the church, rather than trying to extract non-Christians out of the world into the church;
6. A deep commitment to social justice, ecology, and diversity, and corresponding rejection of the narrow political agenda of the Religious Right;
7. A "postmodern" resistance to firm theological boundaries with a preference for provisional, inclusive, "both/and" ways of thinking.

Of course, not all participants in the ECM will share every one of these traits, nor emphasize particular qualities to the same degree, but there is enough overlap for participants to see themselves in conversation with one another over such issues and thus as part of the same broad movement. This conversational aspect is a key defining quality of the ECM—from the beginning participants have seen the Emerging Church more as a conversation among friends than as an institution or even a "movement."[12] In this

---

11. Bielo, *Emerging Evangelicals*, 5–6; Flory and Miller, *Finding Faith*, 36–37; Lee and Sinitiere, *Holy Mavericks*, 79–80; Marti, *Deconstructed Church*, 25–31; Packard, *Emerging Church*, 6.

12. In his PhD dissertation, *The Church Is Flat* (11–21), ECM leader Tony Jones does argue, however, that the Emerging Church should also be seen as a new social movement.

sense, the Emerging Church might be best understood by reference to John Swales' definition of a discourse community, which in this case is united by common questions and concerns about the practices, polity, theology, and politics of the contemporary church in light of a perceived shift from modernity to postmodernity in the broader culture.[13] The various (and usually provisional) answers arrived at by participants in this conversation may differ, but they share the common goals of deconstructing current forms of Christianity and exploring together new ways forward.

In trying to get a handle on the diverse range of discourses within the ECM, it may be helpful to think of Emerging Christians as grouped into three broad and overlapping streams depending on which aspect of contemporary Christianity they are primarily engaged in rethinking: spiritual practices, polity/ecclesiology, or theology. Those focused primarily on reimagining the practices of the church—whether in the realm of corporate worship and liturgy, personal spirituality, or ministry methodologies—are driven by a desire for missional *relevance* within a postmodern, post-Christendom culture. Maintaining the closest connection to conservative evangelicalism, often these "Relevants" will argue that it is not the message of the church (i.e., its understanding of the gospel) that needs to change in any fundamental way, but rather the methods by which that message is communicated that must to be updated for twenty-first-century society.[14] Informed by missional theology, they argue that churches must become more outward oriented, serving the needs of the communities around them rather than simply trying to attract individuals into the church. Within the church community they are also more likely to encourage experimental and culturally contextual practices of worship and spirituality, often utilizing art, technology, ancient liturgies, historic spiritual practices, and cutting edge innovations in order to cultivate diversity in the ways that both individuals and communities can experience the divine.[15]

A second stream identifies the institutional structures of the church themselves as the primary roadblock to a thriving Christian life and thus seek to *reconstruct* the polity and underlying ecclesiology of the church in various ways. Depending on the context these "Reconstructionists"

---

13. Swales, *Genre Analysis*, 21–32.

14. The labels I am using here—Relevants, Reconstructionists, and Re-Envisionists—are adapted from a taxonomy first proposed by the Southern Baptist missiologist Ed Stetzer in his article "Understanding the emerging church."

15. For examples of this stream, see Baker, Gay, and Brown, *Alternative Worship*; Kimball, *The Emerging Church* and *Emerging Worship*; Taylor, *The Out of Bounds Church*.

INTRODUCTION

critique both the large, institutional mega-churches and their perceived overemphasis on numbers and programming, as well older, more traditional church structures that seem more interested in maintaining dying and Spirit-quenching bureaucracies than in pursuing the mission of Christ in the world. Many in this stream have been influenced by Neo-Anabaptist ecclesiologies, and thus emphasize the distinct, counter-cultural nature of the church in contrast to its surrounding culture.[16] The Reconstructionist response is often to look for smaller and more demanding expressions of Christian fellowship with more collaborative models of leadership: house churches, "organic" or simple churches, small groups within larger bodies, as well as neo-monastic communities among the poor.[17]

Finally, there are those who share many of the same desires as those in the first two streams to reimagine church practices and polities, but also go beyond these issues to *re-envision* underlying theologies as well, and especially certain core evangelical beliefs such as penal substitutionary atonement, literal notions of Hell, the inerrancy of scripture, the sinfulness of homosexuality, and sometimes even classical conceptions of God's own nature.[18] Among Emerging Christians, these "Re-Envisionists" are perhaps the ones most influenced by postmodern notions of subjectivity and the need for epistemic humility, leading them not merely to replace former beliefs with new ones, but to question a posture of theological certainty that would declare any doctrine off-limits for re-examination in the first place.[19] Most significantly, many post-evangelical Re-Envisionists have questioned their former understanding of the gospel as focused solely on individualistic salvation to post-mortem rewards, and moved instead toward seeing the Kingdom of God as an imminent reality that includes both social and personal redemption and renewal. This fresh theological understanding has led many Re-Envisionists to reevaluate their political assumptions as well, whether those of conservative evangelicalism or the moderate mainline, and to move in more radically progressive and liberationist directions.[20]

16. See, for instance, Fitch's *The Great Giveaway*.

17. See, for instance, Bean, *How to Be a Christian without Going to Church*; Cole, *Organic Church*; Heath and Duggins, *Missional, Monastic, Mainline*; Viola, *Reimagining Church*; Wilson-Hartgrove, *New Monasticism*.

18. For examples of this stream, see Bell, *Velvet Elvis* or *Love Wins*; McLaren, *A New Kind of Christianity*; Pagitt, *A Christianity Worth Believing*; Bass, *Grounded*.

19. Dark, *Sacredness of Questioning Everything*; Franke, *Manifold Witness*.

20. Claiborne and Haw, *Jesus for President*; Clawson, *Everyday Justice*; McLaren, *Everything Must Change*; Wallis, *The Great Awakening*.

INTRODUCTION

Clarifying Terminology

Understanding these three types—Relevants, Reconstructionists, and Re-Envisionists—as discrete though sometimes converging streams helps elucidate the distinction made by some between "emerging" and "emergent." Most often this distinction has been made by more theologically conservative participants in the ECM, especially those located exclusively within the Relevant or Reconstructionist streams. By calling themselves "emerging," they affirmed certain aspects of the movement while still disassociating themselves from the more controversial theological explorations of those in the Re-Envisionist stream. These latter were instead dubbed "emergent" because of the affiliation many in that stream had with the non-profit organization Emergent Village.[21] Few within the "emergent" portion of the movement, however, wished likewise to disassociate themselves from the more conservative members, preferring instead to affirm the inclusive and relational nature of the movement.[22] In the view of "emergent" Re-Envisionists, many of whom also embrace concerns found in the Relevant and Reconstructionist streams, the ECM is an expansive movement in which all aspects of the Christian faith are open for re-examination, including core theological affirmations, and unity is based on friendship rather than doctrinal agreement. Those who prefer to identify as "emerging but not emergent," on the other hand, favor a more limited emergence, in which certain doctrines are simply not on the table to be questioned and unity is based on adherence to these perceived essentials.

For the purposes of this volume, the term *Emerging Church Movement* will refer to all three of the streams described above, including those considered "emergent." To prevent any confusion, the term "emergent" will generally be avoided, except when referring specifically to the organization Emergent Village, in which case it will be capitalized. *Emerging Christians* (or *ECM participants*) will be used to refer to individuals or collections of individuals within the movement, and *Emerging church(es)* will refer to specific faith communities. Please note that in each of these cases "Emerging" will be capitalized in order to make it clear that the movement itself

---

21. Devine, "The Emerging Church," in Henard and Greenway, eds., *Evangelicals Engaging Emergent*, 4–46. Driscoll, *Confessions*, 21–23; Dunbar, "Missional, Emerging, Emergent"; Kimball, "Origins of the Terms 'Emerging' and 'Emergent' Church—Part 2"; McKnight, "Emerging and Emergent."

22. Clawson, "Claiming Emergent"; Jones, "Emerging vs. Emergent"; McLaren, "Emergent in *Publisher's Weekly*."

is being referenced. On those rare occasions where "emerging" is not capitalized it should be understood in the usual dictionary sense of the word rather than referring to the ECM.

A final distinction does need to be made, however, between the Emerging Church Movement and "Emergence Christianity," a phrase coined by the late Phyllis Tickle.[23] The difference here is between a broader trend (Emergence Christianity) happening in many different ways across multiple traditions as each adapts and evolves in response to new realities in twenty-first-century society, and those parts of the church that are more conscious of and welcoming toward this evolution (the Emerging Church Movement). In other words, Emergence is happening all over the place, not just among those who self-identify as part of the ECM. This is why some in the ECM prefer to talk about "the church which is emerging" rather than "the Emerging Church," a term which may wrongly make it appear as just another competing denomination, rather than a movement happening within and around the edges of the whole Church.[24] That said however, within this broader Emergence Christianity, self-identified Emerging Christians are the ones most likely to recognize and deliberately try to shape what is emerging. Our suggestion is that scholars should use the term "Emergence Christianity" to refer to the broad trend, and "Emerging Church Movement" to refer to that more self-consciously engaged segment within Emergence Christianity. Both of these, furthermore, should be carefully distinguished from Emergent Village, which is but one of many formal networks within the ECM.

What You Will Find in This Book

Because the ECM involves multiple overlapping attempts to reimagine the practices, institutional structures, and theology of contemporary Christianity, this volume brings together scholars from diverse disciplines to examine each of these aspects in detail. In keeping with the interdisciplinary purpose of this project, rather than grouping these contributions by discipline, we have instead gathered them according to two overarching and complementary themes arising out the chapters themselves. The first set aims at defining the boundaries and characteristics of ECM, describing where it came from, what it is, and what sets it apart. Paradoxically, however, one of these

23. Tickle, *The Great Emergence*.
24. Clawson, "Should the Emerging Church Settle?"

defining characteristics of the ECM is their very resistance to hard and fast boundaries. Participants in the ECM frequently see themselves as reaching across traditional divides, eschewing labels, categories, and affiliations that would limit their ability to engage in the kind of creative reimagining the believe is necessary for the church. Thus our second section is about the various ways the ECM crosses such conceptual boundaries. And this serves as yet another argument for the interdisciplinary nature of this book. Just as the ECM is described in part by its tendency toward boundary-crossing, so does this volume seek to cross the boundaries between disciplines in order to more fully examine the ways in which this happens.

The first section "Defining Boundaries," opens with a historical overview of the Emerging Church Movement in the United States provided by Michael Clawson. While brief narratives of the ECM's origins and evolution since the 1990s have been offered previously by various observers and participants, Clawson's account is the first to dig more deeply into the roots of the movement, showing how evangelical trends from a generation prior produced the movement that emerged in the late 1990s.[25] He looks in particular at the rise of "new paradigm" seeker-oriented churches out of the Jesus People Movement of the late-1960s and early 70s, the development of missional church theology from the work of David Bosch, Lesslie Newbigin, and others, and the rise, fall, and resurgence of politically progressive evangelicalism from the 1970s until today, showing how each has helped to produce and shape the current Emerging movement.

In Chapter 2, sociologist Gerardo Marti draws on the concept of institutional entrepreneurship in order to conceptualize core processes of the Emerging Church Movement. He suggests that the ECM exemplifies collective religious institutional entrepreneurship across disparate social groups and wide geographical spaces. Chapter 3 continues the descriptive effort as anthropologists Jon Bialecki and James Bielo suggest that both the rejection of Constantinianism and the focus on being "missional" are demonstrative of how Emerging Christians perceive temporality. Utilizing Gilles Deleuze's work on cinematic shifts and his concept of a "time-crystal," Bialecki and Bielo suggest a framework for understanding temporality in the ECM and how it differs from other expressions of Christian temporality.

In Chapter 4, Xochitl Alvizo brings an evaluative lens to bear on the movement, providing one of the first analyses of the ECM from a feminist theological perspective. Basing her conclusions on research conducted

25. Jones, *New Christians*; Tickle, *Emergence Christianity*.

while visiting twelve Emerging churches across the United States, Alvizo compares the stated desire of many within the ECM to re-envision Christian theologies and practices with the lived ecclesiology of actual congregations. Ultimately, she points to ways that the ECM must explicitly engage with feminist theologies if they wish to fulfill their own vision of transforming the church.

Chapter 5 serves as a bridge between "Defining Boundaries" and "Crossing Boundaries" as Timothy Snyder explores issues of conflict and identity through a case study into the congregational culture of one Emerging church in Saint Paul, Minnesota. He looks in particular at their experience of transitioning from an American Baptist to Evangelical Lutheran denominational affiliation. While on the surface this seems like a clear example of boundary crossing, Snyder draws on both ethnographic fieldwork, practical theology, and Ann Swidler's theory of "culture in action" to argue that the conflicts arising from such unsettling of ecclesial cultures occasioned by Emergence Christianity actually allow for the possibility of unresolved strangeness, of two parties knowing one another in differentiated otherness. In other words, Snyder demonstrates that defining boundaries may in fact be essential to the work of crossing boundaries.

The second half of the volume, "Crossing Boundaries," opens with Chapter 6 as sociologist Lloyd Chia moves us "From Boundaries to Borderlands." Chia specifically explores the concept of "mapping" as it relates to the ways in which Emerging Christians imagine and foster relationships with other social and religious groups. In Chapter 7, another sociologist, Jason Wollschleger, looks at conceptual boundary crossings. There he argues that the boundary between (or differentiation of) the sacred and the secular is the primary aspect of modern society against which the ECM is reacting.

The values and institutional structures of a religious movement nearly always find embodiment and expression in liturgical and musical practices, and here too Emerging congregations are characterized by boundary-crossing. In Chapter 8, April Stace continues to explore the (non)boundary between the sacred and the secular as expressed in the liturgical/musical practices of several Emerging congregations in the Washington, DC area. She argues that using secular music in worship is one way that Emerging congregations embody and practice a thoroughly sacralized worldview. Heather Josselyn-Cranson examines similar practices in Chapter 9 as she shows how the liturgical/musical practices of an Emerging congregation in Portland, Oregon illustrate the postmodern tendency to draw from a variety of stylistic sources in order to create a new work (a "pastiche").

The final chapter crosses international boundaries, taking the focus beyond North America as Argentinian scholar Juan José Barreda Toscano and North American scholar and former missionary Dee Yaccino introduce us to *La Red del Camino para la Misión Integral*. This Latin American network of churches, which arose independently, though not in isolation from the global movement, illustrates one of the many forms the ECM has taken outside of the Western world, and explores how cross-cultural contacts between the *RdC* and the North American ECM have shaped both in significant ways. They demonstrate that while enough commonalities exist to see the *Red del Camino* as part of a broader global Emerging movement, the particularities that exist within differing cultural contexts mean we should never assume that what is happening elsewhere can be best understood in terms of the ECM in the United States. Indeed, Toscano and Yaccino leave open the question of whether terms like "Emerging" are even rightly applied to movements outside of the West unless those terms are understood in reference to emergence from their own unique ecclesial, cultural, and postcolonial contexts.

Each of these authors adopt distinct methodologies and provide diverse viewpoints on a single though multifaceted subject. Only the shared focus on the Emerging Church as a definable yet boundary-crossing movement unites these chapters. Instead of smoothing out the plurality of perspectives and inevitable differences that arise among our contributors, we have instead embraced this disciplinary otherness, believing that it is in fact more appropriate to the nature of the ECM itself. Our hope is that this approach will prove useful to scholars in each of these fields, as well as to church leaders, seminarians, and Emerging Christians themselves as they seek a more thorough understanding of this important phenomenon within twenty-first-century religion.

—Michael Clawson and April Stace, Editors

INTRODUCTION

Bibliography

Baker, Jonny, et al. *Alternative Worship: Resources from and for the Emerging Church.* Grand Rapids: Baker, 2003.

Bass, Diana Butler. *Grounded: Finding God in the World—A Spiritual Revolution.* New York: HarperCollins, 2015.

Bean, Kelly. *How to Be a Christian without Going to Church: The Unofficial Guide to Alternative Forms of Christian Community.* Grand Rapids: Baker, 2014.

Bell, Rob. *Love Wins: A Book About Heaven, Hell, and the Fate of Every Person Who Ever Lived.* New York: HarperOne, 2011.

———. *Velvet Elvis: Repainting the Christian Faith.* Grand Rapids: Zondervan, 2005.

Bielo, James. *Emerging Evangelicals: Faith, Modernity, and the Desire for Authenticity.* New York: New York University Press, 2011.

Brewin, Kester. *Signs of Emergence: A Vision for Church That Is Organic/Networked/Decentralized/Bottom-up/Communal/Flexible/Always Evolving.* Grand Rapids: Baker, 2007.

Carson, D. A. *Becoming Conversant with the Emerging Church: Understanding a Movement and Its Implications.* Grand Rapids: Zondervan, 2005.

Claiborne, Shane, and Chris Haw. *Jesus for President.* Grand Rapids: Zondervan, 2008.

Clawson, Julie. "Claiming Emergent." *onehandclapping* (blog), 8 September 2008. http://julieclawson.com/2008/09/08/claiming-emergent/.

———. *Everyday Justice: The Global Impact of Our Daily Choices.* Downers Grove, IL: InterVarsity, 2009.

Clawson, Michael. "Should the Emerging Church Settle?" *EmergingPensees* (blog), 15 January 2008. http://emergingpensees.blogspot.com/2008/01/should-emerging-church-settle.html.

Cole, Neil. *Organic Church: Growing Faith Where Life Happens.* San Francisco: Jossey-Bass, 2005.

Dark, David. *The Sacredness of Questioning Everything.* Grand Rapids: Zondervan, 2009.

Driscoll, Mark. *Confessions of a Reformission Rev: Hard Lessons from an Emerging Missional Church.* Grand Rapids: Zondervan, 2006.

Dunbar, David G. "Missional, Emerging, Emergent: A Traveler's Guide." *Missional Journal* 2, nos. 4–5 (2008).

Fitch, David E. *The Great Giveaway: Reclaiming the Mission of the Church from Big Business, Parachurch Organizations, Psychotherapy, Consumer Capitalism, and other Modern Maladies.* Grand Rapids: Baker, 2005.

Flory, Richard, and Donald E. Miller. *Finding Faith: The Spiritual Quest of the Post-Boomer Generation.* New Brunswick, NJ: Rutgers University Press, 2008.

Franke, John R. *Manifold Witness: The Plurality of Truth.* Nashville: Abingdon, 2009.

Gibbs, Eddie, and Ryan Bolger. *Emerging Churches: Creating Christian Communities in Postmodern Cultures.* Grand Rapids: Baker, 2005.

Heath, Elaine A., and Larry Duggins. *Missional. Monastic. Mainline.: A Guide to Starting Missional Micro-Communities in Historically Mainline Traditions.* Eugene, OR: Wipf and Stock, 2014.

Henard, William D., and Adam W. Greenway, eds. *Evangelicals Engaging Emergent: A Discussion of the Emergent Church Movement.* Nashville: B and H, 2009.

Jones, Tony. *The Church Is Flat: The Relational Ecclesiology of the Emerging Church Movement.* Minneapolis: JoPa, 2011.

INTRODUCTION

———. "Emerging vs. Emergent." *Theoblogy*, 15 April 2008. http://www.patheos.com/blogs/tonyjones/2008/04/15/emerging-vs-emergent/.

———. *The New Christians: Dispatches from the Emergent Frontier*. San Francisco: Jossey-Bass, 2008.

Kimball, Dan. *The Emerging Church: Vintage Christianity for New Generations*. Grand Rapids: Zondervan, 2003.

———. *Emerging Worship: Creating Worship Gatherings for New Generations*. Grand Rapids: Zondervan, 2004.

———. "Origins of the Terms 'Emerging' and 'Emergent' Church—Part 2." *Dan Kimball: Vintage Faith* (blog), 21 April 2006. https://web.archive.org/web/20140819172100/http://dankimball.typepad.com/vintage_faith/2006/04/origins_of_the_.html.

Lee, Shayne, and Phillip Luke Sinitiere. *Holy Mavericks: Evangelical Innovators and the Spiritual Marketplace*. New York: New York University Press, 2009.

Marti, Gerardo, and Gladys Ganiel. *The Deconstructed Church: Understanding Emerging Christianity*. Oxford: Oxford University Press, 2014.

McKnight, Scot. *The Blue Parakeet: Rethinking How You Read the Bible*. Grand Rapids: Zondervan, 2008.

———. "Emerging and Emergent: Our New Network." *Jesus Creed* (blog), 24 September 2008. http://www.patheos.com/community/jesuscreed/2008/09/24/emerging-and-emergent-our-new-network/.

McLaren, Brian D. "Emergent in *Publisher's Weekly*." *Brian McLaren* (website), 1 September 2008. http://www.brianmclaren.net/archives/blog/emergent-in-publishers-weekly.html.

———. *Everything Must Change: Jesus, Global Crises, and a Revolution of Hope*. Nashville: Nelson, 2007.

———. *A Generous Orthodoxy*. Grand Rapids: Zondervan, 2004.

———. *A New Kind of Christian: A Tale of Two Friends on a Spiritual Journey*. San Francisco: Jossey-Bass, 2001.

———. *A New Kind of Christianity: Ten Questions That Are Transforming the Faith*. New York: Harper, 2010.

Myers, Joseph R. *Organic Community: Creating a Place Where People Naturally Connect*. Grand Rapids: Baker, 2007.

———. *The Search to Belong: Rethinking Intimacy, Community, and Small Groups*. Grand Rapids: Zondervan, 2003.

Packard, Josh. *The Emerging Church: Religion at the Margins*. Boulder, CO: First Forum, 2012.

Pagitt, Doug. *A Christianity Worth Believing: Hope-Filled, Open-Armed, Alive-and-Well Faith*. San Francisco: Jossey-Bass, 2008.

———. *Church Reimagined: The Spiritual Formation of People in Communities of Faith*. Grand Rapids: Zondervan, 2003.

Stetzer, Ed. "Understanding the Emerging Church." *Baptist Press*, 6 January 2006. http://www.sbcbaptistpress.org/bpnews.asp?ID=22406.

Swales, John M. *Genre Analysis: English in Academic and Research Settings*. Cambridge: Cambridge University Press, 1990.

Taylor, Steve. *The Out of Bounds Church: Learning to Create a Community of Faith in a Culture of Change*. Grand Rapids: Zondervan, 2005.

Tickle, Phyllis. *Emergence Christianity: What It Is, Where It Is Going, and Why It Matters*. Grand Rapids: Baker, 2012.

INTRODUCTION

———. *The Great Emergence: How Christianity is Changing and Why*. Grand Rapids: Baker, 2008.

Viola, Frank. *Reimagining Church: Pursuing the Dream of Organic Christianity*. Colorado Springs: Cook, 2008.

Wallis, Jim. *The Great Awakening: Reviving Faith and Politics in a Post-Religious Right America*. New York: HarperCollins, 2008.

Webber, Robert E. *Ancient-Future Faith: Rethinking Evangelicalism for a Postmodern World*. Grand Rapids: Baker, 1999.

Wilson-Hartgrove, Jonathan. *New Monasticism: What It Has to Say to Today's Church*. Grand Rapids: Brazos, 2008.

Part 1: Defining Boundaries

1

A Brief History of the Emerging Church Movement in the United States

Michael Clawson

BRIAN MCLAREN'S FIRST PUBLISHED work began with this provocative statement: "If you have a new world, you need a new church. You have a new world."[1] The new world McLaren referred to was that of postmodernity, which he identified as a *historical* shift away from the worldview and culture of modernity.[2] From the beginning, a motivating assumption of the ECM has been that changing historical circumstances demand new responses from the church. For a movement so dependent on historical claims for its very *raison d'être*, it is odd then that so little scholarly work has yet been done on the history of this movement itself. While some brief overviews of the ECM's immediate origins in the 1980s and 90s and subsequent development over the past several decades do exist,[3] deeper historical questions—e.g., What are the ideological and institutional roots of this movement and from where, exactly, has it emerged?—remain largely untouched.[4]

1. McLaren, *Church on the Other Side*, 11.
2. Of course, using the term "postmodernity" as a historical period is itself contentious, and some scholars prefer to refer to "late modernity" rather than postmodernity. What is important for the purposes of this study, however, is that ECM participants self-consciously adopted the language of postmodernity and defined themselves in relation to their understandings of it, regardless of the accuracy of such usage.
3. See, for instance: Jones, *New Christians*, 41–59; or Stetzer, "The Emergent/Emerging Church," in Henard and Greenway, eds., *Evangelicals Engaging Emergent*, 47–90.
4. The one significant exception to this are the pair of books by the late Phyllis Tickle, *The Great Emergence* and *Emergence Christianity*. Especially in the latter book Tickle attempts to trace the ideological roots of what she calls "Emergence Christianity," a broader category than the Emerging Church Movement that this volume deals with.

If the ECM does indeed reflect a common desire to deconstruct and reimagine various aspects of contemporary Christianity for a postmodern world, it is important to recognize that this critical-yet-creative stance did not arise in a historical vacuum. Since at least the middle of the last century, various movements within evangelicalism, both in the United States and globally, have critiqued the dominant practices, theology, and politics of that tradition, providing new perspectives and practical alternatives. It is from this soil that the ECM has emerged. In particular I will focus on three currents among evangelicals during the second half of the twentieth century that helped produce and give shape to the ECM: 1) the methodologically experimental "new paradigm" churches of the late-twentieth century emerging out of the evangelical youth sub-culture, the Jesus People Movement, and Church-Growth methodologies during the 1960s and 70s; 2) the missional theology developing out of the works of Leslie Newbigin and David Bosch; and 3) the movement of socially and politically progressive evangelicals produced by the political upheavals of the 1960s and informed by integral mission theology coming out of Latin America. The ECM in the United Sates has largely arisen from the confluence of these earlier trends.[5] It brings together, both through selective appropriation and constructive critique, ideas and practices from movements that were previously discrete. Going further however, ECM participants reshape these preceding influences through their own postmodern tendencies toward eclecticism and epistemic humility, producing a new movement greater than the sum of its parts.

The Evangelical Youth Subculture and New Paradigm Churches

The Emerging Church Movement in the United States was born in the mid-1990s as young, innovative, evangelical pastors (and especially youth pastors) gathered to discuss how their churches, primarily large, "seeker-sensitive"

Unfortunately, Tickle deals primarily in broad strokes rather than scholarly detail, and casts her nets wide, pulling in numerous trends in religion, the sciences, economics, and society to aid her narrative of how Emergence Christianity came to be. This brief history will attempt something much less ambitious but hopefully more focused.

5. While the ECM is a global phenomenon, this chapter focuses on its presence within the United States. It is important to note, however, that the earliest expressions of the ECM arose elsewhere and that they continue to evolve in dozens of countries all over the world, often with only peripheral connection to the ECM in North America.

megachurches, could attract more Gen Xers, people in the eighteen to thirty-five age range who seemed increasingly disinterested in the church. This concern for adopting new methods to evangelize younger generations was already well established among evangelicals by the end of the twentieth century, having begun with an explosion of church-based and parachurch youth ministries in the immediate post-war era.[6] Already these World War II-generation evangelical innovators showed their willingness to adapt the methods of popular culture to their purposes. As historian Joel Carpenter notes, evangelistic rallies held by these ministries were "wrapped in a contemporary idiom borrowed from radio variety shows and patriotic musical revues."[7] Youth groups utilized parties, games, and popular music to inculcate evangelical beliefs and habits of regular bible study.[8] Such youth ministries proved over the subsequent decades to be an ideal setting for inventive practitioners to experiment with new and more culturally attuned methods. Change could be tested and potentially "dangerous" cultural accommodations quarantined, while also allowing successful innovations an eventual route into the wider church.[9] Furthermore, by creating a parallel Christian subculture alongside the mainstream youth culture, post-war evangelicals effectively protected their young people from corruption by "the world," while still offering them some of its enjoyments.

No evangelical youth movement had more success with this adopt-and-adapt strategy than the Jesus People of the late-1960s and early 1970s. What the youth ministers of the 1940s and 50s did tentatively and apologetically, the Jesus Kids did with enormous gusto and creativity, freely adapting the styles, music, lingo, and methods of the hippie counterculture to communicate their message that Jesus was the "One Way" through the bewildering morass of spiritual values and lifestyle options offered by the era. (As just one example, the widely read and frequently imitated *Hollywood Free Paper*, known for adopting the slang of the youth culture, sometimes to the point of absurdity, once wrote: "We're rapping about a Person—Jesus Christ. And if you can dig Him (that means to depend on Him to put your head together) then you're in for some heavy surprises!! He'll turn you on

---

6. Pahl, *Youth Ministry*, 56–60.

7. Carpenter, "Youth for Christ and the New Evangelicals," in Sherrill, ed., *Religion and the Life of the Nation*, 135.

8. Bergler, *Juvenilization of American Christianity*, 148–50.

9. Ibid., 6.

to a spiritual high for the rest of forever.")[10] In so doing the Jesus People effected a widespread revival of conservative religion among their peers, one that ultimately aimed to rescue young people from the degradation of secular society. As one observer noted, the Jesus People were "not as much counterculture as counter-counterculture" in their critique and subversion of many of the secular counterculture's values and lifestyles.[11]

The Jesus Movement began independently of the mainstream evangelical youth culture, sometimes through the work of Pentecostal evangelists but just as often through recently converted hippies themselves. Immersed as they already were in the counterculture, these leaders were able to adapt its styles and themes to their newfound Christian message with authenticity. By bridging both worlds, the Jesus Movement served as a means of eventually integrating countercultural youth back into mainstream society by way of the evangelical church.[12] When the secular counterculture itself began to dissipate in the 70s, the Jesus Movement gradually faded out as well, but the Jesus People did not simply disappear. Rather, as they matured, got jobs, and started families, they increasingly settled into more mainstream religious settings—evangelical churches, overseas missions, campus ministries, and seminaries.[13]

These Jesus Freaks-turned-evangelicals still carried with them, however, many of the lessons and much of the passion acquired in the Jesus Movement, ultimately transforming evangelicalism itself in ways that would set the stage for the Emerging Church Movement a generation later. Two interrelated changes stand out in this regard. First, the charismatic/Pentecostal roots of the Jesus Movement renewed within evangelicalism experientially oriented and emotionally expressive practices of worship and devotion that harkened back to earlier days of camp meetings and tent revivals. Two common aspects of this—contemporary praise and worship songs, a direct outgrowth of Jesus People music; and a therapeutic approach to Christianity, one that focuses on subjective religious experiences, a "personal relationship with Jesus," and individual self-improvement—have proven particularly effective for drawing multitudes of religious seekers into churches that embrace this new expressive spirituality.

10. Pederson, "Jesus Is Better Than Hash," 1.
11. Streiker, *The Jesus Trip*, 89.
12. Ellwood, *One Way*, 23; Hargrove, *Religion for a Dislocated Generation*, 129.
13. DiSabatino, *The Jesus People Movement*, 16–17; Plowman, "Whatever Happened to the Jesus Movement?," 46.

Second, the evangelistic passion and anti-establishment ethos of the Jesus People led the evangelical churches and ministries into which they eventually settled to adopt a highly flexible and iconoclastic approach to ministry methods. Rather than feeling bound to traditional forms and institutions, these new evangelicals felt free, even spiritually called, to rethink such "dead" and "spirit-quenching" structures and experiment with new approaches. In this effort the grown-up Jesus People continued to apply their adopt-and-adapt strategy of engaging with popular culture. Both the multi-billion dollar Contemporary Christian Music industry (along with the related commercialization of "Christian" movies, "Christian" bookstores, "Christian" clothing, etc.), and the rapid growth and proliferation of "seeker-sensitive" megachurches, with their relaxed, informal vibe and rejection of many of the traditional symbols and rituals of Christianity, are testament to the power of this strategy for creating a thriving evangelical sub-culture that could mirror the ways of the world while still preaching a conservative theological message.

The Jesus People qualities of expressive spirituality and methodological adaptability soon merged with the contemporaneous Church Growth Movement coming out of Fuller Seminary, which applied sociological insights and business marketing strategies to evangelistic efforts, to produce thousands of fast-growing, innovative evangelical churches across the United States over the past four decades. Sometimes known to sociologists as "new paradigm churches," the first wave of these, notably the Calvary Chapel, Vineyard, and Willow Creek Associations, were all directly influenced by the Jesus People Movement.[14] While tapping into the anti-establishment attitudes of the Sixties Jesus Generation by largely eschewing denominational affiliations, external authorities, and church traditionalism, these new paradigm churches ironically often foster top-down, bureaucratic leadership models borrowed directly from the corporate business world. Their methodological flexibility and concern for numerical growth also frequently lead such churches to appeal to a consumeristic culture by offering an increasing array of religious goods and services: church sports leagues, bookstores and coffee shops, concerts and seminars, retreats and mission trips, counseling services, business directories, youth programs, etc. These new paradigm churches have spawned many imitators, and so successfully marketed their techniques to other church leaders, that by the

---

14. Miller, *Reinventing American Protestantism*, 11–12.

end of the century their approach had become the norm for evangelicals in North America.

The Emerging Church Movement evolved in the 1990s as the rebellious off-spring of this brand of evangelical Christianity. Through the influence of postmodern theory, with which evangelical intellectuals gradually began engaging throughout the 1990s, they selectively appropriated some aspects of the new paradigm, while rejecting or modifying others. As with their new paradigm, seeker-sensitive parents, young ECM leaders in the United States wanted to communicate the gospel to post-Boomer generations in ways that would resonate with the broader culture and were more than willing to experiment with new ministry methods to do so. These shared impulses account for much of the ECM's affinity for innovative, multi-sensory, and participatory worship experiences.

However, like the Jesus People before them, these Emerging Christians also placed a high value on spiritual authenticity and more organic forms of community.[15] Disillusioned with what they saw as the over-produced, over-marketed, overly slick business models of the new paradigm churches, ECM leaders sought more than just new methods for drawing young people into their churches. They also started rethinking the forms and structures of church altogether. This desire for authenticity led many early participants back to more ancient and traditional forms, symbols, and rituals in their practices of worship and personal devotion—the very things the new paradigm pioneers had been so keen to strip away—though their postmodern sensibilities also lent them the freedom to reinterpret, remix, and modify such rituals to fit their own contemporary needs. In many ECM congregations it would not be uncommon to experience, in the same service, an eclectic mash-up of contemporary praise songs, eighth-century hymns, and sixteenth-century liturgies, together with community created art on the walls and abstract visuals projected onto a screen throughout. The purpose in this eclecticism is both to cultivate diversity in the ways that communities can experience and worship God together, along with an evangelistic desire to contextualize the gospel in ways effective for reaching a postmodern culture.[16]

The desire for more authentic and organic forms of organization rather than the top-down businesslike models of the new paradigm, has also led those in the ECM to move, however imperfectly, toward smaller, less

---

15. Rabey, *In Search of Authentic Faith*, 52, 71.
16. Gay, *Remixing the Church*, 49, 61–67.

institutionalized, and more collaborative forms of religious community with more horizontal and open-source models of shared leadership. Whereas new paradigm churches have been concerned primarily with attracting ever greater numbers into their religious institutions, the ECM critiques such goals, instead emphasizing more intimate and outwardly focused spiritual communities. The ways and degree to which such values are actually lived out vary greatly among Emerging communities, which can include large congregations, small house churches, theology pub discussion groups, and neo-monastic residential communities among the urban poor.

The ECM has reacted strongly against the sacred-secular dualism innate to evangelicalism and amplified to even greater degrees by the Jesus Movement, instead choosing to "see the whole culture and creation as one big mess in which God is moving."[17] Rather than attempting to create an alternative Christianized culture alongside the presumably corrupt secular culture, those in the ECM assume that aspects of God's truth and beauty can be found in both the church and secular society. Ironically, while the Jesus People themselves maintained a more dualistic mindset, it was their willingness to adapt at least the external forms and styles of popular culture to Christian purposes that paved the way for a more radical return to culture by the ECM. If the counsel of earlier evangelicals was total avoidance ("good Christians shun the world"), the Jesus People's adopt-and-adapt approach ("good Christians can use the trappings of the world to preach God's truth") served as the stepping stone to the ECM's rediscovery of the broader culture ("when we looked to the world, we discovered that God's truth is already there!"). The sacred-secular divide preached by mainstream evangelicalism thus rang increasingly false to Emerging Christians' actual experiences of the world, thereby feeding their desire for change.

The means for germinating these emerging seeds of discontent was the same tool that had created the new paradigm in the first place: evangelical youth ministry. By the 1990s evangelical youth and youth ministers had established within mainstream churches an internal culture that had its own music, literature, leaders, and norms—often starkly contrasted with that of the wider church community. Furthermore, youth ministry often created a kind of pluralistic, evangelical ecumenism as young people from a wide diversity of Christian traditions met and worshipped together at Christian concerts and Bible camps, on short-term mission trips with non-denominational agencies, and through parachurch ministries like Youth for

17. Jones, *New Christians*, 75.

Christ and Young Life. The result was the formation of a countercultural, interdenominational, passionately spiritual, and activist-oriented cohort of younger evangelicals.

Having been raised with such high expectations, it seems inevitable that the adult church, even new paradigm churches, would prove unable or unwilling, at least in the eyes of idealistic young Christians, to live up to their desires for authentic Christian community. An enormous disconnect seemed to exist between the kind of Christianity practiced in their youth ministries and that of the broader church. With such discontent rumbling beneath the surface for years among youth and youth ministers, it is not surprising that much of the original ECM conversation began within this same demographic, and that, as will be seen, evangelical youth ministry organizations provided the original institutional base for the Emerging movement.[18] In ways similar to the Jesus People before them, evangelical youth ministry lent to early ECM leaders its passion, activism, interdenominational character, hunger for authenticity, and institutional base, even as those Emerging leaders carried their critique in directions not envisioned by the original Jesus radicals.

Missional Church

A second major stream of influence on the ECM has been the development of missional church theology. This term as it is currently used was coined in a 1998 book entitled *Missional Church: A Vision for the Sending of the Church in North America*, published by a working group of six Protestant theologians concerned with extending and applying what they saw as an emerging missiological consensus in the late twentieth century.[19] In contrast to traditional Western views which have seen mission as merely one activity of the church among others, the emerging paradigm argued that mission is rooted in the *missio dei*, the Trinitarian God's initiative to heal and restore all of creation, and that the church has been instituted by God to participate in this mission as its central and all-encompassing task. With this new understanding, missiologists were then also able to recognize and critique the Euro-centric nature of much missionary activity and the ways in which Western churches tended to shape the gospel according to their own cultural context and make the propagation of these culturally

18. Ibid., 36–37.
19. Guder, *Missional Church*, 3–7.

bound churches their top priority in foreign missions. By contrast, the new paradigm suggests that the church should be seen not as the purpose or goal of God's gospel mission, but as its instrument and witness, and thus is able to contextualize the gospel within a multiplicity of cultures.[20]

Missiologist David Bosch describes in his masterwork, *Transforming Mission*, how this new paradigm emerged over several generations, perhaps beginning with Karl Barth, with his emphasis on mission as an activity of God's own self. Bosch suggests that Barth's influence was most clearly seen at the Willingen Conference of the International Missionary Council in 1952, and that since then this understanding of mission as *missio Dei* has been embraced widely—by Catholics, Eastern Orthodox, and both evangelical and ecumenical Protestants. He also notes that many have used this concept to expand the scope of the *missio Dei* to the whole world and in ordinary human history, not just in or through the work of the church, though the church is privileged to participate in it.[21] This move would later be embraced by many within the ECM as further theological justification for their rejection of sacred-secular dualism.

The innovation of the *Missional Church* authors in particular was to apply these missiological insights beyond the scope of foreign mission to the circumstances of the church in late-twentieth century North America as well. These authors were primarily inspired by the work of missionary statesman Bishop Lesslie Newbigin who first began to analyze the challenge posed by the post-Christian British society that he had returned to after decades of missionary service in India. The book itself arose as a research project under the auspices of the North American branch of Newbigin's own Gospel and Our Culture Network. As part of their process, the authors also consulted with four other seminal theologians, Justo Gonzalez, Douglas John Hall, Stanley Hauerwas, and John Howard Yoder for help formulating a missional ecclesiology. Specifically, the *Missional Church* sought to respond to the crisis of Christian decline in North America by redefining the identity and nature of the church in relation to mission. For them the church was primarily constituted by its calling to mission not just overseas but within its own society as well, in the cultures in which it is embedded, including the postmodern, post-Christendom cultures of the West. They further argued against the assumption that mission's purpose and aim was to draw people into the church, and instead proposed

20. Ibid., 4–5.
21. Bosch, *Transforming Mission*, 399–401.

that the church served as an instrument and witness of the gospel's larger purpose of bringing about the reign of God in all creation.[22] The missional church was to equip and send out its members to incarnate the gospel in their surrounding communities and cultures rather than merely trying to extract non-members out of their communities and attract them into the church. For this reason the missional church is often contrasted with approaches that have been critiqued as the "attractional church," especially late-twentieth century church growth methodologies.[23]

The language of missional church caught on quickly among church leaders and ministry practitioners, especially among white evangelical and mainline Protestants throughout North America and in many other English-speaking countries. *Missional Church* itself has sold tens of thousands of copies since its initial publication, a remarkable number for a book of its kind. In addition, dozens of books utilizing missional concepts have been published since 1998, numerous ministry conferences have been held to teach church leaders how to help their congregations become missional, and missional language is now ubiquitous among denominational literature across the English-speaking Protestant world. Indeed many of the original voices in the missional church movement now worry that the term has become faddish—that its meaning has not fully been grasped and is instead applied in inappropriate ways to practices that are not in fact missional.[24] Nevertheless, the term itself has enjoyed wide acceptance and has very few serious detractors.

From its inception the ECM has embraced missional ecclesiology. Early books by ECM authors frequently advocated for a missional understanding of the church. While this language and its explicit formulation came directly from the *Missional Church* book, which was widely read by ECM leaders, the ground had already been prepared for many by their own familiarity with Newbigin's work.[25] Indeed, the ECM represents one of the earliest and most thorough practical outworking of the *Missional Church*'s call for a more culturally contextual, incarnational expression of the church in postmodern societies.

---

22. Guder, *Missional Church*, 5.
23. Frost and Hirsch, *The Shaping of Things to Come*, 18–19.
24. Van Gelder and Zscheile, *Missional Church in Perspective*, 1–5.
25. Jones, *Postmodern Youth Ministry*, 237; Kimball, *Emerging Church*, 68–70; Long, *Generating Hope*, 229; McLaren, *Church on the Other Side*, 127, 175, 183.

The ECM is distinct from other missional movements, however, in their largely appreciative and constructive engagement with postmodernity in ways that could potentially lead to radical changes within their churches. Whereas others have used missional concepts to revamp but essentially maintain existing aspects of church life—e.g. charitable work, church planting, community life, discipleship, leadership, preaching, etc.—in light of missional ecclesiology, those within the ECM heard missional theology as a call to innovate drastically new (or reinvent ancient and widely forgotten) ministry practices, theologies, and forms of church in order to better incarnate the gospel in a postmodern, post-Christendom society.[26] The missional church conversation provided ECM practitioners and writers with both inspiration and theological rationale for their deconstruction of traditional church practices, structures, politics, and doctrines.[27] Each of these were relativized to the missional call for the church to incarnate itself within the culture of postmodernity, though which of these aspects of church life were primarily focused on for deconstruction, and the extent to which their reimagining was taken varied among those within the ECM. Eventually these differences would lead to fragmentation within the broader movement.

Progressive Evangelicalism

In addition to missional theology and the adaptive ethos of the new paradigm churches, many within the ECM have also inherited a deep commitment to diversity, social justice, and other politically progressive concerns from another stream of evangelicalism dating from the 1960s and 70s. Best referred to as progressive evangelicalism, it sprang from two distinct yet interconnected roots: 1) young evangelical radicals in the United States reacting to the volatile political issues of that era, especially civil rights, Vietnam, feminism, and poverty; and 2) the holistic or integral mission theology being developed by evangelicals in the Two-Thirds World, calling for a more complete integration of both evangelism and social concern for the poor and oppressed within a holistic understanding of the gospel.

---

26. Roxburgh and Boren, *Introducing the Missional Church,* 53–54.

27. Jones, *Postmodern Youth Ministry,* 68–69; Kimball, *Emerging Church,* 95–97; McLaren, *New Kind of Christian,* 153.

PART 1: DEFINING BOUNDARIES

The Young Radicals

Though the neo-evangelical movement emerged out of fundamentalism in the 1940s in part from a desire to reengage with social concerns, few considered these to be of the same importance as personal evangelism.[28] Neither were the social concerns they did express in any way progressive. On Civil Rights, Vietnam, gender roles, and the ideologies of free market capitalism, mainstream evangelicals during the 1960s were decidedly conservative.[29] Nevertheless, as the controversies of that pivotal decade heated up, a younger cohort of evangelicals did indeed find themselves caught up in the passions of the Civil Rights, feminist, and anti-war movements, and as a result began to influence the trajectory of evangelicalism in a more leftward direction. The convergence of radical politics with evangelical faith produced a breed of Christians who learned to apply their evangelical theology not just to issues of personal salvation and individual morality, but also to socially structured crises like racial injustice, militarism, poverty, gender issues, and ecology. In contrast to the older generation of evangelical leaders, these progressive evangelicals tended to look beyond the usual assumption that changed individuals alone can bring about a transformed society,[30] and began asking what specific social transformations such changed individuals might legitimately begin working toward.

The message of these progressive leaders resonated with many other younger evangelicals who had been exposed to broader realities through increasingly common short term mission experiences in the Two-Thirds World. Through typically focused on "soul-winning," the extreme poverty and challenging social conditions these young missionaries encountered motivated them to engage with social and political issues back home as well, often in ways that led beyond the bounds of conservatism. But even for those remaining at home, exposure to Two-Thirds World perspectives came by way of mission conferences, Christian colleges, and student ministries that hosted and highlighted international voices with their condemnations of American imperialism, consumerism, and apathy towards social justice. Though such voices did not represent the dominant message coming from evangelical institutions at the time, the very fact of their difference

---

28. See, for instance, Henry, *Uneasy Conscience*; or Moberg, *Inasmuch*.

29. Carpenter, "What's New?," in Steensland and Goff, eds., *The New Evangelical Social Engagement*, 268.

30. Graham, "A Clarification," 416.

from the mainstream guaranteed that their dissonant message would be even more noticed.

The Thanksgiving Workshop on Evangelicals and Social Concern held in Chicago in 1973 was a watershed moment for this new progressive movement. Attended by nearly fifty evangelical leaders, including many rising stars among the younger progressive evangelicals—Tony Campolo, Sharon Gallagher, John Perkins, Ron Sider, and Jim Wallis among them—as well as a handful of influential older leaders, including Carl Henry himself, this workshop produced a historic declaration clearly condemning racism, sexism, militarism, civil religion, materialism, and economic injustice. This statement marked a major turning point in evangelical social thought by placing specific emphasis on structural and institutional injustice, not just individual sin.[31] Results of the Thanksgiving Workshop also included the formation of Evangelicals for Social Action, organized to implement the vision of the Chicago Declaration, along with numerous other ministries focused on issues of social justice and racial reconciliation. Though this cadre of progressive evangelicals would remain a minority within the larger evangelical movement, they maintained a consistent prophetic counterbalance to the Christian Right, and continued to make their presence known within evangelical institutions over the next several decades.

Integral Mission Theology

At the same time that younger evangelicals in the United States were moving toward more progressive politics, evangelicals in the Two-Thirds World, and especially Latin America, began developing a theology to promote a holistic vision of the church's mission, what they called *misión integral*, arguing that both personal evangelism and socio-political involvement on behalf of the poor and oppressed were equally central to the Christian gospel. These global evangelicals provided the young progressive evangelicals in the United States with a theology to undergird and express their shared concerns. More importantly, they opened space within the worldwide evangelical movement for such concerns to enter the mainstream dialogue.

Integral mission theology originated in the late 1960s among Latin American theologians in response to what they perceived as the excessive influence of North American evangelicals over Christianity in their

---

31. Sider, *The Chicago Declaration*, 1–2.

region.³² They created the *Fraternidad Teológica Latinoamericana* (FTL) to develop and promote an integral theology of mission which would relate their evangelical understanding of the gospel and the mission of the church to the Latin American experience of extreme poverty, political oppression, and widespread despair. By so doing they deliberately sought to move beyond the individualistic and otherworldly emphasis inherited from North American fundamentalist missionaries—one that promised extra-worldly spiritual rewards beyond this life of suffering rather than political, social, or economic justice in the present world.³³ Their alternative emphasized a holistic and kingdom-centered Christology. Integral mission, FTL cofounder René Padilla wrote, is "the concrete expression of a commitment to Jesus Christ as Lord of the totality of life and of all creation."³⁴ Because Jesus is Lord over *all* of creation and *all* spheres of life, they argued, there is no real distinction between serving "spiritual" needs and serving "physical" needs, thus the mission of the church cannot simply be reduced to making religious converts but must include action on behalf of the poor and in service of social justice.

Integral mission theology burst onto the worldwide evangelical scene at the International Congress on World Evangelization held in Lausanne, Switzerland in 1974 (Lausanne '74), and attended by nearly 2500 participants and 1000 observers from 150 countries and 135 Protestant denominations.³⁵ Though originally conceived as a challenge to the World Council of Churches' emphasis on social concerns rather than personal conversion,³⁶ the integral relationship between evangelism and social concerns quickly became a recurring and prominent theme at Lausanne, due in large part to provocative and widely discussed plenary addresses given by FTL-members Samuel Escobar and René Padilla.³⁷ Because of their influence, along with many other representatives from the Two-Thirds World, the final form of the Lausanne Covenant itself included not just one sentence on social concerns, as some of the more conservative conveners

---

32. Escobar, "Heredero de la Reforma Radical," in Padilla, ed., *Hacia Una Teología Latinoamericana*, 51–71.

33. Núñez and Taylor, *Crisis in Latin America*, 374–79.

34. Yamamori and Padilla, *Local Church*, 20.

35. "A Challenge from Evangelicals," *Time*.

36. "Do We Really Need Lausanne?," 36–37.

37. Gill, "Christian Social Responsibility," in Padilla, ed., *The New Face of Evangelicalism*, 90–91.

had originally intended, but an entire section on "Christian Social Responsibility," which affirmed that "evangelism and socio-political involvement are both part of our Christian duty . . . the salvation we claim should be transforming us in the totality of our personal and social responsibilities."[38] While such a statement was less radical than what some had hoped for, it was nevertheless seen by many as indicative of a new direction for the evangelical movement.[39]

Subsequent years saw the proliferation of integral mission ideas throughout the evangelical world, aiding the development of progressive evangelicalism in the United States by legitimating engagement in social ministries and progressive political activism within the broader evangelical movement. With major evangelical leaders like Billy Graham and John Stott lending their stamp of approval to the Lausanne statement on Christian Social Responsibility, such concepts entered the mainstream evangelical dialogue and became acceptable theological possibilities for both Two-Thirds World Christians and North American evangelicals as well.

The Emerging Church and the Reemergence of Evangelical Progressivism

Despite this mainstream acceptance, the meteoric rise of the New Christian Right during the 1980s and 90s overshadowed progressive social concerns among evangelicals in the United States.[40] These politically conservative evangelicals focused primarily on issues of sexual morality and religious freedom, typically seeing progressive concerns—poverty, militarism, gender and racial equality, ecology, etc.—as part of a "liberal agenda" that in their view was to blame for the moral and spiritual decline of American society. Their organizing prowess proved wildly effective among a majority of evangelicals, such that by the late 1990s progressive evangelical leaders were lamenting a perceived disconnect between more moderate, socially concerned mission organizations and colleges, and the broader, more socially conservative "evangelical rank and file."[41]

What pessimistic progressive leaders failed to see was that their own presence within evangelical colleges and mission organizations was already

---

38. "The Lausanne Covenant," in Douglas, ed., *Let the Earth Hear His Voice*, 4–5.
39. Scherer, *Gospel, Church, and Kingdom*, 173; Van Engen, *Mission on the Way*, 136.
40. Schäfer, *Countercultural Conservatives*, 114–21; Swartz, *Moral Minority*, 233–34.
41. Sine, *Mustard Seed versus McWorld*, 132–33.

helping to produce a new generation of evangelicals who would bring their set of social concerns back to the forefront. Leaders from the first generation of progressive evangelicalism continued to speak regularly at Christian colleges and youth rallies throughout the closing decades of the twentieth century. They continued to teach at prominent evangelical colleges and seminaries—places like Eastern College in Philadelphia, Wheaton College in Illinois, and Fuller Seminary in Pasadena, among many others. And many went on to lead campus ministries and mission organizations where they continued to introduce students to the realities of global poverty and social injustice through short term mission experiences. The theological and institutional groundwork laid by this earlier generation thus provided younger evangelicals at the turn of the millennium easier access to a well-developed theology and practice of integral mission and progressive politics. This in turn helped produce a resurgence of progressive social concerns among evangelicals in the first decade of the twenty-first century—a fact easily seen both in the slew of books and articles documenting the phenomenon,[42] as well as the steady stream of official statements by mainstream evangelical leaders urging their followers to embrace a wider range of social concerns.[43]

Though the Emerging Church conversation in the late 1990s centered more on innovative ministry methods for a changing culture than social justice or progressive politics, this would soon change. Conversation about contextualizing worship styles and ministry methods for a postmodern culture quickly moved into the deeper waters of postmodern epistemology, which led in turn to a broad theological re-evaluation of core evangelical doctrines. One key question was the nature of the gospel itself, and with the help of scholars like Dallas Willard, NT Wright, and John Howard Yoder,[44] many in the ECM soon came to emphasize the kingdom of God as lived reality in the present world, often over and against a gospel of merely per-

---

42. Gushee, *The Future of Faith*; Krattenmaker, *The Evangelicals You Don't Know*; Pally, *The New Evangelicals*; Pew Forum on Religion and Public Life, "Assessing a More Prominent 'Religious Left'"; Steensland and Goff, *The New Evangelical Social Engagement*.

43. See for instance the series of statements issued by the National Association of Evangelicals between 2005 and 2011: "For the Health of the Nation: An Evangelical Call to Civic Responsibility," "An Evangelical Declaration Against Torture," "Immigration," "Lowering the Debt, Raising the Poor." See also the 2008 statement signed by over seventy prominent leaders, "An Evangelical Manifesto: A Declaration of Evangelical Identity and Public Commitment."

44. Willard, *The Divine Conspiracy*; Wright, *Jesus and the Victory of God*; Yoder, *The Politics of Jesus*.

sonal salvation to a post-mortem reward.[45] As they fleshed out the meaning of this "kingdom" reality, especially in the context of Jesus' first-century ministry within the Roman Empire, ECM participants frequently connected the counter-imperial message of the early church to potential political implications within their twenty-first-century American context. This discovery left the ECM open to the revival of progressive concerns among evangelicals and in turn to become some of its strongest exponents.[46] Indeed, the rise of the ECM and the reemergence of evangelical progressivism happened so simultaneously, and involved so many of the same personalities, that it is hard to draw clear lines of demarcation between the two trends.

The ECM's turn toward social justice, progressive politics, and a more integral understanding of mission and the kingdom of God was not mere coincidence, but was in fact directly influenced by the older generation of progressive evangelicals—people like Tony Campolo, John Perkins, Tom Sine, Jim Wallis, and others—with whom ECM leaders were in frequent conversation and partnership. Jim Wallis, founder of the progressive evangelical organization Sojourners, impacted the movement directly through his friendship with key ECM leaders like Brian McLaren and especially through his contributions to the 2004 Emergent Convention which Tony Jones recalls as having a "big effect" on the movement.[47] Wallis' bestselling 2005 book, *God's Politics: Why the Right Gets it Wrong and the Left Doesn't Get It*, made an enormous splash among those in the ECM whose newfound theology of the kingdom of God, a peaceable kingdom opposed to imperialistic violence, was seen to be at odds with the warlike policies of the Bush administration. Following the success of Wallis' book, ECM authors produced a flood of similar volumes encouraging the church toward practices of social justice and lifestyles of radical discipleship.[48] In recent years, major ongoing expressions of the ECM have defined themselves by this kind of social justice activism, including the TransFORM and Convergence Networks, as well as the annual Wild Goose Festival.

45. Gibbs and Bolger, *Emerging Churches*, 47–49.
46. McKnight, "Five Streams of the Emerging Church," 35.
47. Tony Jones, email to the author, 10 November 2011.
48. See, for instance: Claiborne, *Irresistible Revolution* (2006); Samson and Samson, *Justice in the Burbs* (2007); McLaren, *Everything Must Change* (2007); Claiborne and Haw, *Jesus for President* (2008); Barker, *Make Poverty Personal* (2009); Clawson, *Everyday Justice* (2009); McLaren, Padilla, and Seeber, eds., *The Justice Project* (2009); Salvatierra and Heltzel, *Faith-Rooted Organizing* (2014).

Campolo too, through his position as a professor of sociology at Eastern University, had a strong influence on the pioneers of the "new monastic" branch of the ECM, a movement of intentional residential communities among the urban poor, many of whom leaders studied with Campolo at Eastern.[49] Many of these neo-monastic communities also soon connected themselves to the racial reconciliation work of John Perkins and his Christian Community Development Association (CCDA), providing yet another link between earlier and newer generations of progressive evangelicals.

The progressive political turn of the ECM also was shaped by direct exposure to the integral mission theology of the Latin American Theological Fellowship (FTL). This first occurred through a series of small annual gatherings for Emerging leaders known as La Mesa. Beginning in the early 2000s, these were convened in the Bahamas by Clint Kemp of New Providence Community Church in Nassau, to bring together key ECM leaders from the United States. They were joined by Latin American church leaders who had already begun organizing their own network, *La Red del Camino para La Misión Integral en America Latina*, to promote the practice of integral mission in their contexts.[50] At these gatherings many prominent ECM leaders first became aware of the pioneering theological work done by Latin American evangelicals before them.[51]

Brian McLaren, arguably the single most influential leader within the ECM, provided another route through which the movement was introduced to Latin American integral mission theology. McLaren first became aware of integral mission ideas in the 1970s through reports on the Lausanne gathering, and describes the contemporary ECM as, in part, a fulfillment of that earlier vision.[52] McLaren also became personally acquainted with the Padilla family when René's daughter Elisa attended his church in Maryland from 2002–2004.[53] She challenged him to address issues of economic justice more substantially and eventually introduced McLaren to her father. The elder Padilla invited McLaren to travel with him in Latin America for several months in 2005 and 2006, mentoring him in Latin American theology

49. Claiborne, *Irresistible Revolution*, 117–26.
50. La Red del Camino, "What is the Del Camino Network?"
51. Tom and Dee Yaccino, interview with the author, June 20, 2014; Darin Peterson, interview with the author, September 26, 2015.
52. McLaren, et al., *The Justice Project*, 14.
53. Brian McLaren, email to the author, 2 May 2010 and 15 November 2011. Most of the other personal details in this paragraph were also communicated through these correspondences.

and also introducing him to leaders of *La Red del Camino*. According to McLaren, these connections have been highly significant to the development of his thought and writing since at least the publication of his most thorough work on social justice and integral mission to date, *Everything Must Change: Jesus, Global Crises, and a Revolution of Hope*, which he completed while traveling with Padilla in Latin America.[54] Through McLaren's books and numerous speaking engagements, these ideas have been put in wide circulation throughout the North American ECM, establishing the ECM as a direct, North American descendant of both the Latin American theology of the 1970s and the progressive evangelicalism which it inspired and informed.[55]

The Evolving Movement

Each of these three earlier streams –new paradigm churches, missional ecclesiology, and progressive evangelicalism—coalesced in the late-1990s and early 2000s through Christian leaders and laypersons as they were catalyzed by the ideas of postmodernity to produce what became the Emerging Church Movement in North America. The most visible (though not exclusive) early expression of the North American ECM was the Young Leaders Network (YLN) created by Leadership Network in the late-1990s to address the difficulty many churches were having in attracting rising the generations of Gen Xers and Millennials. Tension soon arose however as Leadership Network was primarily interested in furthering conversations strictly around practical ministry issues, while those involved with YLN had quickly turned to theological matters after identifying the cultural shift to postmodernity to be of greater significance than mere generational differences. By 2001, these leaders had separated from Leadership Network and reorganized as Emergent Village, a 501c3 which defined itself as "a growing, generative friendship among missional Christians seeking to love our world in the Spirit of Jesus Christ." Emergent Village saw itself as one hub of the Emerging Church conversation, and sought to serve the broader movement by convening national conferences and local cohorts, writing books in partnership with major evangelical publishing houses, and hosting online conversations through its website and member blogs. Even prior to

---

54. McLaren, "Family Letter From Latin America."

55. Jones, *New Christians*, 49–51; McLaren, "Emergent Past and Future"; McLaren, "Everything Must Change Tour 2008."

these developments, however, robust conversation around postmodernity and Emerging ministry had begun taking place at numerous online blogs and several popular message boards, especially theOoze.com, a heavily trafficked site founded by Spencer Burke in 1998, and Next-Wave, an e-zine founded by Charlie Wear in 1999. These kind of online portals provided an entry point for thousands more lay people to enter into the discussion about the changing shape of Christianity in a postmodern world.

From 2001–2005 the ECM gained increasing momentum and visibility within North American evangelicalism. Brian McLaren's *A New Kind of Christian*, published in 2001, articulated well the kind of deconstructive questions Emergent leaders were asking about evangelical theology and approaches to church ministry, soon becoming a touch point for many disillusioned evangelicals who had been wondering if they were the only ones out there with such thoughts. The book would go on to sell well over one hundred thousand copies and point many to the ECM as a safe community in which to converse about these topics.[56] A plethora of books by ECM leaders in subsequent years would bring even more attention to the movement.

At the same time, Emergent Village was becoming increasingly more visible thanks to a strategic partnership with Youth Specialties, an evangelical parachurch organization for equipping youth ministers. This partnership led to an explosion of ECM-related books through the *emergentYS* line with Zondervan, one of the largest evangelical publishing houses. It also allowed for a national Emergent Convention, held bi-annually for three years (from 2003–2005) in conjunction with the National Pastor's Convention, regularly attended by thousands of evangelical pastors who were perhaps introduced to the ECM for the first time through this event. Likewise, Youth Specialties repeatedly invited ECM leaders to speak at its annual National Youth Worker Conventions from the late-1990s onward, introducing their ideas to thousands of evangelical youth ministers. In addition, Emergent Village had already been hosting smaller gatherings, including semi-annual theological conversations with highly influential contemporary theologians, as well as the unstructured Glorieta Gatherings outside of Santa Fe, New Mexico, convening from 2001–2007 and again in 2011. Apart from Emergent Village, Spencer Burke had also been hosting annual "Soularize" learning parties with theologians and innovative practitioners from 2000–2007 (with a final reunion in 2011). Smaller local or regional

---

56. Jones, *The New Christians*, 51.

gatherings—ministry associations, denominational meetings, seminary lectures, etc.—also frequently hosted ECM speakers during these years. This ECM presence at church events both large and small did much to raise awareness of the movement among mainstream evangelicals and beyond. By November 2004 the Emerging Movement was the feature cover article for both *Christianity Today* and *The Christian Century* magazines, flagship publications of evangelical and liberal mainline Protestantism respectively, and in February 2005 *TIME* magazine recognized Brian McLaren as one of "The 25 Most Influential Evangelicals in America."[57]

Increased notoriety naturally brought greater scrutiny, leading to a period of growing criticism of the ECM within evangelical circles, commencing in 2005 with the publication of D.A. Carson's *Becoming Conversant with the Emerging Church* and soon followed by many others.[58] In response to these critiques, some of the more theologically conservative within the ECM began making a distinction between the terms "emerging" and "emergent," identifying the former with those like themselves who primarily wished to reimagine ministry methods, forms of worship, or church structures while leaving evangelical theology intact. "Emergent," on the other hand, was used to designate the more theologically experimental elements within the ECM.[59] As attacks multiplied, it became increasingly costly for many within evangelical institutions to identify with either label. It was not uncommon to find ECM leaders disinvited from speaking engagements, and for ministers to face discipline, loss of funding, or even termination for their involvement with the movement. Evangelical publishers discovered that marketing new books as "emerging/emergent" was counterproductive and gradually phased out such imprints. Arguments also arose from those within the movement over a host of (sometimes contradictory) issues, provoking many heated online conversations over the nature, inclusivity, and direction of the movement.[60] And many found they

---

57. Crouch, "The Emergent Mystique," 36–41; Bader-Saye, "The Emergent Matrix," 20–31.

58. For example, Smith, *Truth and the New Kind of Christian* in 2005; MacArthur, *The Truth War* in 2007; DeYoung and Kluck, *Why We're Not Emergent* in 2008; Belcher, *Deep Church* in 2009; Henard and Greenway, *Evangelicals Engaging Emergent* in 2009.

59. Devine, "The Emerging Church: One Movement—Two Streams," in Henard and Greenway, eds., *Evangelicals Engaging Emergent*, 4–46; Driscoll, *Confessions*, 21–23; Dunbar, "Missional, Emerging, Emergent"; Kimball, "Origins of the terms 'Emerging' and 'Emergent' church—Part 2"; McKnight, "Emerging and Emergent."

60. Jones, "Death of Emergent Round-Up."

PART 1: DEFINING BOUNDARIES

were simply spending too much time defining and defending the terminology rather than getting on with the work it was supposed to describe. This period of both external and internal critique reached its zenith between 2008 and 2010 when several prominent participants publically distanced themselves from the movement[61] and some critics (and a few insiders) began declaring the "death of the Emerging Church."[62] Subsequent controversies over Brian McLaren's *A New Kind of Christianity* (2010), in which he took a more definitive stance on several controversial topics, and Rob Bell's *Love Wins* (2011) which called into question traditional evangelical notions about Hell, led even more to declare the movement outside the bounds of evangelicalism.[63]

This rejection by the gatekeepers of evangelicalism, and widespread discord within the movement itself produced several results. First, the ECM began gaining traction beyond evangelical circles, and especially within progressive mainline denominations, as post-evangelical Emerging Christians sought more hospitable institutional environments for their theological explorations, and stagnant mainline churches sought the kind of missional energy and innovative spirit intrinsic to the Emerging Movement. Though mainline clergy had been involved with the ECM from the earliest days, these connections multiplied from around 2007 onward with the rise of numerous "hyphenated" groups—Presbymergent, Anglimergent, Luthermergent, Baptimergent, etc.—seeking to merge an emergent ethos with ongoing commitment to their mainline denominational heritage.[64]

Another result was increased fracturing of the ECM into various subgroups. As with many reform movements, once the initial unity around a perceived need for change faded, participants in the ECM found that they often differed on both their diagnoses of the problem and their proposed solutions. While the ECM had always been a "network of networks," with

---

61. See, for instance, Bouma, "Goodbye Emergent: Why I'm Taking the Theology of the Emerging Church to Task"; Claiborne, "The Emerging Church Brand"; Clark, "Beyond the Emerging Church?"; Hyatt, "Look Who's Done with Words Like 'Emergent'?"; Jones, "Emerging Church: You Say Dump It"; Jones, "Goodbyes to Emergent Village"; Toderash, "A New Kind of Conversation: Why I Might Be Neo-Emergent."

62. Bradley, "Farewell Emerging Church: 1989–2010"; Jones, "Emerging Church Movement (1989–2009)?"; Scaramanga, "R.I.P. Emerging Church"; Smith, "The End of the Emergent Movement?"

63. Bailey, "Rob Bell's Upcoming Book"; Galli, "Review: Rob Bell's Bridge Too Far"; McKnight, "Review: Brian McLaren's 'A New Kind of Christianity.'"

64. Snider, *The Hyphenateds*, xiii–xvii.

the growing fragmentation and dissatisfaction by many with Emergent Village's previously assumed role as a "hub" of sorts for the movement, new groups emerged to focus more deliberately on whichever issues they felt were most important for the ongoing movement. Those with more evangelical leanings formed networks like the Origins/ReGeneration Project, Ecclesia, and Missio Alliance to emphasize evangelism, mission, and church planting within a postmodern culture.[65] Those on the more theologically and politically progressive end of the spectrum, groups like Transform and ConvergenceUS, organized to equip, multiply, and organize Christian communities around social justice and collective liberation.[66] Somewhere in between these stood the New Monastic movement, which had existed as one stream within the broader ECM (though not always claiming that identity) since the late 1990s, and continues to inspire conversations about social justice and intentional community formation within both evangelical and progressive circles. Other more focused initiatives, events, and networks with an Emerging-ethos and organized by those within the ECM, have also continued to pop-up, from the short-lived Outlaw Preachers collective, to the long-running Homebrewed Christianity podcast, to Pete Rollins' radically iconoclastic Pyrotheology project, among many others. Perhaps the most vibrant expression of the ECM in recent years has been the Wild Goose Festival, which has met annually in North Carolina since 2011. Attended by thousands of evangelical, mainline, and unaffiliated Christians, the Wild Goose represents a convergence of many of these streams for ongoing conversations about faith, justice, spirituality, and art.

Few of these new groups bother to label themselves "emerging" or "emergent" anymore, most finding these terms to be too highly contested and carrying too much prior baggage. Indeed, even Emergent Village had discontinued its 501c3 status and shut down its website by 2014. Nevertheless, each of these groups still continue to exhibit the ECM's central concern to explore new ways forward for the church in a postmodern world, and each continue to extend various aspects of that exploration. Thus, perhaps ironically, even as fewer and fewer care to self-identify as "emerging" or "emergent," the movement itself continues to be more prolific than ever. Indeed, many of its ideals—innovative liturgical expressions, reclamation of ancient spiritual practices, new forms of church community, missional

---

65. http://www.regenerationproject.org/; http://ecclesianet.org/; http://www.missio-alliance.org/.

66. http://transformnetwork.org/; http://www.convergenceus.org/.

PART 1: DEFINING BOUNDARIES

theology and practice, and an emphasis on social justice, for instance—have now become widely accepted and implemented within existing churches and denominations, both evangelical and mainline. It can thus be argued that the decreased visibility of explicitly "Emerging" churches in recent years is due in large part to the ECM successfully achieving its goal of transforming existing churches while also maintaining ongoing conversation for further transformation.

Bibliography

"The 25 Most Influential Evangelicals in America." *Time*, 7 February 2005.
"A Challenge from Evangelicals." *Time*, 5 August 1974.
Bader-Saye, Scott. "The Emergent Matrix." *Christian Century*, 30 November 2004, 20–31.
Bailey, Sarah Pulliam. "Rob Bell's Upcoming Book on Heaven and Hell Stirs Blog, Twitter Backlash on Universalism." *Christianity Today* (website), 26 February 2011. http://www.christianitytoday.com/gleanings/2011/february/rob-bells-upcoming-book-on-heaven-hell-stirs-blog-twitter.html.
Barker, Ash. *Make Poverty Personal: Taking the Poor as Seriously as the Bible Does*. Grand Rapids: Baker, 2009.
Belcher, Jim. *Deep Church: A Third Way beyond Emerging and Traditional*. Downers Grove, IL: InterVarsity, 2009.
Bell, Rob. *Love Wins: A Book About Heaven, Hell, and the Fate of Every Person Who Ever Lived*. New York: Harper, 2011.
Bergler, Thomas E. *The Juvenilization of American Christianity*. Grand Rapids: Eerdmans, 2012.
Bielo, James. *Emerging Evangelicals: Faith, Modernity, and the Desire for Authenticity*. New York: New York University Press, 2011.
Bosch, David J. *Transforming Mission: Paradigm Shifts in Theology of Mission*. 20th Anniv. Ed. Maryknoll, NY: Orbis, 2011.
Bouma, Jeremy. "Goodbye Emergent: Why I'm Taking the Theology of the Emerging Church to Task." *vintage faith made relevant* (blog), 8 February 2010. http://www.jeremybouma.com/goodbye-emergent-why-im-taking-the-theology-of-the-emerging-church-to-task/.
Bradley, Anthony. "Farewell Emerging Church: 1989–2010." *World Magazine* (website), 14 April 2010. http://www.worldmag.com/2010/04/farewell_emerging_church_1989_2010.
Carson, D. A. *Becoming Conversant with the Emerging Church: Understanding a Movement and Its Implications*. Grand Rapids: Zondervan, 2005.
Claiborne, Shane. *The Irresistible Revolution: Living As An Ordinary Radical*. Grand Rapids: Zondervan, 2006.
Claiborne, Shane. "The Emerging Church Brand: The Good, the Bad, and the Messy." *The Simple Way* (website), 13 April 2010. http://www.thesimpleway.org/index.php/resources/ content/the-emerging-church-brand-the-good-the-bad-and-the-messy.
Claiborne, Shane, and Chris Haw. *Jesus for President*. Grand Rapids: Zondervan, 2008.

Clark, Jason. "Beyond the emerging church?" *Jason Clark* (blog), 24 September 2008. http://www.jasonclark.ws/2008/09/beyond-the-emerging-church/.

Clawson, Julie. *Everyday Justice: The Global Impact of Our Daily Choices.* Downers Grove, IL: InterVarsity, 2009.

Crouch, Andy. "The Emergent Mystique." *Christianity Today,* November 2004, 36–41.

DeYoung, Kevin, and Ted Kluck. *Why We're Not Emergent (By Two Guys Who Should Be).* Chicago: Moody, 2008.

Di Sabatino, David. *The Jesus People Movement: An Annotated Bibliography and General Resource.* Westport, CT: Greenwood, 1999.

"Do We Really Need Lausanne?" *Christianity Today,* 15 March 1974, 36–37.

Douglas, J. D., ed. *Let the Earth Hear His Voice: International Congress on World Evangelization Lausanne, Switzerland.* Minneapolis: World Wide, 1975.

Driscoll, Mark. *Confessions of a Reformission Rev: Hard Lessons from an Emerging Missional Church.* Grand Rapids: Zondervan, 2006.

Dunbar, David G. "Missional, Emerging, Emergent: A Traveler's Guide." *Missional Journal* 2, nos. 4–5 (2008). https://www.biblical.edu/images/stories/missional-journal/missional-journal-2-4.pdf. Accessed July 27, 2016.

Ellwood, Robert S. *One Way: The Jesus Movement and Its Meaning.* Englewood Cliffs, NJ: Prentice-Hall, 1973.

Eshelman, Paul. *The Explo Story: A Plan to Change the World.* Glendale, CA: G/L, 1972.

Eskridge, Larry. *God's Forever Family: The Jesus People Movement in America.* Oxford: Oxford University Press, 2013.

Flory, Richard, and Donald E. Miller. *Finding Faith: The Spiritual Quest of the Post-Boomer Generation.* New Brunswick, NJ: Rutgers University Press, 2008.

Frost, Michael, and Alan Hirsch. *The Shaping of Things to Come: Innovation and Mission for the 21st Century Church.* Peabody, MA: Hendrickson, 2003.

Galli, Mark. "Book Review: Rob Bell's Bridge Too Far." *Christianity Today,* April 2011.

Gibbs, Eddie, and Ryan Bolger. *Emerging Churches: Creating Christian Communities in Postmodern Cultures.* Grand Rapids: Baker, 2005.

Graham, Billy. "A Clarification." *Christianity Today,* January 19, 1973, 416.

Guder, Darrell L., ed. *Missional Church: A Vision for the Sending of the Church in North America.* Grand Rapids: Eerdmans, 1998.

Gushee, David. *The Future of Faith in American Politics: The Public Witness of the Evangelical Center.* Waco, TX: Baylor University Press, 2008.

Hargrove, Barbara. *Religion for a Dislocated Generation.* Valley Forge, PA: Judson, 1980.

Henard, William D., and Adam W. Greenway, eds. *Evangelicals Engaging Emergent: A Discussion of the Emergent Church Movement.* Nashville: BandH, 2009.

Henry, Carl F. H. *The Uneasy Conscience of Modern Fundamentalism.* Grand Rapids: Eerdmans, 1947.

Hyatt, Bob. "Look Who's Done with Words Like 'Emergent' . . . " *bob.blog* (blog), 1 September 2008. http://bobhyatt.typepad.com/bobblog/2008/09/my-entry.html.

Jones, Andrew. "Emerging Church: You Say Dump It." *Tallskinnykiwi* (blog), 2 September 2008. http://tallskinnykiwi.typepad.com/tallskinnykiwi/2008/09/emerging-chur-1.html.

———. "Emerging Church Movement (1989–2009)?" *Tallskinnykiwi* (blog), 30 December 2009. http://tallskinnykiwi.com/2009/12/emerging-church-movement-1989-2009/.

———. "Goodbyes to Emergent Village." *Tallskinnykiwi* (blog), 7 January 2010. http://tallskinnykiwi.com/2010/01/goodbyes-to-emergent-village/.

PART 1: DEFINING BOUNDARIES

Jones, Tony. *The Church Is Flat: The Relational Ecclesiology of the Emerging Church Movement*. Minneapolis: JoPa, 2011.

———. "Death of Emergent Round-Up." *Theoblogy*, 7 June 2009. http://www.patheos.com/blogs/tonyjones/2009/06/07/death-of-emergent-round-up/.

———. *The New Christians: Dispatches from the Emergent Frontier*. San Francisco: Jossey-Bass, 2008.

———. *Postmodern Youth Ministry*. Grand Rapids: Zondervan, 2001.

Kennedy, Courtney, and Michael Dimock. "Bush's Troubles Shake the GOP Base." *Pew Research Center Publications*, June 6, 2006. http://pewresearch.org/pubs/226/bushs-troubles-shake-the-gop-base.

Kimball, Dan. *The Emerging Church: Vintage Christianity for New Generations*. Grand Rapids: Zondervan, 2003.

———. "Origins of the Terms 'Emerging' and 'Emergent' Church—Part 2." *Dan Kimball: Vintage Faith* (blog), 21 April 2006. https://web.archive.org/web/20140819172100/http://dankimball.typepad.com/vintage_faith/2006/04/origins_of_the_.html.

Krattenmaker, Tom. *The Evangelicals You Don't Know: Introducing the Next Generation of Christians*. New York: Rowman and Littlefield, 2013.

La Red del Camino. "What is the Del Camino Network?" *Red del Camino* website. http://lareddelcamino.net/en/images/Articles/what%20is%20the%20del%20camino%20network_.pdf.

Lee, Shayne, and Phillip Luke Sinitiere. *Holy Mavericks: Evangelical Innovators and the Spiritual Marketplace*. New York: New York University Press, 2009.

Long, Jimmy. *Generating Hope: A Strategy for Reaching the Postmodern Generation*. Downers Grove, IL: InterVarsity, 1997.

MacArthur, John. *The Truth War: Fighting for Certainty in an Age of Deception*. Nashville: Nelson, 2007.

Marti, Gerardo, and Gladys Ganiel. *The Deconstructed Church: Understanding Emerging Christianity*. Oxford: Oxford University Press, 2014.

McKnight, Scot. "Emerging and Emergent: Our New Network." *Jesus Creed* (blog), 24 September 2008. http://www.patheos.com/community/jesuscreed/2008/09/24/emerging-and-emergent-our-new-network/.

———. "Five Streams of the Emerging Church." *Christianity Today*, February 2007, 35.

———. "Review: Brian McLaren's 'A New Kind of Christianity.'" *Christianity Today*, March 2010.

McLaren, Brian D. *The Church on the other Side: Doing Ministry in the Postmodern Matrix*. Grand Rapids: Zondervan, 1998.

———. "Emergent Past and Future." Seminar session, Emergent Convention, Nashville, TN, May 2005. Audio CD.

———. *Everything Must Change: Jesus, Global Crises, and a Revolution of Hope*. Nashville: Nelson, 2007.

———. "Everything Must Change Tour 2008." *Brian McLaren* (website). http://www.brianmclaren.net/archives/schedule/everything-must/.

———. "Family Letter from Latin America." *Brian McLaren* (website). http://brianmclaren.net/archives/resources-archive/family letter-from-latin-america.html.

———. *A New Kind of Christian: A Tale of Two Friends on a Spiritual Journey*. San Francisco: Jossey-Bass, 2001.

———. *A New Kind of Christianity: Ten Questions That Are Transforming the Faith*. New York: Harper, 2010.

McLaren, Brian, et al., eds. *The Justice Project*. Grand Rapids: Baker, 2009.
Miller, Donald E. *Reinventing American Protestantism: Christianity in the New Millennium*. Los Angeles: University of California Press, 1997.
Moberg, David O. *Inasmuch: Christian Social Responsibility in the Twentieth Century*. Grand Rapids: Eerdmans, 1965.
Núñez, Emilio A., and William D. Taylor. *Crisis in Latin America: An Evangelical Perspective*. Chicago: Moody, 1989.
Packard, Josh. *The Emerging Church: Religion at the Margins*. Boulder, CO: First Forum, 2012.
Padilla, C. René, ed. *Hacia Una Teología Latinoamericana: Ensayos en Honor a Peter Savage*. San José, Costa Rica: Caribe, 1984.
———. *The New Face of Evangelicalism: A International Symposium on the Lausanne Covenant*. Downers Grove, IL: InterVarsity, 1976.
Pahl, Jon. *Youth Ministry in Modern America: 1930 to the Present*. Peabody, MA: Hendrickson, 2000.
Pally, Marcia. *The New Evangelicals: Expanding the Vision of the Common Good*. Grand Rapids: Eerdmans, 2011.
Pederson, Duane. "Jesus Is Better than Hash." *Hollywood Free Paper* 3, no. 7 (1971) 1.
Pew Forum on Religion and Public Life. "Assessing a More Prominent 'Religious Left.'" 5 June 2008. http://pewforum.org/Politics-and-Elections/Assessing-a-More-Prominent-Religious-Left.aspx.
Plowman, Edward E. "Whatever Happened to the Jesus Movement?" *Christianity Today*, October 24, 1975, 46–48.
Rabey, Steve. *In Search of Authentic Faith: How Emerging Generations are Transforming the Church*. Colorado Springs: Waterbrook, 2001.
Roxburgh, Alan, and M. Scott Boren. *Introducing the Missional Church: What It Is, Why It Matters, How to Become One*. Grand Rapids: Baker 2009.
Rutba House, The, ed. *School(s) for Conversion: 12 Marks of a New Monasticism*. Eugene, OR: Wipf and Stock, 2005.
Salvatierra, Alexia, and Peter Heltzel. *Faith-Rooted Organizing: Mobilizing the Church in Service to the World*. Downers Grove, IL: InterVarsity, 2014.
Samson, Will, and Lisa Samson. *Justice in the Burbs: Being the Hands of Jesus Wherever You Live*. Grand Rapids: Baker, 2007.
Scaramanga, Url. "R.I.P. Emerging Church." *Leadership Journal* (blog), 19 September 2008. http://www.christianitytoday.com/le/2008/september-online-only/rip-emerging-church.html.
Schäfer, Axel R. *Countercultural Conservatives: American Evangelicalism from the Postwar Revival to the New Christian Right*. Madison: University of Wisconsin Press, 2011.
Scherer, James A. *Gospel, Church, and Kingdom: Comparative Studies in World Mission Theology*. Minneapolis: Augsburg, 1987.
Sherrill, Rowland A., ed. *Religion and the Life of the Nation: American Recoveries*. Urbana: University of Illinois Press, 1990.
Sider, Ronald J. *The Chicago Declaration*. Carol Stream, IL: Creation House, 1974.
Sine, Tom. *Mustard Seed versus McWorld: Reinventing Life and Faith for the Future*. Grand Rapids: Baker, 1999.
Smith, Adam. "The End of the Emergent Movement?" *Neue Magazine*, April 2010. http://www.relevantmagazine.com/god/church/features/21181-the-end-of-emergent.

Smith, R. Scott. *Truth and the New Kind of Christian: The Emerging Effects of Postmodernism in the Church*. Wheaton, IL: Crossway, 2005.

Snider, Phil, ed. *The Hyphenateds: How Emergence Christianity Is Re-Traditioning Mainline Practices*. St. Louis: Chalice, 2011.

Steensland, Brian, and Philip Goff, eds. *The New Evangelical Social Engagement*. Oxford: Oxford University Press, 2014.

Streiker, Lowell D. *The Jesus Trip: Advent of the Jesus Freaks*. Nashville: Abingdon, 1971.

Swartz, David R. *Moral Minority: The Evangelical Left in an Age of Conservatism*. Philadelphia: University of Pennsylvania Press, 2012.

Tickle, Phyllis. *Emergence Christianity: What It Is, Where It Is Going, and Why It Matters*. Grand Rapids: Baker, 2012.

———. *The Great Emergence: How Christianity Is Changing and Why*. Grand Rapids: Baker, 2008.

Toderash, Brent. "A New Kind of Conversation: Why I Might be Neo-Emergent." *Subversive Influence* (blog), 16 February 2010. http://subversiveinfluence.com/2010/02/a-new-kind-of-conversation-why-i-might-be-neo-emergent/.

Van Engen, Charles. *Mission on the Way: Issues in Mission Theology*. Grand Rapids: Baker, 1996.

Van Gelder, Craig, and Dwight J. Zscheile. *The Missional Church in Perspective: Mapping Trends and Shaping the Conversation*. Grand Rapids: Baker, 2011.

Wallis, Jim. *God's Politics: Why the Right Gets It Wrong and the Left Doesn't Get It*. San Francisco: HarperCollins, 2005.

———. *The Great Awakening: Reviving Faith and Politics in a Post-Religious Right America*. New York: HarperCollins, 2008.

Willard, Dallas. *The Divine Conspiracy: Rediscovering Our Hidden Life in God*. San Francisco: HarperCollins, 1997.

Wilson-Hartgrove, Jonathan. *New Monasticism: What It Has to Say to Today's Church*. Grand Rapids: Brazos, 2008.

Wright, N. T. *Jesus and the Victory of God*. Vol. 2 of *Christian Origins and the Question of God*. Minneapolis: Fortress, 1996.

Yamamori, Tetsunao, and C. René Padilla, eds. *The Local Church, Agent of Transformation: An Ecclesiology for Integral Mission*. Buenos Aires: Kairós, 2004.

Yoder, John Howard. *The Politics of Jesus*. 2nd ed. Grand Rapids: Eerdmans, 1994.

2

Emerging Christianity through a Social Scientific Lens: The ECM as a Case of Religious Institutional Entrepreneurship

Gerardo Martí

When it comes to the Emerging Church Movement (i.e., the ECM), social scientists are not interested in theological disputes or intra-Christian dialogues, nor are they caught up in debates about Emerging Christians as evangelicals-in-disguise, liberal Protestants, religious consumers, or simply "heretical." Instead, social scientists note that Emerging Christians' religious orientations and practices situate them squarely within the modern/postmodern social landscape. The ECM's practices of "flat" leadership, communication, and dissemination of ideas echo the experience of "networking" that most of us already experience in everyday realms of work and leisure. More importantly, ECM churches, gatherings, and "meet ups" provide settings where pluralism is embraced and an otherwise isolated "self" finds meaning and fulfillment in relationship with others (what has been characterized as "cooperative egoism").[1] While this chapter cannot pursue the fullness of ECM dynamics, it does highlight that such complex processes do not occur on their own. The ECM is a product of uniquely purposeful activity by highly inventive people who create liturgical spaces and routines for the renegotiation of their religious lives. Variety and fluidity are characteristic of the movement—yet what makes the ECM different from the many other heterogeneous branches of contemporary Christianity is that all this variety and fluidity consists of a highly intentional effort to

---

1. Marti and Ganiel, *The Deconstructed Church*.

craft religious structures that legitimate new and uniquely contemporary religious practices.

In *The Deconstructed Church: Understanding Emerging Christianity*, Gladys Ganiel and I highlight the ongoing micro-politics of challenge and confrontation found among ECM groups. Our large-scale and cross-national analysis led us to define Emerging Christianity as a religious orientation built on the continual practice of deconstruction. This "deconstructing" is not merely a negative or critical exercise but consists of an ongoing preparing toward a fundamental rebuilding. Emerging Christians are renegotiating standard forms of Christianity, fighting against what they see as the dangers of conventional Christianity while simultaneously generating opportunities to change it. Emerging Christians react primarily against conservative/evangelical/fundamentalist Protestantism, but also against other forms of "traditional," "established," or "mainstream" Christianity experienced as spiritually stifling and inauthentic. As Emerging Christians push away from certain established forms, they simultaneously and proactively appropriate practices from a wide range of Christian traditions to nourish spirituality and enhance their religious communities. More radically than mere adjustments or adaptations to social change,[2] Emerging Christians strive to create Christian communities that allow a religious autonomy where freedom of individual belief and religious conviction reign. Using a social scientific perspective, these dynamics of the Emerging Church Movement can be productively examined using a conceptual lens arising from a surge of research on *institutional entrepreneurship*.[3]

In approaching the ECM, social scientists like myself readily affirm that we strive to grasp a set of groups that resist definition.[4] Some who are affiliated with the ECM passionately and obsessively fight against being boxed into labels. The act of resisting definition is a fundamental dynamic of this religious group. Indeed, social scientists see that resisting definition in-and-of-itself is an important activity for the ECM because resistance to definition is an implicit strategy to create "breathing space" for creating new religious frameworks in the face of more public and powerful definitions of

---

2. See ethnographic studies of congregations in Marti, *A Mosaic of Believers*; Marti, *Hollywood Faith*; and Marti, *Worship across the Racial Divide*.

3. Hardy and Maguire, "Institutional Entrepreneurship," 198–217.

4. See Bielo, *Emerging Evangelicals*; Marti and Ganiel, *The Deconstructed Church*; Packard, *The Emerging Church*.

Christianity. In short, resisting definition is part of their activity as *religious institutional entrepreneurs*.

My goal in this chapter is not to define the ECM but to conceptualize a set of core processes inherent to the movement. To understand the ECM is to see how its identities, beliefs, and activities are oriented around changing broad institutional structures associated with Christianity, specifically reframing institutional logics and practices. By drawing on the concept of *institutional entrepreneurship*, I emphasize the innovative, creative, and experimental actions of the ECM. Further, I offer a description of *religious institutional entrepreneurship* to provide conceptual handles for grasping the Emerging Church Movement. In highlighting the role of religious institutional entrepreneurs, I do not mean to emphasize the enterprising work of isolated individuals; instead, the activity among ECM groups indicates the presence of *collective religious institutional entrepreneurship*. Ultimately, the ECM represents a broad base of religiously entrepreneurial activity operating in synchrony among larger networks of people.

Defining Institutional Entrepreneurship

Institutional entrepreneurs are actors (organizations and/or individuals) who desire to change institutional arrangements by mobilizing people and resources both to transform existing institutions and to create new ones.[5] As institutional entrepreneurs, Emerging Christians are embedded within *institutions* and engage in *entrepreneurship* in a quest for *legitimacy* for Emerging practices in the creation of new *organizational forms*. Each term used here is meaningful and understood as sociological (rather than "common sense") processes. To grasp the ECM through this perspective requires going over these terms in more detail.

Among sociologists, *an institution* is an observable pattern of collective action (i.e., sets of social practices).[6] The workings of institutions rely on culturally embedded understandings among actors such that institutions are firmly rooted in taken-for-granted rules, norms, and routines

---

5. Sotarauta and Pulkkinen, "Institutional Entrepreneurship for Knowledge Regions," 96–112. See also Battilana, "Agency and Institutions," 653–76; Battilana et al., "How Actors Change Institutions," 67.

6. Berger and Luckmann, *The Social Construction of Reality*; Scott, "The Adolescence of Institutional Theory," 493; Scott, "Conceptualizing Organizational Fields," 203–21.

that indicate appropriate actions and appropriate actors.[7] Institutions are not merely orderly but regulative because they govern social behavior; deviations from institutionalized practices activate social controls that make nonconformities costly.[8] The enforcement of conformity can be formal (legal sanctions) but are most often informal. Normative controls are more powerful in that they define what is appropriate or expected.[9] Institutions are therefore not run by individual people but by inherent principles or *institutional logics*, which are the organizing principles that provide guidelines for practice based on legitimacy and familiarity.[10]

Grasping the normative regulation of religious institutions is key to understanding the ECM. While some Emerging Christians say they are rebelling against their previous Christian traditions, in practice they remain dependent on playing against established structures for actualizing their "deconstructed" religious orientation. Norms include scripts for performance, and institutions are firmly rooted in taken-for-granted rules, norms, and routines that involve formal rule sets,[11] *ex ante* agreements,[12] less formal shared interaction sequences,[13] and taken-for-granted assumptions that organizations and individuals are expected to follow.[14] It is precisely the taken-for-granted aspects of Christianity that the ECM attempts to make obvious in order to play and subvert. For example, ECM's apparent "casualness" in so many settings can be seen as an attempt to generate "slack" in rule-following and create a space for experimentation. Even "church in a pub" where the drinks appear to allow for a great reduction in sanctity, drinks can actually be familiar objects to hide behind (e.g., drinking with

---

7. See Barley and Tolbert, "Institutionalization and Structuration," 99; Czarniawska, "Emerging Institutions," 423–41.

8. See Jepperson, "Institutions, Institutional Effects, and Institutionalism," 145.

9. On normative institutional regulations, see Wicks, "Institutionalized Mindsets of Invulnerability," 659–92; Caronna, "The Misalignment of Institutional 'Pillars,'" 45–59; Hoffman et al., "Cognitive and Institutional Barriers to New Forms of Cooperation on Environmental Protection," 820–45.

10. Friedland and Alford, "Bringing Society Back In" 232–63; Zucker, "Organizations as Institutions," 1–42; Zucker, *Institutional Patterns and Organizations*.

11. North, *Institutions, Institutional Change and Economic Performance*.

12. Bonchek and Shepsle, *Analyzing Politics*.

13. Jepperson, "Institutions, Institutional Effects, and Institutionalism."

14. Meyer and Rowan, "Institutionalized Organizations: Formal Structure as Myth and Ceremony."

friends on a night out) while new normative imperatives flex their way into the scene.

Through activities like "pub church," Emerging Christians seek to change conventional Christianity by engaging in *institutional entrepreneurship*.[15] As Hardy and Maguire write, "institutional entrepreneurship is all about altering deeply embedded norms, values, and practices."[16] *Institutional entrepreneurs* are people responsible for new or changed institutions and who leverage resources to develop alternative models of social arrangements (i.e., altering schemas, scripts, templates, and logics of action) to create new institutions or transform existing ones.[17] Institutional entrepreneurs are insiders from a particular institutional field and use their close understanding of that institution toward transformation.

While institutional entrepreneurs seek change, change does not happen easily because the creation, transformation, and diffusion of institutions require *legitimacy*, a condition where competing alternatives are less appropriate, desirable, or viable.[18] All principled action—even when it seems rational and rooted in individual conviction—takes its force from being legitimated. Moreover, the assumption that the beliefs and behaviors are desirable, proper, and appropriate does not come from within individuals; they come from groups. Finally, if legitimation is to hold over time, groups providing legitimation must themselves remain coherent over time. In short, groups that legitimate ethical and religious principles must become *organized* to sustain the power required for individual adherents to lay stakes into their convictions. The actor stands on the sense that their beliefs and behaviors are right, good, and true; in other words, that they are *legitimated*.

Grasping processes of legitimation is extremely useful for approaching phenomena like the Emerging Church Movement. What appears on the

---

15. Hardy and Maguire, "Institutional Entrepreneurship."

16. Ibid.

17. Battilana, et al., "How Actors Change Institutions"; Beckert, "Agency, Entrepreneurs, and Institutional Change"; DiMaggio, "Interest and Agency in Institutional Theory"; Greenwood and Suddaby, "Institutional Entrepreneurship in Mature Fields"; Kraatz and Moore, "Executive Migration and Institutional Change"; Leblebici, et al., "Institutional Change and The Transformation of Interorganizational Fields"; Maguire, et al., "Institutional Entrepreneurship in Emerging Fields"; Sherer and Lee, "Institutional Change in Large Law Firms."

18. Dacin, et al., "Institutional Theory and Institutional Change," 47. See also Hargadon and Douglas, "When Innovations Meet Institutions."

surface to be a free-wheeling heterodoxy reacting to the established institutions of contemporary Christianity is on closer investigation an intriguing case in the construction of religious agency. To be more specific, Emerging Christians are not simply striving for an "authentic" self; they are negotiating for a type of "legitimized" self. There are many competing religious organizations in the world, and individuals come to find that the emergence of new institutions that align with new formations of ideals will inevitably conflict with others, necessitating a vigorous attempt by every person to justify their choices in rationalized ways as they are confronted with those alternatives. As the ECM attempts to renegotiate the rules of the Christianity amidst this broader social system, they negotiate the desire to discover an "authentic" self, one that is not fully institutionalized. This resonates with the frequent claims of Emerging Christians to escape institutionalized Christianity (that is often viewed as an escape from the chains of a delegitimized faith). As Brian McLaren writes in *Naked Spirituality*, "Doctrinal correctness, institutional participation, and religious conformity won't suffice anymore."[19] The ECM strives as a religious community to avoid inauthentic, "standardized" spirituality and cultivate new affinities, some of which start with reading books like those by Brian McLaren. Participating in ECM structures might be understood as stepping aside from standardized agency, especially what many experience as the oppressive structures of fundamentalist piety. In doing so, they cannot merely do whatever they want. People seek places where they can pursue an alternative approach to religious engagement that is legitimized.

The institutional entrepreneurs of the ECM are "agents of legitimacy."[20] Of course, none of the practices within the ECM are radically "new." What we see in practice is a "selective adoption and deployment of available institutional logics that legitimize and mobilize political action against incommensurate institutional logics."[21] It lies in the nature of legitimation for the people developing new logics, arrangements, and congregations to borrow and hybridize already accepted practices.[22] If legitimation is to hold, newly established groups that provide legitimation must themselves remain relatively coherent over time. This makes it necessary for Emerging

---

19. McLaren, *Naked Spirituality*, 3.
20. Dacin, et al., "Institutional Theory and Institutional Change," 47.
21. Seo and Creed, "Institutional Contradictions, Praxis, and Institutional Change," 237.
22. Ibid.; Clemens and Cook, "Politics and Institutionalism."

Christians to reinvent congregations as they have known them from past experience. Emerging Christians find newly legitimated ways to move out of conventional expectations in their attempt to form new structures to support alternative ways of enacting their religious agency.

In sum, the ECM is a form of organized legitimation of convictions that strives to renegotiate beliefs and practices of orthodox Christianity. Emerging Christians create religious communities with loose boundaries of belonging and belief (so that pluralism is not just tolerated, but celebrated), while at the same time encouraging people to follow individualized religious paths. Using theoretical language, the ECM is attempting to remodel modern Christianity as a network of historically distinctive and newly rationalized purposive associations. Leaders who identify with the ECM are those willing to develop strategies for religious change and shape new institutions.[23] "To qualify as *institutional entrepreneurs*, individuals must break with existing rules and practices associated with the dominant institutional logic(s) and institutionalize the alternative rules, practices or logics they are championing."[24] These are not just entrepreneurs but *religious entrepreneurs* seeking to draw on the symbolic power of their religious orientation to change it.

Processes Inherent to Religious Institutional Entrepreneurship

Readers of this book will likely know that *Emerging Christians consistently characterize themselves as anti-institutional*. Using empirical data, anthropologist James Bielo and sociologist Josh Packard both argued that the ECM's anti-institutional stance is central to its identity and its appeal.[25] Yet, through the lens of institutional entrepreneurship it is crucial to note that Emerging Christians are "embedded agents,"[26] which means that they

---

23. Leca and Naccache, "A Critical Realist Approach to Institutional Entrepreneurship," 627.

24. Garud and Karnøe, "Path Creation as a Process of Mindful Deviation"; Battilana, "Agency and Institutions."

25. Bielo, *Emerging Evangelicals*; Packard, *The Emerging Church*; see also Marti and Ganiel, *The Deconstructed Church*.

26. On the "paradox of embedded agency," see Battilana, "Agency and Institutions"; Holm, "The Dynamics of Institutionalization"; Seo and Creed, "Institutional Contradictions, Praxis, and Institutional Change"; DiMaggio and Powell, "Introduction"; Friedland and Alford, "Bringing Society Back In"; Sewell, "A Theory of Structure."

are simultaneously enabled and constrained by the institutions they seek to change.[27] Caricatures of institutional "rebels" as autonomous "advocates" who are disembodied from the constraints of context should be avoided because all institutional entrepreneurs are firmly rooted within their contexts.[28] Moreover, newly shaped beliefs (heterodoxies) require the creation of new organizational forms (alternative movements and congregations), and the selective, hybridized, and pluralist practices of these ECM congregations remain embedded within the wider Christian field.

The notion of *embedded agency* reveals how actors embedded within institutional fields come to envision new practices. Emerging Christians are embedded in the institution of conventional Christianity and yet simultaneously challenging such structures to change this religious institution from within.[29] As change agents, they use their embeddedness to their advantage by drawing on the strong working knowledge of their organizational and institutional contexts to determine actions to take.[30] Conventional Christians who are embedded within their religious systems are so fully institutionalized (i.e., full of recipes) as to be unable to consider alternative approaches.[31] In contrast, Emerging Christians are neither so embedded as to lack the motivation to change the system yet not so peripheral so as to be deprived of an imagination to change it.

Provoking change among the norm-constrained majority is the quintessential work of religious institutional entrepreneurs. Emerging Christians seek to dislodge habitual, familiar, and conditioned forms of religion within mainstream Christianity. The ECM is rife with creating practices that are both disruptive and defensive; Remember that institutions by definition involve deeply entrenched, taken for granted assumptions, institutions are remarkably stable and resistant to change. Therefore, institutional entrepreneurs engage in purposive disruptive institutional work to undermine

---

27. See Weik, "Institutional Entrepreneurship and Agency."

28. van Dijk, et al., "Micro-Institutional Affordances and Strategies of Radical Innovation," 1509.

29. Battilana, "Agency and Institutions"; Holm, "The Dynamics of Institutionalization"; Seo and Creed, "Institutional Contradictions, Praxis, and Institutional Change"; DiMaggio and Powell, "Introduction"; Friedland and Alford, "Bringing Society Back In"; Sewell, "A Theory of Structure."

30. Reay, et al., "Legitimizing a New Role," 994.

31. Maguire, "Institutional Entrepreneurship"; Greenwood and Suddaby, "Institutional Entrepreneurship in Mature Fields," 29.

meanings.³² They envision alternative ways of accomplishing religious tasks and leverage resources to manipulate structures in which they are already embedded to reintroduce fluidity, tensions, and hybridity.³³ The spread of the ECM is dependent on such advocates—people who represent and recruit on behalf of the movement—and a network of affiliates allow dispersed flows of information. Particularly significant for the spread of a movement is a densely connected network of core leaders,³⁴ something that was characteristic of the now-defunct Emergent Village. Institutional entrepreneurs usually already occupy key positions in social networks, thus possessing "a high level of 'reach centrality,' defined as access to a large number of field members through a limited number of intermediaries."³⁵ They enjoy high levels of "social capital," able to command the trust of others in their networks and to garner information and political support.³⁶ These religious institutional entrepreneurs "champion and orchestrate collective action."³⁷ Anyone part of the movement, even if they are less central to the core network, carry the movement further because, ultimately, institutional change is a collective endeavor.

Disruptive institutional work undermines assumptions and beliefs about practices, disassociate their moral foundations, and disconnect sanctions from practices.³⁸ Institutional entrepreneurs participate in "the gradual undermining of the moral foundations of institutions, rather than their wholesale turnover."³⁹ Existing practices must become seen as inappropriate; at the same time, alternative practices must be equally seen as legitimate. Since so much is done to sustain *status quo*,⁴⁰ institutional entrepreneurs are left to struggle among those who are nominally on the same "team" of Christianity in the face those who aim to discredit all forms of religion. Christianity is also subject to various forms of delegitimization,

32. Lawrence and Suddaby, "Institutions and Institutional Work."

33. Garud, et al., "Institutional Entrepreneurship in the Sponsorship of Common Technological Standards."

34. Burt, *Brokerage and Closure*. See also Kim and Bearman, "The Structure and Dynamics of Movement Participation"; Andrews and Biggs, "The Dynamics of Protest Diffusion"; Marwell and Oliver, *The Critical Mass in Collective Action*.

35. Battilana, et al., "How Actors Change Institutions," 84–85.

36. Ibid.

37. Ibid.

38. Lawrence and Suddaby, "Institutions and Institutional Work," 235.

39. Ibid., 236.

40. Oliver, "The Antecedents of Deinstitutionalization."

and that means that outsider-driven change may be absorbed by the ECM as part of their arsenal of tools for changing the institution of Christianity. Therefore, while institutional entrepreneurs of the ECM are indeed insiders, certainly they draw on and address critiques from outsider Christianity.

The key process of religious institutional entrepreneurship lies in building new bases of legitimacy for religious identity and behavior, at times re-defining what is appropriately "religious." A core mechanism in the use of *discourse* is *theorization*. *Theorization* involves how institutional entrepreneurs specify problems with existing practices and justify new ones as solutions.[41] Hardy and Maguire call these "discursive interventions to create and communicate convincing rationales."[42] Discussion among institutional entrepreneurs is not systematic as much as polemical and opportunistic. Books, messages, and blog posts provide a variety of entrepreneurial accounts or legitimating accounts for the manner of institutionalizing practices that frame changes with the intention to generate collective action.[43] The framing of legitimation is typically done in terms of existing categories and schema that draw on available discourses to make the change meaningful to other actors, enlist allies, and build coalitions.[44] Discursive frames justify new practices and legitimize them as indispensable.[45] Framing and theorization discredits the status quo while presenting alternative practices. Alternative practices are championed as necessary, valid, and appropriate.[46] Legitimating accounts often come as stories or narratives used strategically both orally as well as the production and distribution of texts.[47]

41. Strang and Meyer, "Institutional Conditions for Diffusion"; Greenwood, et al., "Theorizing Change."

42. Hardy and Maguire, "Institutional Entrepreneurship," 209–10.

43. See Colomy, "Neofunctionalism and Neoinstitutionalism"; Creed, et al., "Clothes Make the Person?"; Benford and Snow, "Framing Processes and Social Movements." See also Lounsbury, et al., "Social Movements, Field Frames and Industry Emergence"; Garud, et al., "Institutional Entrepreneurship in the Sponsorship of Common Technological Standards."

44. Hargadon and Douglas, "When Innovations Meet Institutions"; Hardy and Phillips, "No Joking Matter"; Rao, "Caveat Emptor"; Rao, et al., "Power Plays."

45. Rao, "Caveat Emptor."

46. Ibid.

47. Lounsbury and Glynn, "Cultural Entrepreneurship"; Suddaby and Greenwood, "Rhetorical Strategies of Legitimacy"; Philips, et al., "Discourse and Institutions"; Fligstein, "Social Skill and the Theory of Fields," 113; Colomy, "Neofunctionalism and Neoinstitutionalism."

Emerging Christians place priority on intentionally provoking reflexivity.[48] So it is not surprising that their prognostic framing values conversation as key to overcoming the perceived shortcomings of existing religious institutions. For Emerging Christians, dialogue simply means listening to others' points of view or positions *without trying to change them*. In a manner that echoes the traditional "testimonies" of being converted or "born again" within evangelicalism,[49] people are encouraged to share stories about their personal experiences of faith with others, publicly or in small groups. As Harrold has noted, often these are stories of disillusionment or "de-conversion."[50] Such reflexivity through conversation is constant and ongoing as Emerging Christians believe that within mainstream expressions of Christianity there is *not enough space for conversation*.

Therefore, the resources to evoke change are largely cultural and symbolic,[51] which involve entrepreneurs' ability to "make meaning," to "frame" new ideas, and employ "discursive strategies" as key to instigating change.[52] Institutional entrepreneurs rework already existing "institutional vocabularies" consisting of commonly understood words, expressions and meanings. Such work requires "expert theorizers"—like Bell, McLaren, Jones and Rollins—who exhibit high levels of reflexivity and creativity.[53] Because they are altering definitions of "reality," they must go beyond simply selecting among existing cultural beliefs; they must actively propagate new explanations of reality.[54] The critical role of *expert theorizers* emerges

---

48. Jones, *The New Christians*, 155.

49. Mitchell and Ganiel, *Evangelical Journeys*.

50. Harrold, "Deconversion in the Emerging Church."

51. See Creed, et al., "Clothes Make the Person?"; Hardy and Phillips, "No Joking Matter"; Hensman, "Social Movement Organizations"; Lawrence and Philips, "From Moby Dick to Free Willy"; Maguire and Hardy, "The Emergence of New Global Institutions."

52. Battilana, et al., "How Actors Change Institutions," 94; Morrill and Owen-Smith (2002), Munir and Phillips, "The Birth of the 'Kodak Moment,'" Phillips, et al., "Discourse and Institutions,"; Creed, et al., "Clothes Make the Person?"; De Holan and Phillips, "Managing in Transition"; Fligstein, "Social Skill and Institutional Theory"; Fligstein, "Social Skill and the Theory of Fields"; Maguire, et al., "Institutional Entrepreneurship in Emerging Fields"; Rao, "Caveat Emptor"; Rao, et al., "Power Plays."

53. Strang and Meyer, "Institutional Conditions for Diffusion"; Battilana, et al., "How Actors Change Institutions," 82; Morrill and Owen-Smith, "The Emergence of Environmental Conflict Resolution"; Greenwood, et al., "Theorizing Change"; Maguire, et al., "Institutional Entrepreneurship in Emerging Fields"; Rao et al., Suchman, "Managing Legitimacy."

54. See Aldrich and Fiol, "Fools Rush In?"; Ashforth and Gibbs, "The Double-edge

because of the high level of reflexivity, complexity, and creativity needed to accomplish discursive theorization.[55] Moreover, the skills of institutional entrepreneurs include core aspects of social movement leadership. "*Developing a vision* encompasses activities undertaken to make the case for change including sharing the vision of the need for change with followers. *Popularization* is "promoting comprehensibility by explicating new cultural formulations."[56] Institutional entrepreneurs develop alternative models of social arrangements (e.g., schemas, scripts, templates, logics of action). From the social movement literature, this involves a shift in frames for approaching phenomena.[57] For example, part of institutionalization of the ECM is the process of "*normalization of problematizations*."[58] These are the "amens" that occur when Emerging Christians agree with the various agreed upon problems or issues with conventional Christianity. Previously taken-for-granted conclusions about Christianity (like positions on gay rights) become rich points of contrast to draw out a new orientation of appropriate faith. Over time, such collective agreements build a winning coalition of co-religionists "whose conceptions of socially desirable activity set the terms for subsequent moral debate."[59] Some researchers using a critical realist framework suggest that the capacity to operate as an institutional entrepreneur comes through the process of reflexivity, the ability to look back upon oneself and cognitively disembed oneself from institutional commitments. Indeed, reflexivity is so key to the ECM that some of the most prominent representatives within the movement define their entire posture toward ministry among Emerging Christians as the intentional provocation of reflexivity (e.g, Rob Bell, Nadia Bolz-Weber, Brian McLaren, and Peter Rollins).

Since the ECM often views itself as a "conversation," it is relevant to discuss the interpretive struggles inherent to institutional entrepreneurship. Institutions are not just practices but also meanings that are shared and taken for granted. While some mainstream church leaders would rather see hard and fast lines of "doctrine" or "liturgy," the diffusion of

of Organizational Legitimation," 77–194.

55. Strang and Meyer, "Institutional Conditions for Diffusion."

56. Suchman, "Managing Legitimacy," 592.

57. Gamson, "The Social Psychology of Collective Action"; McAdam, et al., "Social Movements"; Snow and Benford, "Master Frames and Cycles of Protest."

58. Maguire and Hardy, "The Emergence of New Global Institutions," 56.

59. Suchman, "Managing Legitimacy," 592.

liturgical practices are never accomplished as singular, monolithic entities put in place by homogenized actors but always involves struggles over meanings, specifically meanings (myths, logics, discourses) that legitimate practices.[60] Discourse on a broad level (through books, sermons, lectures, blog posts, podcasts, workshops, etc.) is inevitably translated at the micro-level. Local actors do not diffuse intact and unchanging meanings associated with practices; instead, all local actors become active interpreters of practices whose meaning is both transmitted and negotiated. A more fluid approach to institutional meanings and practices allows us to account for the variety and diversity of Emerging Church "congregations." Out of the rich heritage of Christian tradition, a diverse set of meanings are accessed as resources to support positions and undermine those opposed to new thoughts and practices.[61] While the Christian faith is not infinitely pliable, there is plenty for local actors to draw on to support the legitimation of alternative approaches.

Beyond purely discursive skills are also *social skills* such that religious institutional entrepreneurs both create a new collective identity and the structural means to maintain it. Entrepreneurial efforts include coalescing social groups with heterogeneous interests.[62] Such skills include creating new networks and alliances. The social skills of institutional entrepreneurs include the ability to motivate the cooperation and activism of others by facilitating "communities of practice."[63] Both the meanings and the means of action are constructed.[64] Cooperation is so essential to institutional entrepreneurship that the research strongly asserts "that institutional entrepreneurs have unique political and social skills."[65] Certainly we can detect such skills in some of the public figures of the ECM. For example, *mobilizing people* includes activities undertaken to gain others' support for and

---

60. Zilber, "The Work of the Symbolic in Institutional Processes."

61. Ibid.

62. Lounsbury and Glynn, "Cultural Entrepreneurship"; Aldrich and Fiol, "Fools Rish In?"; Sotarauta and Pulkkinen, "Institutional Entrepreneurship for Knowledge Regions," 102.

63. Brown and Duguid, "Organizational Learning and Communities-of-Practice"; Wenger, *Communities of Practice;* Jarzabkowski, "Strategy as Practice."

64. Fligstein, "Social Skill and Institutional Theory"; Fligstein, *Fields, Power, and Social Skill.*

65. Perkmann and Spicer, Fligstein, "Institutional Entrepreneurs and Cultural Frames," 112, Fligstein, "Social Skill and the Theory of Fields."

acceptance of new routines, and *motivating others to achieve and sustain the vision* consists of activities undertaken to institutionalize change."[66]

Overall, the creation of newly legitimated religious identities and the organizational forms to sustain them essentially consists of an *institutionalization project*.[67] As such, institutional entrepreneurship involves processes of institutionalization, which comprises several different activities: *Framing reality* and *engaging others* at an interpersonal level; *theorizing practices* and *bridging relational networks* at an organizational level; *legitimating morally acceptable forms* and *connecting broader relevance structures* at a macro-level. Although analytically distinct, these activities are intertwined in a fluid and ongoing process.[68]

Collective Religious Institutional Entrepreneurship

Even a casual observer will note that the ECM deliberately creates "anti-institutional" structural forms that are collective in nature, including pub churches, transitory gatherings, experimental congregations, and neo-monastic communities. The variety of assemblies represents an experimental, entrepreneurial dynamic that propels leaders and participants to connect with other leaders and participants through both face-to-face and online conferences and networks. More than just the work of high profile leaders, religious institutional entrepreneurship is a *collective process* in which cooperation and collective action are fundamental,[69] requiring political and social skills for building collaborations, coalitions, and partnerships.[70] Religious institutional entrepreneurship therefore is not simply the act of individuals but rather a *collective institutional entrepreneurship*.[71] Whenever

---

66. Battilana, et al., "How Actors Change Institutions," 78.

67. DiMaggio, "Interest and Agency in Institutional Theory," 14.

68. Tracey, et al., "Bridging Institutional Entrepreneurship and the Creation of New Organizational Forms."

69. Sotarauta and Pulkkinen, "Institutional Entrepreneurship for Knowledge Regions," 102.

70. Perkmann and Spicer, "Healing the Scars of History." See also Fligstein, "Institutional Entrepreneurs and Cultural Frames," 112; Fligstein, "Social Skill and Institutional Theory"; Fligstein, "Social Skill and the Theory of Fields"; King and Soule, "Social Movements as Extra-institutional Entrepreneurs"; Lawrence et al., "Institutional Effects of Interorganizational Collaboration"; Zucker, *Institutional Patterns and Organizations*.

71. Wijen and Ansari, "Overcoming Inaction through Collective Institutional Entrepreneurship."

institutional entrepreneurialism is widely dispersed, it takes on features of a social movement, giving impetus to the standard terminology of talking about the Emerging Church as a *movement*.

In the context of Emerging Christians' understanding of themselves, we see how the discursive practices of the ECM "conversation" can be considered a paradigmatic example of collective institutional entrepreneurship. The ECM's on-going conversation is a mechanism that sustains a plurality of identities and positions within Emerging congregations. At the same time, the ECM conversation allows Emerging Christians to develop ideas that support their desire to change institutions and legitimate their attempt to redefine themselves and their congregations. Those who participate in the ECM "conversation" are working together, even if they do not consider themselves leaders or attend any type of planning meetings. Cooperation is essential to the process of the religious institutional entrepreneurship, and forging alliances is critical so as to stimulate collaborations, coalitions, and partnerships.

The ECM institutional entrepreneurs collectively "frame"[72] their change projects in particular ways to "define the grievances and interests of aggrieved constituencies, diagnose causes, assign blame, provide solutions, and enable collective attribution processes to operate."[73] Recall from above that "Institutional entrepreneurs are called upon to articulate a vision for the divergent change they are promoting and mobilize allies to support its implementation."[74] Such legitimization necessitates mobilization of coalitions of diverse groups to generate the collective action to substantiate a broad base of support for institutional change.[75] A broader more process-oriented discussion of entrepreneurship recognizes the diverse and spatially dispersed actors.[76] Today, the Internet and occasional conferences provide ways to overcome the natural limitations of coordinating collective action among dispersed network effectively.[77]

---

72. Khan, et al., "A Dark Side of Institutional Entrepreneurship."

73. Snow and Benford, "Master Frames and Cycles of Protest," 150.

74. Battilana, et al., "How Actors Change Institutions," 79.

75. Fligstein, "Social Skill and the Theory of Fields"; Wijen and Ansari, "Overcoming Inaction through Collective Institutional Entrepreneurship."

76. Lounsbury and Crumely, "New Practice Creation."

77. See Wijen and Ansari, "Overcoming Inaction through Collective Institutional Entrepreneurship."

PART 1: DEFINING BOUNDARIES

By understanding the necessarily collective nature of institutional entrepreneurship, it becomes clear that *all those who participate in ECM communities are entrepreneurs to the extent they actively work to build and maintain their communities.* Indeed, I found many rank-and-file Emerging Christians participating in "the conversation" have not read or listened to so-called "leaders" and are completely unaware of the wider ECM.[78] As Battilana, Leca, and Boxenbaum state:[79] Agents without any grand plan for altering their institutions, or even awareness that they are contributing to changes that diverge from existing institutions, might thus end up acting as institutional entrepreneurs. We thus define institutional entrepreneurs as change agents who, whether or not they initially intended to change their institutional environment, initiate, and actively participate in the implementation of changes that diverge from existing institutions.

Overall, these are "network actors intentionally spreading heterodoxy across institutional settings," and in the case of the ECM, that means places like churches, seminaries, and denominational bodies.[80]

Central actors to the spread of ECM are *bridge leaders*, dedicated advocates who take the ECM orientation outward to their own particularistic locations.[81] Bridge leaders are not necessarily high profile or famous, but they make innovations contagious. Diffusing the creative dissent of the ECM is achieved in part through conventional means like books and conferences as well as the Internet via blogs, podcasts, video feeds, and social media networks. Conferences like the TransFORM and regional happenings like the Wild Goose Festival in addition to key communities like Solomon's Porch in Minneapolis and IKON in Belfast become "critical communities" who "convince potential change agents of their conceptualization of a problem, advocate new social values, and export heterodox ideas" to broader constituents.[82] More importantly, Emerging Christians who come to conferences and actively participate in online networks are agents of diffusion, and by openly discussing heterodox and uncomplimentary views of mainstream Christianity, they risk the dangers associated with agitation. These include students, pastors and ex-pastors, dedicated lay people, and

---

78. Marti and Ganiel, *The Deconstructed Church.*

79. Battilana, et al., "How Actors Change Institutions," 70.

80. Kim and Pfaff, "Structure and Dynamics of Religious Insurgency," 209.

81. Robnet, *How Long? How Long?*, 19. See also Kim and Pfaff, "Structure and Dynamics of Religious Insurgency."

82. Kim and Pfaff, "Structure and Dynamics of Religious Insurgency," 190.

those who have left previous churches who become jointly embedded in global and local dissident religious communities. They "deliver insurgent ideas to a local arena, convert local actors, and instigate insurgency"[83] by taking the sentiments and ideals from hot centers of the movement and diffusing them outward to their particularistic localities. Even the most seemingly inconsequential members of the movement who live and work in the most remote locations carry forward ideals and principles of the ECM in places otherwise untouched. Of course, "exposure to new ideas alone is rarely enough to trigger extensive collective action, much less remake the institutional order."[84] It is not ideas that are effective but rather *the diffusion of ideas through dense relational networks of trust.*[85]

The activities of an institutionalization process involve establishing a new group of legitimated actors who simultaneously delegitimate and deinstitutionalize institutional forms that had previously provided legitimacy.[86] Due to the challenge of embeddedness, the ECM does not recruit those who are deeply entrenched within mainstream Christianity. Nevertheless, there is a difference between those who want to *change* a system and those who want to *break* a system. The religious institutional entrepreneurs of the ECM attempt to "loosen" institutional embeddedness to mobilize support and take advantage of those who are already "loosened" from their institutional commitments. Such work involves persuasion, aligning interests, and building consensus.[87] It also involves mobilizing others to collective action and adopting new practices. The emphasis of religious institutional entrepreneurship involves a realignment of both materials and discourse, is concentrated within organizational structures, is spread through networked relationships, and ultimately legitimizes new identities, beliefs, and practices.[88]

---

83. Ibid., 209.

84. Ibid., 192.

85. Ibid., 209. See also Kim and Bearman, "The Structure and Dynamics of Movement Participation"; Rogers, *Diffusion of Innovations*; Valente, *Network Models of the Diffusion of Innovations*; Watts, *Small Worlds.*

86. DiMaggio, "Interest and Agency in Institutional Theory," 13; see also Singh, Tucker, and Meinhard, "Institutional Change and Ecological Dynamics."

87. Dew, "Institutional Entrepreneurship"; Garud, et al., "Institutional Entrepreneurship in the Sponsorship of Common Technological Standards"; Demil and Bensédrine, "Processes of Legitimization and Pressure Toward Regulation."

88. Levy and Scully, "The Institutional Entrepreneur as Modern Prince."

PART 1: DEFINING BOUNDARIES

The Emerging Church Movement as Institutional Entrepreneurship

The ECM does not represent merely the introduction of a few interesting people or religious organizations; rather the ECM involves an earnest attempt to fundamentally redefine contemporary Christianity. In short, the ECM involves institutional entrepreneurship.[89] The approach described here highlights the role of institutional entrepreneurial skills to mobilize institutional logics and resources from a heterogeneous institutional environment to legitimize and support change. This is difficult and challenging, involving not only a high degree of reflexivity and creativity but also "the unlearning of what has been ingrained over history and embedded into structures, policies, metrics, rhetoric, and practice."[90] Seo and Creed write, "Initiating collective social reconstruction of institutional arrangements requires many complex, creative, and multidimensional skills. Theoretically, it entails at least the challenging of taken-for-granted belief systems, the reasoned analysis of the limitations and latent possibilities of existing social patterns, the framing of alternatives, and the mobilization of resources for the social construction of those alternatives."[91] Any institutional field is full of inconsistencies and conflict,[92] and the realm of Christianity is so broad that the ECM can be conceived as an instance of a field with multiple, competing logics. Institutional tensions and contradictions are themselves an impetus for institutional change.[93] At the same time, institutional entrepreneurs like those of the ECM intentionally encourage contradictions and ironies by tying together disparate institutional logics (bridging established logics[94]) and practices together.

---

89. For an extended discussion, see Marti and Ganiel, *The Deconstructed Church*.

90. Hoffman and Ventresca, "The Institutional Framing of Policy Debates," 1386.

91. Seo and Creed, "Institutional Contradictions, Praxis, and Institutional Change," 242.

92. Friedland and Alford, "Bringing Society Back In"; Holm, "The Dynamics of Institutionalization"; Hoffman, "Institutional Evolution and Change"; Clemens and Cook, "Politics and Institutionalism"; Seo and Creed, "Institutional Contradictions, Praxis, and Institutional Change"; DiMaggio and Powell, "Introduction"; Sewell, "A Theory of Structure"; Jepperson, "Institutions, Institutional Effects, and Institutionalism."

93. Rao and Giorgi, "Code Breaking"; Seo and Creed, "Institutional Contradictions, Praxis, and Institutional Change."

94. Tracey, et al., "Bridging Institutional Entrepreneurship and the Creation of New Organizational Forms," 77.

Understanding the dynamics and counter-dynamics of institutional entrepreneurialism help us understand the difficulty and ambiguity frequently pointed out in the ECM. The work of problemization destabilizes the institution and provokes defensive work from those invested in institutions as they exist. Also, destabilization affects the existing organizational filed by making discourse about practices less structured. Further translation and reinterpretation of new discourses create variety and contradictions, which make the emerging institutional forms less coherent. As Maguire and Hardy write, "a range of new actors produce texts that support and promote problematizations; existing actors begin to produce counter texts; and the number of both problematizing texts and counter texts increases."[95]

While institutional entrepreneurs in other organizational fields may have the goal of institutionalizing their innovations, the ECM maintains a much more ambivalent approach towards institutions in and of themselves. Essentially, *deinstitutionalization* occurs when previously institutionalized practices are no longer taken for granted and abandoned.[96] In a sense, deinstitutionalization is inherent to the work of institutional entrepreneurship as certain meanings and practices become displaced, delegitimized, and decommissioned.[97] Deinstitutionalizing discourse uses various claims, arguments, stories, illustrations, examples to "substantiate and dramatize the ineffectiveness and injustice of existing practices."[98] In all cases, the goal is to delegitimize the *status quo*.[99] Emerging Christians do this by claiming that the changes they advocate facilitate a more authentic living out of the gospel and that they help people to make better religious sense of pluralist and postmodern contexts. Institutional entrepreneurs may become convinced of the need for change by external factors such as "social upheaval, technological disruption, competitive discontinuity, and regulatory changes that might disturb the socially constructed, field-level consensus and invite the introduction of new ideas." Internal tensions (as between "ideals" and "reality") may also stimulate a need for change. But institutional entrepreneurs must legitimize new or changing institutions by

95. Maguire and Hardy, "The Emergence of New Global Institutions," 170.

96. Davis, et al., "The Decline and Fall of the Conglomerate Firm in the 1980s"; Farjoun, "The Dialectics of Institutional Development in Emerging and Turbulent Fields," 851.

97. Ahmadjian and Robinson, "Safety in Numbers"; Scott, *Institutions and Organizations*.

98. Colomy, "Neofunctionalism and Neoinstitutionalism," 289.

99. Pettigrew, "On Studying Organizational Cultures."

connecting them with taken-for-granted beliefs and values. Most important, and most threatening to the legitimizing power of entrepreneurs, is recognizing the difficulty of establishing a new, unified approach to social reality.[100]

To the extent the work of institutional entrepreneurship is successful, over time and as new institutionalization takes root, there arrive new "leaders" enabled to represent the disruptive institutional work by being recognized as legitimate actors who continue creating a flow of messages to problematize previously practices. Such texts accumulate and the problematizations become normalized, which means they become taken for granted truths. Problematization creates room for establishing new identities and new organizations. In the end, institutional entrepreneurship is a predominantly collective process, and Emerging Christians who participate in the ECM will continue to use religious discourses to interrogate conventional Christianity and reconsider religious practices to create congregations where they can affirm each other's more open and fluid personal religiosity.

Bibliography

Ahmadjian, Christina L,. and Patricia Robinson. "Safety in Numbers: Downsizing and the Deinstitutionalization of Permanent Employment in Japan." *Administrative Science Quarterly* 46, no. 4 (2001) 622–54.

Aldrich, H. E., and C. M. Fiol. "Fools Rush in? The Institutional Context of Industry Creation." *Academy of Management Review* 19 (1994) 645–70.

Andrews, Kenneth, and Michael Biggs. "The Dynamics of Protest Diffusion." *American Sociological Review* 71 (2006) 752–77.

Ashforth, Blake E., and Barrie W. Gibbs. "The Double-Edge of Organizational Legitimation." *Organization Science* 1 (1990) 177–194.

Barley, Stephen R., and Pamela S. Tolbert. "Institutionalization and Structuration: Studying the Links between Action and Institution." *Organization Studies* 18 (1997) 93–117.

Battilana, Julie A. "Agency and Institutions: The Enabling Role of Individual's Social Position." *Organization* 13, no. 5 (2006) 653–76.

Battilana, Julie, et al. "How Actors Change Institutions: Towards a Theory of Institutional Entrepreneurship." *Academy of Management Annals* 3, no. 1 (2009) 65–107.

Beckert, Jens. "Agency, Entrepreneurs, and Institutional Change: The Roles of Strategic Choice and Institutionalized Practices in Organizations." *Organization Studies* 20, no. 5 (1999) 777–99.

Benford, Robert D., and David A. Snow. "Framing Processes and Social Movements: An Overview and Assessment." *Annual Review of Sociology* 26 (2000) 611–39.

---

100. On how tightly structured and coherent discourse legitimizes institutional practices, see Phillips, Lawrence, and Hardy, "Discourse and Institutions."

Berger, Peter, and Thomas Luckman. *The Social Construction of Reality: A Treatise in the Sociology of Knowledge*. Garden City, NY: Anchor, 1966.

Berghoef, Brian. "Beer, Conversation and God: Pursuing Faith Over a Pint." Religion Blog, *Huffington Post*, 2013. http://www.huffingtonpost.com/bryan-berghoef/beer-conversation-and-god_b_2885329.html?utm_hp_ref=tw (accessed March 20, 2013).

Bielo, James. *Emerging Evangelicals: Faith, Modernity, and the Desire for Authenticity*. New York: New York University Press, 2009.

Bonchek, M. S., and Shepsle, K. A. *Analyzing Politics: Rationality, Behavior and Institutions*. New York: Norton, 1996.

Brown, John Seely, and Paul Duguid. "Organizational Learning and Communities-of-Practice: Toward a Unified View of Working, Learning, and Innovation." *Organization Science* 2, no. 1 (1991) 40–57.

Burt, Ronald S. *Brokerage and Closure*. New York: Oxford University Press, 2005.

Caronna, Carol A. "The Misalignment of Institutional 'Pillars': Consequences for the U.S. Health Care Field." *Journal of Health and Social Behavior* 45 (2004) 45–59.

Clemens, E. S., and J. M. Cook. "Politics and Institutionalism: Explaining Durability and Change." *Annual Review of Sociology* 25, no. 1(1999) 441–66.

Colomy, Paul. "Neofunctionalism and Neoinstitutionalism: Human Agency and Interest in Institutional Change." *Sociological Forum* 13, no. 2 (1998) 265–300.

Creed, W. E. D., et al. "Clothes Make the Person? The Tailoring of Legitimating Accounts and the Social Construction of Identity." *Organization Science* 13, no. 5 (2002) 475–96.

Czarniawska, Barbara. "Emerging Institutions: Pyramids or Anthills?" *Organization Studies* 30 (2006) 423–41.

Dacin, M. T., et al. "Institutional Theory and Institutional Change: Introduction to the Special Research Forum." *Academy of Management Journal* 45 (2002) 45–57.

Davis, Gerald F., et al. "The Decline and Fall of the Conglomerate Firm in the 1980s: The Deinstitutionalization of an Organizational Form." *American Sociological Review* 59, no. 4 (1994) 547–70.

De Holan, P. M., and N. Phillips. "Managing in Transition: A Case Study of Institutional Management and Organizational Change." *Journal of Management Inquiry* 11, no. 1 (2002) 68–83.

Demil, Benoît, and Jabril Bensédrine. "Processes of Legitimization and Pressure Toward Regulation: Corporate Conformity and Strategic Behavior." *International Studies of Management and Organization* 35, no. 2 (2005) 56–77.

Dew, N. "Institutional Entrepreneurship: A Coasian Perspective." *International Journal of Entrepreneurship and Innovation* 7, no. 1 (2006) 13–22.

DiMaggio, Paul. "Interest and Agency in Institutional Theory." In *Institutional Patterns and Culture*, edited by L. Zucker, 3–22. Cambridge: Ballinger, 1998.

———. "Introduction." In *The New Institutionalism in Organization Analysis*, edited by Walter W. Powell and Paul J. DiMaggio, 1–38. Chicago: University of Chicago Press, 1991.

DiMaggio, P., and W. Powell. "The Iron Cage Revisited: Institutional Isomorphism and Collective Rationality in Organizational Fields." *American Sociological Review* 48 (1983) 147–60.

Farjoun, M. "The Dialectics of Institutional Development in Emerging and Turbulent Fields: The History of Pricing Conventions in the On-line Database Industry." *Academy of Management Journal* 45, no. 5 (2002) 848–74.

Fligstein, N. "Fields, Power, and Social Skill: A Critical Analysis of the New Institutionalism." Paper presented at the German Sociological Association Conference on Power and Organization, Hamburg. 1997.

———. "Institutional Entrepreneurs and Cultural Frames: The Case of the European Union›s Single Market Program." *European Societies* 3, no. 3 (2001) 261–87.

———. "Social Skill and Institutional Theory." *American Behavioral Scientist* 40 (1997) 387–405.

———. "Social Skill and the Theory of Fields." *Sociological Theory* 19, no. 2 (2001) 105–25.

Friedland, Roger, and Robert R. Alford. "Bringing Society Back In: Symbols, Practices, and Institutional Contradictions." In *The New Intuitionalism in Organizational Analysis*, edited by W. W. Powell and P. J. DiMaggio, 232–63. Chicago: University of Chicago Press, 1991.

Gamson, W. A. "The Social Psychology of Collective Action." In *Frontiers in Social Movement Theory*, edited by A. Morris and C. M. Mueller, 53–76. New Haven: Yale University Press, 1992.

Garud, R., and P. Karnøe. "Path creation as a process of mindful deviation." In *Path Dependence and Creation*, edited by R. Garud and P. Karnøe, 1–38. Mahwah, NJ: Earlbaum, 2001.

Garud, Raghu, et al. "Institutional Entrepreneurship in the Sponsorship of Common Technological Standards: The Case of Sun Microsystems and Java." *Academy of Management Journal* 45, no. 1 (2002) 196–214.

Greenwood, Royston, et al. "Theorizing Change: The Role of Professional Associations in the Transformation of Institutionalized Fields." *Academy of Management Journal* 45, no. 1 (2002) 58–80.

Hardy, Cynthia, and Steve Maguire. "Institutional Entrepreneurship." In *The SAGE Handbook of Organizational Institutionalism*, 198–217. Thousand Oaks, CA: Sage, 2008.

Hargadon, Andrew B., and Yellowlees Douglas. "When Innovations Meet Institutions: Edison and the Design of the Electric Light." *Administrative Science Quarterly* 46, no. 3 (2001) 476–501.

Harrold, Philip. "Deconversion in the Emerging Church." *International Journal for the Study of the Christian Church* 6, no. 1 (2006) 79–90.

Hensmans, Manuel. "Social Movement Organizations: A Metaphor for Strategic Actors in Institutional Field." *Organization Studies* 24, no. 3 (2003) 355–81.

Hoffman, A. J. "Institutional Evolution and Change: Environmentalism and the U.S. Chemical Industry." *Academy of Management Journal* 42 (1999) 351–71

Hoffman, Andrew J., et al. "Cognitive and Institutional Barriers to New Forms of Cooperation on Environmental Protection: Insights from Project XL and Habitat Conservation Plans." *American Behavioral Scientist* 45 (2002) 820–45.

Hoffman, A. J., and M. Ventresca. "The Institutional Framing of Policy Debates: Economics versus the Environment." *American Behavioral Scientist* 42, no. 8 (1999) 1368–92.

Holm, Peter. "The Dynamics of Institutionalization: Transformation Processes in Norwegian Fisheries." *Administrative Science Quarterly* 40 (1995) 398–422.

Jarzabkowski, Paula. "Strategy as Practice: Recursiveness, Adaptation and Practices-in-Use." *Organization Studies* 25, no. 4 (2004) 529–60.

Jepperson, R. L. "Institutions, Institutional Effects, and Institutionalism." In *The New Institutionalism in Organizational Analysis*, edited by W. W. Powell and P. J. DiMaggio, 143–63. Chicago: University of Chicago Press, 1991.

Jones, Tony. *The New Christians: Dispatches from the Emergent Frontier*. San Francisco, CA: Jossey-Bass, 2009.

Khan, F. K. Munir, and H. Willmott. "A Dark Side of Institutional Entrepreneurship: Soccer Balls, Child Labour and Postcolonial Impoverishment." *Organization Studies* 28, no. 7 (2007) 1055–77.

Kim, Hyojoung, and Peter S. Bearman. "The Structure and Dynamics of Movement Participation." *American Sociological Review* 62, no. 1 (1997) 70–93.

Kim, Hyojoung, and Steven Pfaff. "Structure and Dynamics of Religious Insurgency: Students and the Spread of the Reformation." *American Sociological Review* 77, no. 2 (2012) 188–215.

King, B. G., and S. A. Soule. "Social Movements as Extra-Institutional Entrepreneurs: The Effect of Protests on Stock Price Returns." *Administrative Science Quarterly* 52 (2007) 413–42.

Kirzner, I. M. "Entrepreneurial Discovery and the Competitive Market Process: An Austrian Approach." *Journal of Economic Literature* 35 (1997) 60–85.

Kraatz, M. S., and J. H. Moore. "Executive Migration and Institutional Change." *Academy of Management Journal* 45 (2002) 120–43.

Lawrence, T. B., et al. "Institutional Effects of Interorganizational Collaboration: The Emergence of Proto-Institutions." *Academy of Management Journal* 45, no. 1 (2002) 281–90.

Lawrence, Thomas B. and Nelson Phillips. "From Moby Dick to Free Willy: Macro-Cultural Discourse and Institutional Entrepreneurship in Emerging Institutional Fields." *Organization*, 11.5 (2004) 689–711.

Lawrence, Thomas B., and Roy Suddaby. "Institutions and Institutional Work." In *Handbook of Organization Studies*, edited by S. R. Glegg et al., 215–54. London: Sage, 2006.

Leblebici, H., et al. "Institutional Change and The Transformation of Interorganizational Fields: An Organizational History of the U.S. Radio Broadcasting Industry." *Administrative Science Quarterly* 36 (1991) 333–63.

Leca, B., and P. Naccache. "A Critical Realist Approach to Institutional Entrepreneurship." *Organization* 13, no. 5 (2006) 627–51.

Levy, D. and M. Scully. "The Institutional Entrepreneur as Modern Prince: The Strategic Face of Power in Contested Fields." *Organization Studies* 28, no. 7 (2007) 971–91.

Lounsbury, M., and L.T. Crumley. "New Practice Creation: An Institutional Perspective on Innovation." *Organization Studies* 28, no. 7 (2007) 993–1012.

Lounsbury, Michael, and Mary Ann Glynn. "Cultural Entrepreneurship: Stories, Legitimacy, and the Acquisition of Resources." *Strategic Management Journal* 22, nos. 6–7 (2001) 545–64.

Lounsbury, Michael, et al. "Social Movements, Field Frames and Industry Emergence: A Cultural-Political Perspective on U.S. Recycling." *Socio- Economic Review* 1 (2003) 71–104.

Maguire, Steve. "Institutional Entrepreneurship." In *International Encyclopedia of Organization Studies*, edited by S. Clegg and J. R. Bailey, 674–78. London: Sage, 2007.

PART 1: DEFINING BOUNDARIES

Maguire, Steve, and Cynthia Hardy. "Discourse and Deinstitutionalization: The Decline of DDT." *Academy of Management Journal* 52:1 (2009) 148–178.

———. "The Emergence of New Global Institutions: A Discursive Perspective." *Organization Studies* 27 (2006) 7–29.

Maguire, Steve, et al. "Institutional Entrepreneurship in Emerging Fields: HIV/AIDS Treatment Advocacy in Canada." *Academy of Management Journal* 47, no. 5 (2004) 657–79.

Marti, Gerardo. *A Mosaic of Believers: Diversity and Innovation in a Multiethnic Church.* Bloomington: Indiana University Press, 2005.

———. *Hollywood Faith: Holiness, Prosperity, and Ambition in a Los Angeles Church.* New Brunswick, NJ: Rutgers University Press, 2008.

———. *Worship across the Racial Divide: Religious Music and the Multiracial Church.* New York: Oxford University Press, 2012.

Marti, Gerardo, and Gladys Ganiel. *The Deconstructed Church: Understanding Emerging Christianity.* Oxford: Oxford University Press, 2014.

Marwell, Gerald, and Pamela E. Oliver. *The Critical Mass in Collective Action.* New York: Cambridge University Press, 1993.

McAdam, D., et al. "Social Movements." In *Handbook of Sociology*, edited by N. J. Smelser, 695–737. Newbury Park, CA: Sage, 1988.

McLaren, Brian. *Naked Spirituality: A Life with God in 12 Simple Words.* New York: HarperCollins, 2011.

Meyer, J., and B. Rowan. "Institutionalized Organizations: Formal Structure as Myth and Ceremony" *American Journal of Sociology* 83 (1977) 340–63.

Mitchell, Claire, and Gladys Ganiel. *Evangelical Journeys: Choice and Change in a Northern Irish Religious Subculture.* Dublin: University College Dublin Press, 2011.

Morrill, Calvin, and Jason Owen-Smith. "The Emergence of Environmental Conflict Resolution." In *Organizations, Policy, and the Natural Environment*, edited by A. J. Hoffman and M. J. Ventresca, 90–118. Stanford: Stanford University Press, 2002.

Munir, Kamal A., and Nelson Phillips. "The Birth of the 'Kodak Moment': Institutional Entrepreneurship and the Adoption of New Technologies." *Organization Studies* 26, no. 11 (2005) 1665–87.

North, Douglas C. *Institutions, Institutional Change and Economic Performance.* New York: Cambridge University Press, 1990.

Oliver, C. "The Antecedents of Deinstitutionalization." *Organization Studies* 13 (1992) 563–88.

Packard, Josh. *The Emerging Church: Religion at the Margins.* Boulder: Lynne-Reinner/First Forum, 2012.

Perkmann, Markus, and André Spicer. "'Healing the Scars of History': Projects, Skills and Field Strategies in Institutional Entrepreneurship." *Organization Studies* 28 (2007) 1101–22.

Pettigrew, Andrew M. "On Studying Organizational Cultures." *Administrative Science Quarterly* 24 (1979) 57–81.

Phillips, Nelson, et al. "Discourse and Institutions." *Academy of Management Review* 29, no. 4 (2004) 635–52.

Rao, Hayagreeva. "Caveat Emptor: The Construction of Non-profit Watchdog Organizations." *American Journal of Sociology* 103 (1998) 912–61.

Rao Hayagreeva, and Giorgi S. "Code Breaking: How Entrepreneurs Exploit Cultural Logics to Generate Institutional Change." *Research in Organizational Behavior* 27 (2006) 269–304.

Rao, Hayagreeva, et al. "Power Plays: How Social Movements and Collective Action Create New Organizational Forms." In *Research in Organizational Behavior*, edited by B. M. Staw and R. I. Sutton, 237–81. New York: Elsevier/JAI, 2000.

Reay, T., et al. "Legitimizing a New Role: Small Wins and Micro-Processes of Change." *Academy of Management Journal* 49, no. 5 (2006) 977–98.

Robnet, Belina. *How Long? African-American Women in the Struggle for Civil Rights*. New York: Oxford University Press, 1997.

Rogers, Everett. M. *Diffusion of Innovations*. New York: Free, 1995.

Schumpeter, J. A. *Capitalism, Socialism, and Democracy*. New York: Harper and Bros., 1942.

Seo, M., and D. Creed. "Institutional Contradictions, Praxis, and Institutional Change: A Dialectical Perspective." *Academy of Management Review* 27 (2002) 222–48.

Scott, W. R. "The Adolescence of Institutional Theory." *Administrative Science Quarterly* 32, no. 4 (1987) 493–521.

———. "Conceptualizing Organizational Fields: Linking Organizations and Societal Systems." In *Systemrationalitat und Partialinteresse*, edited by H. Derlien, U. Gerhardt, and F. Scharpf, 203–21. Baden-Baden: Nomos, 1994.

———. *Institutions and Organizations*. Thousand Oaks, CA: Sage, 2001.

Scott, W. R., P. Mendel Ruef, and C. A. Caronna. *Institutional Change and Healthcare Organizations*. Chicago: University of Chicago Press, 2000.

Seo, Myeong-Gu, and W. E. Douglas Creed. "Institutional Contradictions, Praxis, and Institutional Change: A Dialectical Perspective." *Academy of Management Review* 27, no. 2 (2002) 222–47.

Sewell, William F. "A Theory of Structure: Duality, Agency, and Transformation." *American Journal of Sociology* 98, no. 1 (1992) 1–29.

Sherer, P. D., and K. Lee. "Institutional Change in Large Law Firms: A Resource Dependency and Institutional Perspective." *Academy of Management Journal* 45 (2002) 102–19.

Shane, S., and S. Venkataraman. "The Promise of Entrepreneurship as a Field of Research." *Academy of Management Review* 25 (2000) 217–26.

Singh, J. V., et al. "Institutional Change and Ecological Dynamics." In *The New Institutionalism in Organizational Analysis*, edited by W. W. Powell and P. J. DiMaggio, 390–422. Chicago: University of Chicago Press, 1991.

Snow, D. A., and R. D. Benford. "Master Frames and Cycles of Protest." In *Frontiers in Social Movement Theory*, edited by A. D. Morris and C. M. Mueller, 133–53. New Haven: Yale University Press, 1992.

Sotarauta, Markku, and Riina Pulkkinen. "Institutional Entrepreneurship for Knowledge Regions: In Search of a Fresh Set of Questions for Regional Innovation Studies." *Environment and Planning C:Government and Policy* 29, no. 1 (2011) 96–112.

Strang, D., and J. W. Meyer. "Institutional conditions for diffusion." *Theory and Society* 22 (1993) 487–511.

Suchman, M. C. "Managing Legitimacy: Strategic and Institutional Approaches." *Academy of Management Review* 20 (1995) 571–610.

———. "On the Role of Law Firms in the Structuration of Silicon Valley." Paper presented at the annual meeting of the Law and Society Association, Chicago. 1993.

Suddaby, R., and R. Greenwood. "Rhetorical Strategies of Legitimacy." *Administrative Science Quarterly* 50, no. 1 (2005) 35–67.
Tracey, Paul, et al. "Bridging Institutional Entrepreneurship and the Creation of New Organizational Forms: A Multilevel Model." *Organization Science* 22, no. 1 (2011) 60–80.
Valente, Thomas W. *Network Models of the Diffusion of Innovations*. Cresskill, NJ: Hampton, 1995.
Watts, Duncan J. *Small Worlds: The Dynamics of Networks between Order and Randomness*. Princeton: Princeton University Press, 1999.
Weik, Elke. "Institutional Entrepreneurship and Agency." *Journal for the Theory of Social Behaviour* 41, no. 4 (2011) 466–81.
Wenger, Etienne. *Communities of Practice: Learning, Meaning, and Identity*. Cambridge: Cambridge University Press, 1998.
Whittington, R. "Putting Giddens into Action: Social Systems and Managerial Agency." *Journal of Management Studies* 29 (1992) 493–712.
Wicks, D. "Institutionalized Mindsets of Invulnerability: Differentiated Institutional Fields and the Antecedents of Organizational Crisis." *Organization Studies* 22 (2001) 659–92.
Wijen, F., and S. Ansari. "Overcoming Inaction through Collective Institutional Entrepreneurship: Insights from Regime Theory." *Organization Studies* 28, no. 7 (2007) 1079–1100.
Zilber, Tammar B. "The Work of the Symbolic in Institutional Processes: Translations of Rational Myths in Israeli Hi-tech." *Academy of Management Journal* 45, no. 1 (2006) 81–101.
―――. *Institutional Patterns and Organizations: Culture and Environment*. Cambridge: Ballinger, 1988.
Zucker, Lynne G. "Organizations as Institutions." In *Research in the Sociology of Organization*, edited by S. B. Bacharach, 1–42. Greenwich, CT: JAI, 1983.

3

The Ancient-Future Time-Crystal: On the Temporality of Emerging Christianity

—— Jon Bialecki and James S. Bielo[1] ——

When is Emerging?

What is our relationship to the passing of time? How do we define the nature of time? When do we locate ourselves in time? What effect does this location have on individual experience and community practice? How do our engagements with the past, present, and future cohere and differ with each other? These are questions of temporality. With this chapter, we hope to make matters of temporality explicit for future scholarship on Emerging Christianity. Our primary goal is to outline an ethnographically informed theoretical framework that can accurately apprehend the way Emerging Christians do time.

Christians have worked to define and institutionalize their relationship with time ever since the first moment of anticipating the *parousia* of Christ. Arguably, temporality can be considered a core problematic that helps define what Christianity is and what it means to be a Christian. Christian engagements with time have also proven influential outside the boundaries of Christianity, such as lending modern time a millenarian *telos*.[2] Christians challenged that same *telos* during the nineteenth and twentieth centuries by creating the "willfully mad" discourse of dispensation, standing modernist

---

1. The authors would like to recognize each other as equal contributors and collaborators for this chapter.
2. Boyer, *When Time Shall Be No More*.

time on its head in an eschatological esprit.[3] Of course, Christians need not have a copy of the Scofield Reference Bible (or, Hal Lindsay, or a *Left Behind* novel) tucked under arm to question time's *telos*. And, Christianity should not be reduced to hosting a singular relationship with time. This is particular true for the Emerging Church.

The Emerging movement has been read as an allergic reaction to the modernism of America's politicized, megachurch evangelicalism.[4] And, Emerging Christians have crafted a host of liturgical, evangelistic, and devotional practices they believe will blunt the drive of conservative evangelical modernity. While the Emerging critique certainly involves ethics that are universal in aspiration and that suggest a different vision for what should count as "timeless" ways of being Christian, our aim in this chapter is to illustrate that there is more going on with the Emerging critique. To a large degree the Emerging movement, and the critiques it uses for fuel and orientation, casts evangelical modernism as not so much abjectly wrong as just very poorly aligned with the present historical-cultural moment. This misalignment results from the way that evangelical moderns have failed to recognize how the contemporary has shifted, how the present departs from the immediate past. Consider two examples.

First, there is the Emerging critique of Constantinianism. To some degree this is a universalist critique: the entanglement of the Church with governing powers leads the Church away from its mission (whether to stand against what is broken in the world, gather the saved for The End, or witness to the ends of all the Earth). But, this critique of Constantinianism is also distinctly about temporality. It is not only that Constantianism is a questionable, troubling, or objectionable framework, it is that it is a framework poorly suited for the current moment. In Emerging critiques of Constantinianism there are very specific historical shifts to consider, such as the rise of secularism in the age of pluralistic nation-states. Due to these shifts there is a new unworkability in any rapprochement between the Church and the State, whether formal (as in the classic Northern European Protestant State-Church) or informal (as in a politically activist, non-established Church that operates in cahoots with specific political parties and agendas). For Emerging Christians, the problems of Constantinianism are both categorical and contextual, and they devote as much time to elaborating the latter as the former.

---

3. Harding, *The Book of Jerry Falwell*; Webster, *The Anthropology of Protestantism*.
4. Bielo, *Emerging Evangelicals*; Marti and Ganiel, *The Deconstructed Church*.

Second, there is the concept of being missional, another important ingredient for the Emerging recipe. Discursively, missional functions as an identity marker, to distinguish individuals, institutions, and practices as belonging to one specific kind of Christianity, as opposed to others. (Think for a moment of all those congregational fliers and websites that feature unelaborated, declarative statements that a specific community is "missional"). Beyond the rhetorical circulation of missional, its content can be seen in two ways. One way is dispositional: a recalibration of the evangelical modern imperative towards proselytization, where one rejects the idea that proclaiming truth to a potential convert will be sufficient. Instead, one works to build relationships with non-Christians over an extended period of time. But, missional is also a temporal marker. It exceeds the promise that this is a more effective way to carry out the Great Commission, to "live like Jesus," or whatever other warrant is preferred. Being missional is also a commitment that the present moment is a new historical-cultural era in which older methods of arguing for Christian Truths have become outmoded due to shifts in society's normative relationship with Christianity.[5]

In short, both the rejection of Constantinianism and the self-conscious desire to be missional are temporal indices. As critiques, they highlight troubling conditions about the present segment on a linear time progression. Further, they upset the standard Christian entelechy. They run counter to an important teleological imperative that grounds linear Christian models of temporality by demanding that Christians look back in time. They do this in two ways.

First, they locate the center of temporal gravity "in the past" through a sort of Post-ology. The present is marked to a degree not by its actual qualities, but by what it is after: "Post-Constantinianism," "Post-Christendom," and the ubiquitous signifier we return to below, "Post-Modern." Second, Emerging Christians disrupt evangelical modern models of time by suggesting that we have all, in a way, returned to an earlier age. This return creates an opportunity for Christians to reclaim a lost condition of the Church's collective self. Living in a Post-Constantinian era means that the Church is able to return to its first, second, and third century roots. The significance of being missional tracks in part to the claim that there is something "pagan" about contemporary society; either in the absence of Christian values and knowledge (a more conservative critique), or alternately in society's savage socio-political-economic configuration (a more

---

5. Engelke, *A Problem of Presence*.

progressive critique). To successfully "be the Church" in this new pagan world, contemporary Christians must rediscover how their distant relatives in time engaged the old pagan world. The imperative is temporal to the core: look back, remember, return, rediscover.

A striking expression of this temporal imperative is the Emerging championing of "ancient-future." The term's originator, American theologian Robert Webber used "ancient-future" broadly as a way to characterize faith, evangelism, and worship.[6] His broad sense of the term is carried forward by some, but many Emerging Christians associate ancient-future strictly with liturgical forms that reference, adapt, or incorporate elements of earlier Christian devotional and ritual practices. Given the entanglement of Protestantism and modernity, these practices tend toward Roman Catholicism and Eastern Orthodoxy. For example, we find Emerging Church communities that place heightened emphasis on public creedal recitation, ritually read monastic prayers, burn incense and candles, sing "ancient" songs, chant Orthodox prayers, use ritual icons and devotional art, create prayer labyrinths, closely following the Church calendar for sermon writing and shared readings, read scripture using the method of *lectio divina*, and elevate the role of contemplative silence during worship.

The Emerging attraction to ancient-future has several sources, each stemming from the temporal disjuncture that characterizes Emerging Christianity. There is a generational warrant that echoes the calls to be anti-Constantinian and missional. "Post-Baby Boomers," particularly Millennials, need multi-modal forms of worship that engage multiple senses because their bodies have been socialized by a media culture that is both more relentless and more diverse than that of the Boomers.[7] Then, there is the idea that ancient-future amounts to a literal recouping of worship forms that have up to the present been lost among American Protestants. In one way this also suggests a return to a prior condition, echoing again anti-Constantinian and missional calls. To use the worship forms of an earlier age is to accomplish a multiple return: to needed practices, to a location in time, and to the religious authenticity of that location.

The temporality of ancient-future is clarified by its performance. Consider how the suite of "earlier" worship practices being "rediscovered" are performed amid and through technologies that are perfectly at home, even products of, the present moment. Modern instruments are used to perform

---

6. Webber, *Ancient-Future Faith*.
7. Hirschkind *The Ethical Soundscape*; Reinhardt, *A Christian Plain of Immanence*.

ancient songs; images of icons and art are gathered on a laptop and digitally projected onto a screen; *lectio divina* and creedal readings are done from smart phones; prayer labyrinths are built from popular commodities. Similarly, we should not ignore the pivotal role played by various internet technologies in the making and maintenance of Emerging Church networks, centers, and communities (i.e., the movement itself). These materialities of the contemporary lean in the direction of the future, particularly as they are juxtaposed with their use to convey "ancient" worship practices. Yet, these materialities do not threaten the promise of rediscovery. Ancient-future does not require a wholesale return to the past, only a strategic engagement with the past. And, multiple temporal conditions operate in parallel with one another, not as ordered units in a sequence. We return to this juxtaposition and the idea of parallel temporalities below, but first we dwell a little longer on Emerging treatments of the "modern" and the "post-modern."

Post-Modernism's Modernism

This temporal disjuncture has been observed in the scholarly literature about the Emerging Church, but it remains under-theorized.[8] That is, while we have thick descriptions of how Emerging Christians do time, we lack a framework for understanding how Emerging temporality works and how it differs from other expressions of Christian temporality. Outlining such a framework is the central goal of this chapter, but to do so we need a clearer sense for the temporalities named by Emerging communities, namely "modernity" and "post-modernity."

For popular and scholarly crowds alike, a common way to articulate the temporal disjuncture that characterizes the Emerging Church is to call it "post-modern." This is an articulation that Emerging Christians largely recognize as legitimate, if not affirm as accurate or advocate outright. Emerging communities have marshaled "post-Modern" to a similar effect, and with similar gusto, as they have "being missional." Yet, anthropologically, there is no denying that Emerging Christians continue to display modern dispositions. For example, Emerging discourse practices are shot through with an irony rooted in a commitment that there is something equally necessary and impossible about the sincerity demanded by the

---

8. Bielo, *Emerging Evangelicals*; Marti and Ganiel, *The Deconstructed Church*; Packard, *The Emerging Church*.

semiotic ideology of modern Protestantism.⁹ Practicing irony is a way to hold true to the ethical vision. It is, in fact, a way to intensify that vision by purposefully fulfilling the imperative in a way that reveals its seams and boundaries. We might also recall that, at least in aesthetics, irony is a deeply modernist construct. Frederic Jameson argues strongly in his classic work on postmodernity that there is an implicit modernist universalism in irony as opposed to pastiche.¹⁰ Like satire, irony addresses sidelong what cannot be said outright, but which remains insistent. By way of contrast, pastiche is flat, a logic of simple juxtaposition.

Despite the Emerging movement's continuing modernism, there may be some benefit yet of articulating "ancient-future" as a "post-modern" phenomenon. For example, consider this pictorial depiction on the February 2008 cover of Christianity Today.

Figure 1: February 2008 Christianity Today cover art.

His image claims to convey core features of the Emerging Church. To do so, it marshals several indexical signs. We have the head of a white, millennial, middle-class, contemplative male. This head is sutured to a body that is half ipod. This (cyborgian?) composition has unearthed an ornate

9. Bielo, *Emerging Evangelicals*; Keane, "Sincerity, 'Modernity,' and the Protestants."
10. Jameson, *Postmodernism*.

golden cross, a shovel plunged into the ground off to the side. Framing devices give definition to the image: "Lost Secrets," "Ancient Church," "looking back," "move forward." The framing language works alone, without the aid of any background context. The image is set only against blank white space. With the abandonment of perspective and the simulation of collage, this image could be taken as a Christianized version of the post-modern aesthetic. Returning to Jameson, this image is more like Andy Warhol than it is Van Gogh's painting of peasant shoes.

Another iteration of ancient-future's post-modernism is in the specific material features that are used to produce the sensual panoply of "ancient" practices. Ancient-future worship is performed not just by purposefully confusing temporalities as we noted above (think: icons on ipads), but also by eliding modern binary divisions between high/low, sacred/profane, and religious/secular. An Emerging community that met in Cincinnati, Ohio for several years provides a clear illustration.

"Thinplace" was created by an Emerging Christian named Lilly. Lilly spent most of her life in conservative evangelical churches, including years as a youth and worship pastor. Her deconversion out of conservative evangelicalism was primarily about how worship was imagined and conducted. She was equally opposed to how the spoken sermon and minimal aesthetics are over-valued, while formal liturgies are under-valued. For Lilly, evangelical worship has been reduced to equal musical performance, the noise of which crowds out needed contemplative opportunities for silence.

In 2008, Lilly organized a loosely knit community of ancient-future worshippers in the Cincinnati area. "Thinplace" is a term she adapted from the Celtic Christian tradition; naming, too, is a resource in the Emerging desire to rediscover the lost past. Thin places originally referred to physical spaces on the earth where God's presence could be most readily felt (where the line between heaven and earth was at its most thin). Lilly's adaptation redirects the pursuit from making pilgrimage to thinplaces to creating thinplaces wherever you are; any place can be made thin through strategic ritual action.

Thinplace consisted of three regularly held events: a bi-weekly "Artwalk," in which participants gathered at the Cincinnati Art Museum to perform a prayer walk through the exhibits (framed by a *lectio divina* scripture reading beforehand and an open discussion afterward); a weekly journaling group organized around *lectio divina*, silent reflection, and open discussion;

PART 1: DEFINING BOUNDARIES

and, a monthly "Maproom," a "multi-sensory," "curated" worship space. For Lilly, the focus of all three events is to "experience God."

In February 2010 the Maproom theme aligned with two calendars, the Church's and Hallmark's: "Lenten Hobo Honeymoon." The flyer for the event combined an image (an early Middle age painting of Madonna and Child, devotional art indexing ancient faith) with three lines of framing text:

"Maproom is an experiential worship gathering where you can spend five minutes or three hours.

Maproom is a place where you engage God on your own . . . interacting with prayer stations set up around the room. Each station involves one or more of your senses.

Maproom is a place to be still, and a place to create your prayers in art. Come experience worship beyond preaching and singing."

Lilly's preferred location for Maproom was not a church building, but a coffee shop next to the University of Cincinnati. The pastor who owned the shop was a friend and ministry partner of Lilly's. He was pleased to offer the space as the host for Maproom. For Lilly, the shop's size and the fact that it was closed on Sundays made it a perfect fit. Unlike Artwalk and the journaling group, Maproom was a labor-intensive event and required a relatively large, adjustable meeting space. Like Artwalk and the journaling group, Maproom was open to the public, but was mainly attended by Thinplace regulars.

A take-home sheet available as you first enter the space described the theme:

> "The title of our journey is "Lenten Hobo Honeymoon," inspired by a book by the same name by Edward Hays. What is a Hobo Honeymoon you may ask? A Hobo is a pilgrim working his/her way Home . . .
>
> A Honeymoon . . . it's a special time set aside exclusively for the one you love. So what if we actually take time to FALL in LOVE with JESUS during Lent . . . the days between now and Easter. Where could we be by Easter on our journey with God?"

This theme was repeated in 14 prayer stations, with material items iconically restating the theme throughout (e.g., hiking boots, camping gear, bandanas, maps, walking sticks, and heart-shaped objects). Slow, soft, instrumental music played on overhead speakers as participants proceeded through Maproom: silently, each at their own pace, arriving whenever they want, staying however long they want. Each of the 14 stations provided a different activity for participants. For example, Station 1 featured some phonological play.

Figure 2: Station 1 of Lilly's Maproom.

Dryer lint from Lilly's home dryer is spread on the table, next to lint rollers and cards with self-reflective questions and scriptural texts. The interactive portion of the station asks you to roll the lint brush on your clothes, and consider the removed lint as a representation of how Jesus removes sin from our lives. The remaining stations repeat this refusal of modern binary divisions. High/low, sacred/profane, and religious/secular are creatively scrambled by Lilly, and purposefully engaged by Maproom participants.

Here again, much like the play of irony and sincerity, the Emerging post-modernism of Maproom is not stripped completely of modernist elements. For example, the subjectivity presumed in this expression of ancient-future worship is not the fractured subject of post-modernity. It is, instead, a highly reflexive self-conscious modern subject. Through practices such as journaling and engaging a series of reflexive questions, ancient-future worship encourages a creative self consistently engaged in authoring a narrative about one's life-arc. Further, the materiality here remains locked in the logic of representation. The various dioramas, displays, icons, and readings are all meant and trusted to signify clearly. Despite the emphasis and strategic use of the sensual and the multimodal, the prayer stations still operate within the logic of denotation, the default speech ethic of modern Protestantism. This logic of representation suggests a stability in the operation of the sign. This representational stability directly clashes with high post-modernism's pronouncements about the contingency of the sign and the unmoored play of the signifier.

We have now outlined the core problem that animates this chapter. The discourse and performance of ancient-future marks a key feature of the Emerging movement: temporal disjuncture, such as that between the modernist subjectivities encouraged by worship practices and the post-modern aesthetics that define them. We must now begin outlining a theoretical framework that can make sense of not just individual instances of disjuncture, but the fact that the Emerging orientation is defined by disjuncture. For this, we look to the philosophical work of Gilles Deleuze.

The Virtual

We can begin by articulating a choice. The choice is to understand modernism and post-modernism as temporalities operating at different intensities (or, different speeds), not as qualitatively different temporalities. In short, post-modernism is not a break from modernism, but modernism with the throttle opened all the way up.[11] This choice allows us to ask how ancient-future is a sort of aesthetic high modernism, not a confused or failed modernism. This involves our seeing "post-modern" phenomena as more akin to the modernity that it is usually seen as replacing. Further, this allows us to grasp the disjuncture in the temporality and historical imagination of ancient-future. For this discussion to make the most sense, we must elaborate on a key term, which is the idea of "potential."

Treating ancient-future worship rituals as a kind of high modernism means seeing them as being part of a process of charting a self-consistent system of potentialities. Here, Lilly's choice of the term "Maproom" to name the ritual is very much on point. Consider again the self-reflective questions that are asked throughout Maproom's prayer stations. For example, Station 5, "The Stuff In Your BackPack," asks: "What is weighing down your pack today? What things are making you slow and heavy, slowing you down on your journey?" The point of asking questions like this, questions

---

11. Harvey, *The Condition of Postmodernity*.

that are at once rather specific, yet still rather vague at the same time, is to spur further development and definition of where one "is" in one's life, and where one is "going," while at the same time insuring that the question does not overdetermine what the answer "is." Together, the prayer stations catalyze a narrativizing of life, but only through asking a series of open-ended questions that summon up swaths of one's life, and one's capacities to make determinate choices in one's life, without specifying to any degree of thickness what those circumstances and choices might be. In short, they open up a series of horizons; that is, directions in which one can move while still allowing things to remain relatively unfixed.

To understand why the terms of "potentialities" and "horizons" are useful, we can move briefly from Maproom to scholarship in the anthropology of religion. Scholars have recently been interested in framing ritual and religious practice as either realizing or facilitating the realization of structured but still indeterminate potentials. Put differently, religion and rituals involve iterable problems that give birth to a range of differential solutions.[12]

In this vision, a key purpose of ritual is to take the wealth of potential inherent in any problematic and make its contours visible, to "slow it down" so to speak. This approach has particular promise for the anthropology of Christian populations, which are often predicated on particular problematics. Several scholars have articulated these problematics as "tensions."[13] While this pattern is not unique to Christian populations, the ethnography of Christian populations has been particularly successful in demonstrating how these tensions are never really resolved. Rather, they are more like problems to luxuriate in. Living amid problems leads to an increase in ritual activity, rather than a cessation. Each ritual performance and innovation works as an attempt to address a persistent problem; always effective but never final.

Much of this work on ritual as a form of slowing down open potential is drawn from the writings of Gilles Deleuze. Borrowing the term from the French philosopher Henri Bergson, Deleuze names these swaths of problem-based potential "the virtual."[14] Deleuze contrasted the virtual with

12. Bialecki, "Virtual Christianity in an Age of Nominalist Anthropology"; "After the Denominozoic"; "Diagramming the Will."

13. Tomlinson, *In God's Image*, 12; Bialecki, "Disjuncture"; "No Caller I.D. for the Soul"; Bielo, *The "Emerging Church" in America*, 154–55; Engelke, *A Problem of Presence*; Robbins, *Secrecy and the Sense of an Ending*.

14. Deleuze, *Cinema 2*.

"the actual," but not in the sense that one is real and the other not. Both are perfectly real. Rather, the virtual and the actual differ in the sense that the virtual is defined by potentials that have not gone through any process of actualization. Though not actualized, the virtual is still graspable in a variety of modes. While Deleuze's profession of philosophy meant he often focused on "thought" or "thinking" or "philosophy" as a mode through which the virtual was apprehended, he acknowledged that other human activities have that capacity as well. Deleuze viewed art, for instance, as the production of perceptions and intensities that draw the attention of the individual engaging with art away from the actual and towards the virtual. That is, attention is drawn away from the actualized product in front of the viewer and toward the series of virtual possibilities that were not (or, better, have yet to be) actualized. Rather than simply assert a constant play of signification, Deleuze felt that bringing one's attention from the actual to the more open virtual was an achievement that followed an *askesis*, a purposeful discipline and a concerted effort. Deleuze's most elaborate effort to think through how the virtual worked was his analysis of the cinema. It is Deleuze's reflections on the cinema as an art form that allows us to grasp ancient-future and its temporal disjunctures as a virtual field, full of potential and structuring the actual.

The Time-Crystal

Deleuze's two volume analysis of twentieth century cinema discusses a fundamental shift in films from the "movement-image" to the "time-image."[15] Understanding the difference between these two will help us understand how temporality works as a virtual field, and thus how ancient-future temporality works in the Emerging movement.

Cinema prior to World War II was concerned with the "movement image," which sought to visually capture affect and intensity through the concrete movement of bodies. Cinema used this process to "think" time. This was a cinema that invested its faith in the effect of human agency, both individual (e.g., films produced through the U.S. movie industry, perhaps exemplified by the work of D. W. Griffith) and collective (e.g., classic Soviet cinema, by auteurs such as Sergei Eisenstein). This is the nineteenth century vision of temporality and history: affect and movement are chained

15. Deleuze, *The Time-Image*.

together causally, humans (individually and collectively) are privileged as the agents of change, and time proceeds in a linear fashion.

Cinema then shifted after the rubicon of World War II. Instead of using affect-spurred bodily movement to depicting time as linear, cinema began experimenting with presenting time itself directly through optical and aural representation. This shift to the "time-image" involved overcoming the "objectivity" of classical cinema. Post-WWII cinema could be ordered by "objective and subjective, real and imaginary, physical and mental" poles. This new ordering produced at least three cinematic innovations. First, there is the hallucinatory aspect of much of post-WWII cinema. Second, there are two now very common cinematic tropes: scenes that convey the subjective fantasies or reveries of characters, and scenes where it is unclear as to whether events within the world of a particular film are being depicted as "really" happening. And, third, there is the use of long scene takes that depict either: objects and spaces where there is little or no movement, or do no work to advance a film's "plot" via interlocking kinesthetic actions.

This shift from the movement-image to the time-image has several consequences. First, there is a dilation of focus to broaden agency beyond individual or collective human actors. Second, there is a "subjectification" of cinema. Third, affect hovers unmoored over a scene, rather than being localized in particular characters. And, fourth, there is a greater degree of "break" from linear narratives.

Cinema's practice of adding memory and fantasy to the present works analogically for thinking through the virtual. Just like in time-image cinema, the virtual has multiple temporalities operating as parallel tracks, not as the movement-image's ordered sequence. The time-image depicts potential; that is, a multiplicity of options that are distinguishable from each other. (Still, because they per force share a commonality, this is not a wild juxtaposition of images without any connection whatsoever.) By engaging memory and fantasy as equally real to present time within the world of a film, the time-image gives similar weight to the virtual and the actual. In short, virtual and actual are allowed to "resemble" one another.

Some films in post-WWII cinema pushed the virtual-actual resemblance to an extreme, creating a circuit in which the viewer is constantly shuttled back and forth between the virtual and the actual. This shuttling levels the virtual and the actual without undoing their distinction. This is often represented in film through tropes, such as: using mirrors, the doubling of characters, having different characters echo or "rhyme" with one another, or purposefully marking a difference within the world of the film between "actor" and "character" (e.g. presenting a "film within a film"). The "time-crystal" is what Deleuze called this close circuity between the actual and the virtual. Here, past, present, and future do not collapse into one another, but are different and equivalent facets of the cinematic world.

In the time-crystal, the virtual is the set of potentials inherent in a plurifom past, either through actual events or fantasies. These potentials are restricted to being extrapolations from past events, reconfigured memories that are only partially actualized. The virtual—as a past that may still lead to multiple futures, or as a fantasy pointing to an actualization not taken—is kept open as being "alongside" (or, leveled with) the actual. In short, the past is a live option pointing to other futures, which is equally insistent as the actual present it appears next to.

The Ancient-Future Time-Crystal

What do we gain from outlining Deleuze's writings on cinematic shifts? Our argument is this: Deleuze's time-crystal provides a theoretical language for thinking through the temporality that has been so crucial for the Emerging Church.

We have shown that the ritual spaces created by Lilly, and her Emerging kin, are about charting virtual potentialities. Invoking the time crystal helps us see that the side-by-side, purposeful and marked, uses of "ancient" and "future" technologies is another meditation on potentiality. When these temporal markers are summoned, a sense of history and time is created through various material indexes of the past, such as icons or *lectio divina*, even when placed alongside material indexes of the contemporary (e.g., smart phones). While this is to some degree a disjuncture, the fact that they operate alongside without major disruption suggests a parallel mirroring. Consider Emerging claims that the visual culture of the contemporary media makes the icon visible, or that the current missional church is like the church of the first three centuries. The similarities between objects such as the icon and the avatar, or between Gregorian chants and ambient techno music, are just as important as the differences—and in fact it is only the similarities which allow them to be placed alongside of one another, so that the differences can become visible. Like the time-crystal in the cinema's time-image, Emerging Christians shuttle back and forth among temporal locations.

Thinking about how the time-crystal works in cinema, then, helps us think about how Emerging temporality works. The resonance of this argument rises given the relative absence of Deleuze in discourses about the Emerging movement. There are occasional references to Deleuze by authors working from an explicitly Christian confessional standpoint[16] as well as a few works that consider Deleuze's implications for theological thought.[17] And, Deleuze is occasionally referenced in Emerging-leaning network encounters, both face-to-face and online (though not nearly as much as other popular French intellectuals, such as Derrida or Foucault). However, the Deleuze that appears in these contexts is the Deleuze associated with ideas such as "becoming" or "the rhizomic."[18] The absence of any direct references to Delueze's work on cinematic shifts might suggest that our invocation of the concept is nothing but a theoretical wrong turn. After all, Deleuze did not understand the time-image as a cognitive universal, but a particular historical shift located within a particular art form. Should we turn around and go back? No. Consider two reasons our argument remains worth entertaining.

First, there is the specific, conscious, and marked relation that the Emerging Church has to media. Not only does the Emerging Church have an active interest in media production and late modern theories of mass media, media consumption is to a considerable degree a chief warrant Emerging Christians offer for their existence. This shift is not a neutral one, however. Emerging worship strives to be multimodal in that it sees itself as reaching out to all the senses, including the olfactory (e.g., use of incense), the haptic/tactile, and the iconic presentation of material that emphasizes the haptic and tactile aspects of different materialities.[19] But, all these senses are not weighed equally. The oral/aural is sometimes marked as a problematic mode of conveyance, and the kinesthetic, haptic, and tactile senses offer their own logistical problems as possible privileged sensory modes. As

---

16. See, for example, Raschke, *GloboChrist*.

17. See, for example, Barber, *Deleuze and the Naming of God*; Sherman, "No Werewolves in Theology?"; Shults, *Iconoclastic Theology*.

18. Deleuze is also largely unaddressed in scholarship *about* the Emerging Church. To our knowledge, there is only one social scientific analysis of the Emerging Church that looks to Deleuze. Packard and Sanders, "Emerging Church as Corporatization's Line of Flight," use Deleuze's "lines of flight" to argue that Emerging Christians in the U.S. leverage discontinuities of corporatization processes to avoid reproducing rigid, ultra-rationalized institutions.

19. Bielo, *Emerging Evangelicals*, 95–96.

a result, the visual becomes the sense they lean on most, perhaps returning them to an uncomfortably close position of being more like the conservative evangelical modern forms they seek to leave behind. And, while the expansion of television and the birth of internet video means that celluloid will not be per se the medium through which most visual material is conveyed in the present moment, it seems safe to say that the visual grammar of the cinema has been a predominate force in these non-film media. Given the influence that media in general, and film in particular, has had on the development of Emerging sensibilities, it would not be too surprising if filmic aspects have bled over to the Emerging ritual imaginary.

The other factor that might explain the chance convergence of Deleuze's time-image cinema and Emerging ancient-future ritual practice is this: both are fundamentally about confronting the same problem. We have shown that much of the Emerging Church's core concerns are matters of temporality, often articulated as the sense that the movement has broken with what appeared to be a previous linear progress towards a recognizable *telos*. And, this is undoubtedly an issue that drives a great deal of Emerging thought, as Emerging Christians are deeply invested in "The Church" as an institution, even as they may invest less importance in denominations or other overreaching institutions that have served as placeholders for "The Church" throughout the twentieth century.[20]

This concern with the Church's place in history is no doubt sincerely felt, but a careful look at the Maproom suggests that it may be epiphenomenal to, or even a project of, a concern that strikes much more closely to home. All of Maproom's self-reflective questions are addressed to the individual participants of Maproom. Furthermore, none of these questions have a rhetorical edge. These are questions asked as if the answers are generally unknown. Even the particular imperatives are cast in metaphorical language, which is to say that they are all highly context dependent, and that acting them out requires a higher degree of judgment by the Maproom participant.

This is important because while all ritual may in some way work to make virtualities visible, they do not all have this degree of openness. Anthropologist Rupert Stasch argues that it is useful to see ritual as involving "exceptionally dense representations of spatiotemporally wider categories and principles in an interactional here-now."[21] But, this "dense

20. Packard and Sanders, "Emerging Church as Corporatization's Line of Flight."
21. Stasch, "Ritual and Oratory Revisited," 160.

representation" can just as often be used to constrict the realm of the virtual as to dilate it. Ritual is not always certainty's enemy, as it is with Maproom. If we want to boil the Maproom down to its essentials, it does not state "here is what you should do now," but rather asks, nervously, "what is it that you *can* do now?" It is the expression of a set of anxieties about the present moment, now that the certitudes of a conservative evangelical framing of the world have been set aside as unworkable.

In short, Maproom is an open inquiry into this particular present moment of time. Emerging ritual incorporates visions of the past and future because it is uncertain about what it is doing at the present moment. Paola Marrati, speaking of Deleuze's account of post-WWII cinema, observed that "[i]t is when history is broken that time presents itself in its *pure state* and deploys all the power of its non chronological dimensions."[22] For Emerging Christians at the present moment, both at the level of the Church and the individual believer, time is broken. These post-Baby Boomers are thinking through this brokenness through the argot of their first media language. It is no wonder, then, that the ritual they produce looks so similar to the cinema of a historical moment that found many at a loss about the future's certainties, unclear of where or how to step forward next. Deleuze's cinema and Emerging are similar not only because they share a visual language, but because they are both fundamentally asking about temporality as crisis.

For those who have a personal investment in the Emerging movement, it may be reasonable to ask whether this similarity is healthy. The time-crystal is not necessarily a positive formation, as there is a danger in the way that it levels the virtual and the actual as in some ways coeval and coequal. The reason for this lies in the term "crystal." The danger is inherent in the idea that an overly concretized virtual that is just one "facet" of the present moment alongside the actual can result in what is in effect an endless shuttling between the actual and the virtual, allowing for the illusion of a great deal of movement, but not much actual change. This does not have to be the case.

In discussing various filmic instantiations of the time crystal, Deleuze distinguished between three ways in which the actual and the virtual might resemble one another. This is his typology of "perfect," "cracked," and "degenerate" crystals. In perfect crystals, we have a virtual which is a perfect expression of the actual, but which by force means that it always returns to it. In the cracked crystal, we have a "flaw" in the reflection, where

22. Marrati, *Gilles Deleuze*, 78.

something escapes in either the actual or the virtual: "something is going to slip away in the background, in depth . . . through the crack."[23] Lastly, in the degenerate crystal we have a moment in which the reflection is "too late," where despite a seeming symmetry, some aspect cannot be actualized. The moment of alignment has passed, perhaps always already passed. So, which of these three time-crystals accurately captures the workings of ancient-future? Or, what is the degree of fit between the ancient and the future in the Emerging temporality?

Logics of pure equivalence between the ancient and the future offer no way out, and are the equivalent of Deleuze's perfect crystal, where the doublings of time are conveyed through film. For example, consider especially literal interpretations of "the new monasticism," where this constellation of practices is taken as being fully equivalent to earlier practices coded as "monastic" in origin and character.[24] In these comparably strict re-imaginings, the sense of "new" being used actually offers nothing new, but is novel only in the sense of a return, as when we talk about some reiteration that ends up strengthening the office or institution (such as references to the "new president," where individuality is subsumed to the role being fulfilled). Likewise, versions of ancient-future that stress pure disconnect exemplify Deleuze's degenerate crystal. Here, older forms of Christianity become merely exercises in nostalgia in the original and literal sense of the term, a sickness caused by the past. In this case ancient-future worship would be a form of mourning a loss of Christian plentitude.

What remains is the cracked crystal. Maproom, like other expressions of ancient-future worship, is best apprehended through this version of the time-image. Unlike the perfect and degenerate crystals, the cracked crystal allows for (at least metaphorical) movement, Deleuze's "slipping away into the background." The crystalline element of the Maproom is especially evident in its referencing of Lent, its evocation of "Ash Wednesday," and its use of a "station" model that directly indexes the Roman Catholic devotional practice of walking the Stations of the Cross. Past and present are once again laid alongside each other in an intentional, strategic, and marked manner. But, the very quotidian nature of the materiality that the Maproom relies upon, as well as the wider world that it gestures to, has all sorts of other possible metonymic links. These links draw attention not just back to the present moment, effecting a pure virtual-actual time crystal,

---

23. Deleuze, *Cinema 1*, 85.
24. For example, Bielo, *Emerging Evangelicals*, 117.

but beyond the actual-virtual circuit. For instance, one of the Maproom's stations references the then-topical 2010 Haitian earthquake. Another station, through using images of impoverished Africans and explicitly naming Palestinian refugees, raises issues of political economy. By linking to such global concerns—and by transforming those concerns from being distant and mass mediated to being immanently present in the ritual space of Maproom—it is impossible to see the here and now as a simple iteration of a crystalline early Church past. Rather than merely presenting a simple statement that the contemporary ritual moment is a pure reiteration of a similar, but markedly "past" ritual moment, the Maproom continually gestures to aspects of the contemporary "actual" world that are not obviously mirrors of Lent or of the Stations of the Cross. It is these fleeting gestures that break the symmetry, and thereby constitutes a "crack" in the crystal.

Again, the crack in the crystal is not a flaw, but an additional capacity. The idea of a crystalline relation between the actual and virtual does not foreclose action in the world, but opens up for the possibility of multiple actions by allowing for returns to the past that are askew, that do not require a perfect resemblance between "ancient" and "future," "then" and "now," "past" and "present." This is important. While the Emerging Church seems to have abandoned the teleological edge of evangelical modernity, in its vision of making a difference in the world it has not entirely abandoned the idea of moving forward. That movement, wherever it might be leading, is facilitated by the cracked time-crystal of an ancient-future temporality.

Bibliography

Barber, Daniel Colucciello. *Deleuze and the Naming of God: Post-Secularism and the Future of Immanence*. Edinburgh: Edinburgh University Press, 2014.

Bialecki, Jon. "After the Denominozoic: Evolution, Differentiation, Denominationalism." *Current Anthropology* 55, S10 (2014) S193–S204.

———. "Diagramming the Will: Ethics and Prayer, Text and Politics." *Ethnos* (2014). DOI: 10.1080/00141844.2014.986151

———. "Disjuncture, Continental Philosophy's New 'Political Paul,' and the Question of Progressive Christianity in a Southern Californian Third Wave Church." *American Ethnologist* 36, no. 1 (2009) 110–23.

———. "No Caller I.D. for the Soul—Demonization, Charisms, and the Unstable Subject of Protestant Language Ideology." *Anthropological Quarterly* 84, no. 3 (2011) 679–703.

———. "Virtual Religion." In *Oxford Handbook of the Anthropology of Religion*, edited by Simon Coleman and Joel Robbins. Oxford: Oxford University Press, forthcoming.

PART 1: DEFINING BOUNDARIES

———. "Virtual Christianity in an Age of Nominalist Anthropology." *Anthropological Theory* 12, no. 3 (2012) 295–319.

Bielo, James S. "The 'Emerging Church' in America: Notes on the Interaction of Christianities." *Religion* 39 (2009) 219–32.

———. *Emerging Evangelicals: Faith, Modernity, and the Desire for Authenticity.* New York: NYU Press, 2011.

Bloch, Maurice. "Symbols, Song, Dance and Features of Articulation: Is Religion an Extreme Form of Traditional Authority?" *European Journal of Sociology* 15, no. 1 (1974) 54–81.

Boyer, Paul S. *When Time Shall Be No More: Prophecy Belief in Modern American Culture.* Cambridge, MA: Harvard University Press, 1992.

Deleuze, Gilles. *Cinema 1: The Movement-Image.* Minneapolis: University of Minnesota Press, 1986.

———. *Cinema 2: The Time-Image.* Minneapolis: University of Minnesota Press, 1989.

———. *Difference and Repetition.* London: Continuum, 2001.

Engelke, Matthew. *God's Agents: Biblical Publicity in Contemporary England.* Berkeley: University of California Press, 2013.

———. *A Problem of Presence: Beyond Scripture in an African Church.* Berkeley: University of California Press, 2007.

Harding, Susan F. *The Book of Jerry Falwell: Fundamentalist Language and Politics.* Princeton: Princeton University Press, 2000.

Harvey, David. *The Condition of Postmodernity: An Inquiry into the Origins of Cultural Change.* London: Wiley-Blackwell, 1989.

Hirschkind, Charles. "The Ethical Soundscape: Cassette Sermons and Islamic Couterpublics." New York: Columbia University Press, 2006.

Jameson, Frederic. *Postmodernism, or, The Cultural Logic of Late Capitalism.* Durham, NC: Duke University Press, 1991.

Keane, Webb. "Sincerity, 'Modernity,' and the Protestants." *Cultural Anthropology* 17, no. 1 (2002) 65–92.

Marrati, Paola. *Gilles Deleuze: Cinema and Philosophy.* Translated by Alissa Hartz. Baltimore: John Hopkins University Press, 2008.

Marti, Gerardo, and Gladys Ganiel. *The Deconstructed Church: Understanding Emerging Christianity.* Oxford: Oxford University Press, 2014.

Packard, Josh. *The Emerging Church: Religion at the Margins.* Boulder, CO: Reiner, 2011.

Packard, Josh, and George Sanders. 2013. "The Emerging Church as Corporatization's Line of Flight." *Journal of Contemporary Religion* 28, no. 3 (2013) 437–55.

Raschke, Carl. *GloboChrist: The Great Commission Takes a Postmodern Turn.* Grand Rapids: Baker Academic, 2008.

Reinhardt, Bruno. "A Christian Plain of Immanence: Contrapuntal Reflections on Deleuze and Pentecostal Spirituality." *Hau* 5, no. 1 (2015) 405–36.

Robbins, Joel. "Secrecy and the Sense of an Ending: Narrative, Time, and Everyday Millenarianism in Papua New Guinea and in Christian Fundamentalism." *Comparative Studies in Society and History* 43, no. 3 (2001) 525–51.

Sherman, Jacob Holsinger. "No Werewolves in Theology? Transcendence, Immanence, and Becoming Divine In Gilles Deleuze." *Modern Theology* 25, no. 1 (2009) 1–20.

Schults, F. LeRon. *Iconoclastic Theology: Gilles Deleuze and the Secretion of Atheism.* Edinburgh: Edinburgh University Press, 2014.

Stasch, Rupert. "Ritual and Oratory Revisited: The Semiotics of Effective Action." *Annual Review of Anthropology* 40 (2011) 159–74

Tomlinson, Matt. *In God's Image: The Metaculture of Fijian Christianity*. Berkeley: University of California Press, 2009.

Webber, Robert. *Ancient-Future Faith: Rethinking Evangelicalism for a Postmodern World*. Grand Rapids: Baker Academic, 1999.

Webster, Joseph. *The Anthropology of Protestantism: Faith and Crisis Among Scottish Fisherman*. New York: Palgrave, 2013.

4

A Feminist Theological Analysis of the Leadership Structures of the Emerging Church

Xochitl Alvizo

An analysis of the literature on the Emerging Church,[1] both in works based on research with the Emerging Church (Jones, Marti and Ganiel, Larson and Osborne) and in works written by ministers and participants of Emerging Church congregations (Bolz-Weber, Kimball, Rodkey, Sawyer, Snider, Spellers), reveals the Emerging Church's commitment to form a church that is organic, relational, and inclusive in character.[2] The Emerging Church understands these qualities to be necessary components for an

---

1. The term itself "emerging church" was first introduced by Larson and Osborne in *The Emerging Church*. At the time it did not refer to the Emerging Church of today—as a recognizable genre of Christian congregations that have certain shared qualities, but more generally to the church they saw "emerging" in their time for their changing culture. Today, scholars use different terms for the "Emerging Church," reflecting varying definitions. This project is ecclesiological in nature; the term "Emerging Church" suffices in reference to my subject matter and accords with the literature. I also speak often of "congregation/s" when referring to singular or multiple Emerging Churches. The term reflects my use of a congregational-studies approach in my research. I recognize, however, that not all Emerging Church communities would use such a term, preferring to think of themselves as a collective, gathering, or simply "community," and my use of it is due to the nature of this practical theological project.

2. These reflect only a small sampling of the literature I reviewed: Jones, *The Church is Flat*; Larson and Osborne, *Emerging Church*; Marti and Ganiel, *Deconstructed Church*; Kimball, *Emerging Church*; Snider, *The Hyphenateds* (with essays from Nadia Bolz-Weber, "Innovating with integrity: Exploring the Core and Innovative Edges of Postmodern Ministry," 1–11; Christopher Rodkey, "Satanism in the Suburbs: Ordination as Insubordination," 47–60; Stephanie Spellers, "Monocultural Church in a Hybrid World," 12–25; and Nanette Sawyer, "The Imperative of Imagination," 70–80); and Snider and Bowen, *Toward a Hopeful Future*.

embodiment of church that follows in the way and witness of Jesus Christ. Central to its vision are changes that make for such a church—a church that is alive, uniquely formed at the grassroots, and continually being reformed in response to and in relationship with its community (organic); a church that is relationally centered, having no hierarchy, professional Christians, or second-class citizenship, a church that is characterized first and foremost as a community of mutual trust and participation (relational); and a church open to change, change based on encounters among those within the church as well as with those outside of it, a church that never closes itself off in fear but is always open to questioning and critique (inclusive).[3]

Early in my exploration of the Emerging Church I noted the connection between the Emerging Church's aims and the work and focus of feminist theology. Early feminist theologians, inspired by the women's liberation movement of the late 1960s and early 1970s, called for reforms that today parallel that which the Emerging Church seeks to embody as an organic, relational, and inclusive form of church. They raised charges against the church regarding its habits of exclusion, hierarchy, clericalism, and especially the embedded sexism and misogyny in its structures and habits, as well as its overall obstinacy in the face of the changing times. However, it is a rare exception to encounter references to feminist theology or to the work of prominent feminist theologians either in the literature about the Emerging Church or in Emerging Church related conferences—an omission that seemed contrary to its desires of being relational and inclusive, and responsive to the hurts and negative experiences people have had within church. It was also not long into my research with the Emerging Church that I encountered critiques made against the Emerging Church by people within the movement itself, including concerns similar to those raised by feminist theologians decades earlier. Feminist critiques of church, including those mentioned above, were being raised by women involved in the Emerging Church.[4] Additionally, some popular literature and public conversations

---

3. I chose to use the specific terms—organic, relational, and inclusive—to represent recurring themes that are dominant in the Emerging Church literature. The terms themselves appear often within the literature (and in many of the Emerging Church book titles) along with other synonymous words. I chose these three though other words could have likewise captured the themes.

4. Such critiques were expressed to me in conversation by Emerging Church women —who are loosely organized through a collective blog—in Claremont, CA at the Emergent Village Theological Conversation, January 31–February 2, 2012. As no books have yet been published on the topic of feminism (or women) and the Emerging Church, this information is primarily found in Emerging Church women's blogs and is based on

on blogs, social media, and conferences raised questions about the Emerging Church's predominantly white and predominantly male public presentation, and about practices of exclusion and marginalization within it.

As a researcher, these critiques raised questions for me about the extent to which the Emerging Church was emerging into the new embodiment of church it hoped to be and whether it was sufficiently responding to the complexity of issues that needed addressing in order to be such a body. It was with an eye to these concerns and the characteristics of the Emerging Church as organic, relational, and inclusive that I analyzed the findings that resulted from my own research with twelve Emerging Church congregations across the United States between September 2012 and July 2013.[5] My findings are based on research that includes interviews with the minister/s and lay participants, a review of each congregation's printed material, my own participant observation and notes, and the narrative analysis I applied to the transcripts of the interviews using the *Listening Guide* method of analysis.[6] My research study was not intended to be a full-scale study of these congregations, but was designed to supplement the secondary source data and allow Emerging Church participants to speak for themselves regarding their experiences of church as organic, relational, and inclusive. The research sought to uncover the ecclesiology practiced and embodied by the Emerging Church rather than that intended or written about in the literature by Emerging Church leaders.

While it is important to note that the clearly varied and diverse Emerging Church cannot be reduced to a singular ecclesiology, the intent of my study was to identify the lived ecclesiology that most characterizes the movement and is useful for reflecting on the Emerging Church's faithfulness to its own claims about what it is as church. The selection of the twelve congregations that make up my study sample therefore reflects a cross-section of the broad and varied Emerging Church. To select the participating

---

my conversations with women writers and ministers within the Emerging Church. Julie Clawson stands out as one who has maintained a sustained critique of the Emerging Church inclusion and support of women's participation and leadership. See, for example, http://julieclawson.com/2007/08/12/women-in-the-emerging-church/; and http://julieclawson.com/2007/08/10/to-the-men-of-the-emerging-church/.

5. See Appendix for information on congregations included in this study. Several of the congregations have since experienced changes in pastoral leadership, but the observations I report and the majority of my analysis is based on the congregations as they existed during the time of my research study.

6. Carol Gilligan et al., "On the Listening Guide: A Voice-Centered Relational Method," in Hesse-Biber and Leavy, eds., *Emergent Methods in Social Research*, 253–72.

congregations I began with a cursory review of the literature by and about Emerging Church and its participants. During this initial review of the literature I kept a running tally of all the congregations that were referred to as part of the "Emerging Church" or the "Emerging Church Movement." From this tally I took the fifteen most mentioned churches and contacted the minister or ministers[7] listed on the website to express my interest in including them in the study. Ten of these top fifteen churches agreed to participate in the study. I then also followed two leads I had received from these top ten and made connection with two other churches held in high regard by their peers, though they were not mentioned as frequently in the literature, and added these to my sample.[8] The data I draw from my research with this cross-section of Emerging Church congregations in the United States, together with the literature, serve as the basis from which I determine the ecclesiology that is emerging from the movement. Much of the literature is written by leaders of Emerging Churches themselves, so the qualitative research serves to supplement the literature and is not intended to be a full-scale study of the congregations. Together, the literature and the qualitative study provide a thick description of the Emerging Church, its context, and its theological underpinnings, and serve as the basis from which I identify the ecclesiology that is embodied in the movement and from which I determine whether, and in what ways, Emerging Church congregations do or do not reflect a church that is organic, relational, and inclusive. In this chapter I present the findings related to a subset of my research regarding the *relational* nature of the ecclesiology of the Emerging Church, specifically to the leadership and decision-making structures I saw embodied and practiced among the congregations.

---

7. Theologically, the divide between "minister" and "lay" participant is an artificial one, since the case can be made that all Christian identified people have a call to be ministers. Also, in many cases lay participants are very much leaders and ministers in their respective Emerging Church. However, almost all of these congregations have one or more paid staff/pastor/ minister. I use two criteria to refer to some Emerging Church participants as ministers and others as lay. The first is if the participant is paid, and the other is if the individual is in some way identified or given a title on the church website that denotes and therefore sets them apart as a leader of the church. This includes people ordained to ministries of word and table, individuals identified on the website by the title "pastor," and any member of the staff who officially fulfills pastoral duties, regardless of ordination.

8. The individual list of churches, both the first ten and the two later added, are listed in the Appendix.

I used the *Listening Guide* method of narrative analysis with the transcripts from the interview and focus groups I conducted. The *Listening Guide* was developed collaboratively by Carol Gilligan et al., and designed to keep the researcher open to discovery.[9] In my listening, I noted places in the transcripts where participants spoke of their relationships in the church, both in terms of the social aspects of their relationality and the structural aspects of their leadership and decision-making processes, in order to get at the operational relational nature of their ecclesiology that is highly touted in the literature. Did they speak of sharing their stories and of being vulnerable with one another? Were these exchanges and encounters encouraged and facilitated structurally? Did their clergy/lay structures and relations reflect the relational ecclesiology described in the literature? Was their "democratization" applied to and implemented in their leadership structures and decision-making processes or only to the church space and room arrangement? What was revealed in the stories they shared with me when I applied the deep listening method of analysis and attuned to the contrapuntal voices in the stories they told? My analysis reveals the wide and varied degree to which these characterizations are true in practice.

A Relational, Egalitarian Community

In their recent book, *The Deconstructed Church: Understanding Emerging Christianity*, Gerardo Marti and Gladys Ganiel, both sociologists of religion, describe the Emerging Church Movement as pluralist congregations with dialogue-centered spaces and flatter leadership hierarchies.[10] Tony Jones, in his book *The Church is Flat: The Relational Ecclesiology of the Emerging Church Movement*, describes a flattening of the hierarchies that happens within the Emerging Church as expressed in its "ever-changing relationships between clergy and laity."[11] He sees this demonstrated in part by the lack of elevated pulpits, vestments for clergy, or mics and lights for the preacher. Central to the embodiment of the relational ecclesiology he identifies are the weekly practices of communion and the "open sermon," the exegesis and construction of which is often done collectively during church services. Overlapping what Jones describes, Marti and Ganiel report that the ideal of the Emerging Church's "flat leadership" is based on shared

---

9. Gilligan et al., "On the Listening Guide," 157–72.
10. Marti and Ganiel, *Deconstructed Church*, 195.
11. Jones, *The Church Is Flat*, 179.

responsibility, decentralized leadership and part-time clergy, and an egalitarian form of congregational government that strives to distribute power.[12] They further note that Emerging Church participants make "intentional efforts to reconstruct spaces" and democratize the space, moving away from pews, altars, and elevated pulpits.[13] Preaching in Emerging Church congregations is often communitarian, meaning that it is participatory rather than simply having one speaker and an audience of passive receivers, while keeping scripture central.[14] And as Marti and Ganiel report, worship is not the "typical" evangelical liturgical experience, but instead draws in and creatively reappropriates traditional liturgical practices more closely affiliated with Roman Catholic and Anglican worship[15] and focuses in large part around communion and communal practices.[16]

Broadly speaking, my research confirmed the relational aspects of the Emerging Church reported in the literature. The relational nature of the ecclesiology of the Emerging Church revealed itself in the prominent sociality of the congregations, the importance of vulnerability and of being able to share one's stories, and in the expressed commitment to have collaborative leadership structures and open decision-making processes. The congregations' high valuation of sociality, vulnerability, and the telling and hearing of each other's stories was a ubiquitous theme throughout the interviews with participants and was evident in the stories they told about moments of sharing in such ways and the meaningfulness of such times. Participants repeatedly expressed their assurance that their church was a space in which people could be honest, authentic, and vulnerable with one another. They described their communities as places where they feel free to bring their darkness and their brokenness, where they share their stories not just of joy but also of suffering, pain, and vulnerability. This aspect of their ecclesiology is facilitated through a multiplicity of built-in structures and gathering practices and is a meaningful part of participants' experiences in the Emerging Church. Participants tell stories that highlight the meaningfulness and at times transformative impact of their encounters of vulnerability: stories of being welcomed and "seen" in ways not before

---

12. Marti and Ganiel, *Deconstructed Church*, 117–21. They also note that decentralization of leadership "can lead to oligarchy."
13. Ibid., 132, 128.
14. Ibid., 113–15.
15. Ibid., 122–23.
16. Ibid., 125–28.

experienced in church feature prominently in participants' narratives of why they are drawn to or have chosen to participate in their Emerging Church congregation.

However, it was a more complicated task to get at the relational ecclesiology of the Emerging Church Movement as it concerned leadership and decision-making structures. The relational aspect of the leadership and power-sharing areas of these Emerging Church congregations was not as straightforward as their sociality and vulnerability, and not as straightforward as one might expect from the description in the literature. The literature emphasizes a "flattened-hierarchy" and decentralized leadership demonstrated in part by the arrangement of the room, the lack of elevated pulpits, and the open and conversational format of the sermons, as well as by the distribution of power, an egalitarian form of governance, and shared responsibility. The data confirm some of these characteristics in many of the congregations, while at the same time drawing attention to some areas of tension and contradiction.

Participants made frequent mention of the various forms of shared leadership at work within their churches, among them that: anyone can lead; anyone is free to take the lead with an idea and make it happen; whoever is gifted can lead regardless of sex or gender or ordained status. Structurally, many of the congregations made reference to having: no hierarchy, a flat leadership structure, or having "de-hierarchalized" it; participatory, collaborative, or open-handed leadership; or majority-rule, collective, or group decision-making, if not consensus, processes. Five of the twelve congregations spoke of the importance of giving away power when describing their leadership and decision-making structures.[17] Most of the congregations (nine out of twelve) have some manner of openness in terms of who can preach or lead the collective reflection in the weekly worship service. The degree of openness varies from congregation to congregation.

At Solomon's Porch, Doug Pagitt described their structure by stating, "Most of the life of Solomon's Porch happens in non- . . . non-hierarchical . . . people just do whatever they want. So, if you want to do something, just say 'hey this is what I want to do,' and it's just, 'Great, go do it—it's your place and it's your building.'"[18] At Vintage Faith, Dan Kimball noted that both women and men teach in the church, "if somebody can speak or

---

17. Danielle Shroyer of Journey Church spoke specifically of "ecclesial power" and that ecclesial power is given away.

18. Ellipses here indicate pauses.

teach or if they're gifted in an area [they do so]—we're all in this together." Similarly, during one of my group interviews at The Gathering, participants made it clear that if someone had an idea, they have the church's collective support to make it happen. I visited with them in the season of Lent, during which the church featured a week long interactive Lenten activity that was open to the public: "In His Steps: re-imagining the stations of the cross. A Passion Week project."[19] It was a type of meditative/prayer walk around different stations set up in their meeting place, the Vault. During the interview I learned that the whole plan and structure for this event was one person's idea; she shared the idea with the church, took the lead in planning it, and received time and labor support from the congregation to make it happen. Participants confirmed that this ad hoc process was the way most things took place at The Gathering.

Mosaic had a unique story regarding who gets to have a speaking/preaching role, and how this was decided upon based on the response of the congregation when they had multiple speakers. One of the staff explained of Erwin McManus, Mosaic's "principal visionary and primary communicator"[20]:

> Erwin is a very open-handed person when it comes to influence and power . . . whoever is the most passionate, most talented, most powerful, is the person who gets to lead. So it's all based on your current acumen as opposed to your pedigree. So Erwin always drives us to being like, that, whoever's got the hottest fire in their belly gets to move forward. So, in his—that's just his framework, so at Mosaic he's always been very open-handed. One year, the first year I spoke at Mosaic, there were fifty-five people who spoke that year; at all the different campuses different people spoke at different times, we wanted to move it to a community of voices as opposed to just his voice. It didn't go super well, because people were like, I don't want to hear that guy, and, "What's happening here?" and "I can never know who's speaking." And like, people wanted a voice, frankly. So we worked for years on finding ways to mix-in other voices and I started as a once-every-two- months guy and then a once-a-month guy and then when Erwin made the transition [of consolidating the church from multiple sites to

19. Phil Wyman, "Passion Week at The Gathering—Salem, MA," Phil Wyman YouTube channel, https://www.youtube.com/watch?v=lsOMecS8c-g (accessed March 2, 2015).

20. The phrase "principal visionary and primary communicator" is Erwin McManus's title as listed on Mosaic's website.

PART 1: DEFINING BOUNDARIES

a single site] he created it as like our voices were going to work together and really the church chose that. It was just based on what voice they could follow really.[21]

In Mosaic's case, there is a sense in which input from the people in the church is taken into account; for them this meant a consolidation of voices since the congregations expressed that they did not want multiple voices, but instead wanted "a voice." At the same time, the final decision-making fell to Erwin. So while he is "a very open-handed person" he is still recognized as having the "influence and power."

Similarly, at HFASS, Nadia Bolz-Weber is clear that the content that is proclaimed from the pulpit is her responsibility. She expresses a clear understanding of what her role is and has certain restrictions regarding how open she will be in the democratizing process. As the theologian-in-residence, she understands that part of her job is to guard what people hear, though not what they believe. She makes the point that they "haven't democratized the preaching" as she is "the one that usually does the proclamation." She does note, however, that while she is "set apart to be the preacher" for that particular community and her community gives "ten minutes of their week to listen" to her, she in turn gives "the whole week to listening to them;" she listens to their stories as she reflects on the scripture text for her Sunday sermon. She explains that she takes what she has heard throughout the week and "connect[s] what's going on in the world and what's going on in their lives to [the] text." She is clear that as pastor she does hold a particular role, even an authoritative one, in which she serves as "a theological center that's held" beyond which "there's complete freedom to be whoever you are and believe whatever you want. So it's not krypto-unitarianism where anything is explored and we'll [. . .] talk about Thich Nat Han one Sunday or whatever . . . and yet people are free to just again be who they are in terms of belief." Both Mosaic and HFASS stand out among the others regarding the boundaries of authority that are in place: one in which certain aspects of decision-making and power are shared, but within certain limits; where power is centralized around one person, even while that person opens him or herself to input from the community.

Among the congregations I studied, there are a variety of structures in regard to clergy and the form of leadership their role takes:

---

21. The reference, "whoever is the most passionate, most talented, most powerful, is the person who gets to lead," raises for me questions of how this is determined and by whom; what is the criteria used and who has a say in creating or determining the criteria?

- Eight of the twelve congregations[22] have someone in the traditional pastor role, with three of these in part-time positions.[23] Of these eight congregations, half of them are denominationally affiliated and the other half are not.[24]
- Three of the congregations have co-pastor structures: House of Mercy, Revolution, and Vintage Faith.
- Ikon NYC stands out in that they have no one in the traditional pastor role. Theirs is a collaborative team effort brought together by Peter Rollins and inspired by his writing and the work of Ikon Belfast.

Six of the twelve congregations made references to having a "flat hierarchy" or no hierarchy at all: COTA, House of Mercy, Journey, Solomon's Porch, The Gathering, and Vintage Faith. How this takes shape is different for each of them. For some this was a commitment that existed from the very founding of the church. For others the intention was there but the reality turned out differently. And others continue to reconfigure their structure so as to best reflect their commitments.

House of Mercy was inspired by a conversation between two male friends, who, as they began to talk about starting a church, were conscious of the fact that they were two white men and that they had to be intentional about addressing that fact so as to not fall into the long-established patterns of all-male leadership in the church. Co-pastor/co-founder Russell Rathbun recalls, "And we, very consciously from the beginning, even when it was just me and Mark, we didn't want just men talking. But we were men, so . . . [voice trails off]." Later, he tells the fuller story of how he and his friend Mark, the other of the three co-founders, had the conversation about their vision for the church very early on:

> "We, you know, we have to have, we can't do this without a woman, we can't start a church without a woman." Because we just felt like at the time there, you know, the church was full of . . . white men, you know? And that, one of the parts of our vision was like, you can't have this one white man interpreting scripture for the people every week, you know, a person who represented the dominant

---

22. COTA, Church of the Beloved, Grace Commons, HFASS, Journey, Mosaic, Solomon's Porch, The Gathering.

23. Ryan Marsh of Church of the Beloved, Nanette Sawyer of Grace Commons, and Danielle Shroyer at Journey Church are part-time.

24. Overall, only five of the twelve congregations are denominationally affiliated.

culture, interpreting scripture for the community every week, it just doesn't—no. We didn't want to be a part of that. So I guess we settled for two white men and a white woman [they laugh]. So, we wanted to model, sort of, a non-hierarchical leadership kind of thing, you know, where it's not like, uh, the senior pastor—no one was ever the—there was never a senior pastor, there was just like, we all are the pastor and there's no hierarchy here and we all kind of make decisions mutually and yeah. So yeah, so I met Debbie and we were like, "Yeah, this seems great, let's do it."

For the co-pastors/co-founders of House of Mercy, their vision of a non-hierarchically led church was part of their founding and helped shaped their new church from the start. It is also part of the reason they do not feel as connected with the larger Emerging Church Movement—because the movement seems to fail at actually embodying an 'emerging' structure.[25] Debbie Blue, co-pastor/co-founder, commented that as co-pastors they never identified House of Mercy as an Emerging church, in part because, as she says, "It seemed like from the very beginning . . . it was, more patriarchy." She recalls that, "these women [who started the Emergent Women website] had to try, and—they were always resisting it . . . it's not really truly emerging if it's coming out of a patriarchy that we then have to resist—it's like, undoing it from the beginning." Debbie, Mark, and Russell had a vision to try to do things differently.

At one church,[26] the pastor did admit that at the founding of the church, they had a particular ideal of how they would structure themselves and make decisions but how in the end it did not turn out that way: "Yeah, well, we did a lot of thinking early on about, (pause) about a flattened hierarchy that is . . . that builds consensus on all decisions; that . . . is, you know, permeable and blah blah blah."[27] The "blah, blah, blah" is his segue into the reality of their decision-making structure: "And, you know, honestly, when it comes down to it, we're just like—yeah, um, we're just kind of organized like a church [of our denomination] is organized.[28] You know, we have a council. That council will often try to seek out . . . the consensus of the

---

25. As I noted earlier, the inclusion of House of Mercy, as with the other congregations in my study sample, was due to their repeated mention in the literature.

26. Due to the sensitivity of the information, I have made the church and minister's information anonymous.

27. Ellipses here are inserted to replace the "ums" from the interview transcripts.

28. Here the minister made reference to the denomination the church is part of, which I have left out in order to preserve its anonymity.

community through one-to-ones, or kitchen table talks, or SurveyMonkey, or . . . all-church meetings and stuff like that."[29] Despite the reality of their structure not being what they expected, the pastor comments that there is a lot of trust in their community and that the process seems to work smoothly in comparison to the stories he hears of other churches:

> I was talking to someone the other day and they were telling me about the last three churches that they were a part of and all the different arguments that went on and, and, divisions that went on while they were there—like, just in the last ten years, right? Like how many just nasty battles this person had been a part of. And I was, like, thinking, at [our church] we haven't had that, we haven't had any of those, like, you know, things.

In contrast to these other churches, he told a story of a recent incident of the staff at their church feeling taxed by the two Sunday services they held, when previously they had had only one service. They took the issue to the "guide group" (church council), who then took it to the community for consideration. Two community meetings were held during which people gave their feedback and within two weeks the community reached consensus and decided to go back to one joint Sunday service. The pastor recalls the moment when they reached consensus and a guide group member concluding: "That just seems like where we are in this moment in time [preferring to go back to one service]. So does that sound good to everybody? Okay." With this particular decision, the process seemed to work, though other stories reveal that this is not always the case. There are other decisions that were made without such a process, such as cutting back on the pastor's time and pay:

> Pastor: Um (pause), but then, I mean, like, I don't know, I— I went down 25% in my work here just because . . . we just didn't have the money to pay me. That's part of it, right? So . . . that decision was just made you know. Just (laughs) . . .[30]
>
> Female parishioner: Well it wasn't a decision.
>
> Pastor: No it wasn't. The guide group was just kind of like, "Hey look . . . you may need to go down because this is the reality of our finances." So . . .[31]

29. Ellipses here are inserted to replace the "ums" from the interview transcripts.
30. Ellipses here are inserted to replace the "uhs" from the interview transcripts.
31. Ellipses here are inserted to replace the "ums" or "uhs" from the interview

It is interesting to note that with one concern, multiple services being a tax on the staff, the whole congregation was brought into the trouble-shooting and decision-making process, however, with another concern, being low on finances, the guide team made an executive decision to simply cut down the pastor's time and pay without bringing the congregation in to trouble-shoot. As the female parishioner said, "it wasn't a decision," at least not a decision the congregation was involved in making. How this was determined to be the case is not clear, however, in short, the structure that this congregation adopted for its decision-making process is neither what participants expected it to be nor does it always work in the way that it is designed to function. Finances could have been discussed in the same manner that staff difficulties and the workload of having two services was, but were not.[32]

The leadership and decision-making structure at Journey Church developed over time and was distinctly shaped by a previous experience of conflict that they refer to as "the great elder debate." At the point when the founding pastor was leaving the church he put in place a team of elders to form and serve as the new leadership structure once he left. He chose the structure and selected the specific elders independent of any church-wide discussion or conversation, and, as Danielle Shroyer reports, "Journey went ballistic!" She explains, "[T]hat's just not at all what we are all about. Oh no! So there was like a huge uproar, I mean a massive huge uproar about who decided this. 'Can't we talk about it?' 'How did you decide who the elders are gonna be?'—I mean it was not good." The pastor's executive decision was an affront to the ethos of the community and the community expressed as much. As a result, Journey Church has a very different structure and decision-making process in place now:

> There's me [the pastor], there is a group of elders and there's a group of leaders. The elders keep me accountable, so like, they have to do an annual review, so . . . if there was ever an issue they would be the ones to hold the cards to sort of approach me about it. So the elders and the leaders, they serve annually, they serve a

---

transcripts.

32. I did not specifically inquire about church finances during my research with the congregations. However, I suspect that the denominational structure had something to do with financial decisions. This church is considered a missional congregational of a mainline denomination. With congregations that are not "self-sustaining" the denomination often functions as the "coffers" for the church.

one-year term and they are nominated and confirmed by community members.

Leaders can be either nominated by the community or self-nominated, while elders can only be nominated by the community. Once nominated, a current elder and leader interview each prospective elder, and then the full list of nominees is presented to the larger community. At that point, "The community has a week to say anything to [the pastor] or any of the [current] elders, if they have an issue [with a nominee]." Leader and elder appointments are for one year and for that one-year period they "make a vow to be around more and to help more." Of their current structure, Danielle notes that one of her favorite things is that once someone has served in either a leader or elder capacity for three years in a row, that person must "take a break . . . require[d to take] a sabbatical":

> I just think it's great because otherwise you just have these same people doing all the work all the time, which first of all, it ends up being closed up to other people that maybe can do it if you just gave them the space where they needed to be the person to do it. It also creates groupings . . . like, these are the people who do all the stuff; we are the people that don't. We try to get rid of all those groupings as much as possible. But also, you just do need a break; you don't need to be the person who does all things.

For Journey, their leadership structure has been developed over time as a result of past difficulties. It is designed so that various people will have the opportunity to take the lead, with community support, and likewise, to take a break and make room for others to be able to step into roles that they might not otherwise take if the same people were always in place.

The pattern of having the same few people doing "all the work all the time" and the issue of burnout was not an isolated incident. Vintage Faith has a large team of volunteer leaders, interns, part-time and full-time staff—two of whom are called "staff leads." All staff and volunteers alike are intentionally listed in alphabetical order on the bulletin and the church's website so as to not present a hierarchical ordering of staff or highlight some staff over others. Nonetheless, in my interview with one of the "Protégé" interns,[33] the intern expressed being disheartened and concerned

33. A Protégé intern is a participant of Vintage Faith's internship program, which, according to their website, is "a leadership immersion experience for those desiring to serve on staff in a missional church, learning leadership skills and developing character. The internship is 25 hours per week for either one or two years and is unpaid. We will,

that "within the leadership and the church staff" there was an apparent lack of "good spiritual and emotional health." She explained:

> Everyone's kind of like scrambling around to get things done, or like, the leadership is scrambling to figure out, even, what decisions they need to make next, and like, what, like, "Are we running out of space now?" "Are too many people coming?" "What do we do now, with that?" . . . And like, I just want to—I almost just want to take care of our leaders—like, go off and rest! It's ok, God'll still do his thing. You don't have to, like, put it all on yourself.

Beside the rest she thinks the leaders need, this intern also expressed a need to change the way people viewed leaders, stating,

> We're just all insecure people, and like, I've really learned that instead of putting our leaders up on this pedestal, it's been cool to interact and to see the dynamics of, like—they're so human. They're just—they're like—they have their fears, they have their mistrust, they're carrying the weight of the world on them too.

During my interview with Dan Kimball, he noted that they were currently revisiting its structure and leadership in order to best serve its growing numbers. He noted that while there is an organic aspect to their structure, wherein it develops over time and changes as they change, he concedes that structures must indeed be put in place, especially for a large church, but that this does not preclude it from being organic. Using the example of farming organic spinach as a metaphor for church and church structure, he explains:

> So I think, the spinach is organic, and so is our faith, but the vehicles of administrating the faith and having people— it does form organically, but even organic farming, you know . . . they had to build trellises, like if you just let the plants grow by themselves then that wouldn't work. You had to put up trellises, you have irrigation, you have regular times to irrigate, you know, like . . . so I say organic, but organic I believe can be used as . . . well like, "It can't be bigger than [a certain size]" or "we're organic and you're not." I'm like, no we're organic, but we just want more people to experience the organic, so therefore, you have to get structured, and that's what I was saying . . . does that make sense? So it is

---

however, be providing free housing and utilities (while space is available) in our Protégé House located near downtown Santa Cruz." Vintage Faith website, "Protégé," http://www.vintagechurch.org/protege/ (accessed March, 18, 2015).

organic, but yet you have to have structure and health inspections and, if you don't want to contaminate the spinach, they have to wear uniforms and have heat, and that stuff's measured, so like organic producing has to then have structure for the organic.

However, that the health of the congregation and its leadership was a current concern for Vintage Faith was expressed by both Dan Kimball and the volunteer intern I interviewed. Similarly, at Church of the Apostle, one of the participants I interviewed lamented that too often it is the same small group of people who are always doing the work. She explained: "I feel like so many of us are happy to (pause) come every Sunday, have church put on for us, and then, and then leave. And I feel like there's so much work that goes into that." The challenge she saw in this situation was to figure out how to "more evenly distribute or lessen the workload of the people that are doing a lot of the work." Journey Church developed their structure with the specific aim of distributing the workload and not having the same people do most of the work—even when they wanted to—not only to minimize burn out but also in order to create space for different people to step in and lead, who might not otherwise do so if the opportunity was always met by the same people. Other Emerging Church congregations continue to make efforts to solve the issue of the distribution of labor and leadership.

Role of Clergy

As I listened for participant and leaders' stories of their church structures and leadership, I also listened for whether the "democratization" written about in the literature applied not only to their church space and room arrangement, but to their leadership and decision-making structures. Journey, Solomon's Porch, and The Gathering stood out as having structures and decision-making processes that were communally formed and developed over time. They formed their structures and ways of doing things gradually in a way unique to them and in an effort to facilitate maximum participation. House of Mercy was intentionally founded with a team of three co-pastors so as to counteract hierarchy and male-centered leadership. But this democratization or egalitarian aspect of the operational ecclesiology of these congregations played out in some ways though not in others.

One of the specific areas of analysis I listened for concerned the role of the clergy and how it functioned within the structure of the church and in its relationship with the laity. Were they the typical "professional" clergy

PART 1: DEFINING BOUNDARIES

person tasked with the preaching and the presiding of communion, for example, or did the organic, relational, and inclusive nature of the Emerging Church cause a revisioning of the role of the clergy in the congregation?

Broadly speaking, four congregations have in place clergypersons in the typical pastor role and are also denominationally affiliated. Among those four congregations, there are clergypersons who stay within the denominational rules of their role and some who, though ordained, hold their role a little more loosely. Nadia Bolz-Weber mentioned a few tasks or roles that are part of her particular responsibilities as the pastor of the church. "The language in the liturgy itself and in the proclamation and in the preaching, that's my responsibility, and it, and it is—I'm a really orthodox Lutheran theologian." As she says, "I just do what is my job (laughs), you know? And my job is to be the theologian-in-residence, right, and to be the preacher. And then how everyone else interacts with that, I have curiosity about, but I don't feel responsibility for it." On the other hand, she references the fact that other roles within the liturgy are open to the community; as one walks into the church, one can pick up a bulletin that has directions for filling a particular role in leading the liturgy. She explains: "So when you walk in for the very first time, all these bulletins are laid out that have the jobs: read the gospels, assist the minister, serve communion—I mean you can serve at the altar next to me and say part of the Eucharistic prayer having just walked in—literally—no one has to deem you worthy or ready or competent." Getting to serve at the altar next to her during communion is emphasized to highlight the openness with which they hold their liturgy—though she presides over communion nonetheless.

By contrast, two other mainline-affiliated co-pastors that I interviewed, when I asked about communion and whether presiding over it was restricted to ordained clergy-persons, reported that while as the designated clergy they are often the ones to preside over communion, this was not always the case, that various people preside over communion at their church, both ordained and non-ordained. However, even as one pastor was reporting this to me, the other pastor interrupted to make the point that "the interview is being recorded," to which the first pastor responded by laughing and saying, "well—just don't tell the bishop!" These two contrasting examples, one in which the pastor is very clear about her responsibilities and the boundaries of sharing her authority with others, and the other in which the co-pastors hold that authority much more loosely, even while it may displease the bishop, are both affiliated with mainline denominational structures but reflect divergent approaches to how they regard their role as clergy, in this case, of Emerging Church congregations.

My research study revealed varying degrees to which the Emerging Church is willing to take seriously its claim to a relational ecclesiology when it comes to leadership and decision-making structures, to being more of a living organism than a static institution. Many congregations do indeed hold their structures with openness and demonstrate a willingness to adapt based on the input they receive from within and from outside the church. Journey Church is the best example of that from my study sample. Many likewise hold their theological convictions with openness in acknowledgement that they "could be wrong," and that the church often has been. Other congregations, however, are not so uncertain.

The two congregations that hold a theological center in place, HFASS and Mosaic, through a single person raised for me questions about the extent to which such a model is able to be responsive not only to its changing cultural context but also to the questions and critiques brought to it. Do the questions, doubts, and critiques people bring with them to church actually cause it to change its forms and practices, reflecting organic, relational, and inclusive characteristics, and to examine its theological presuppositions? For example, I wonder whether the "democratization of the space" but not of the preaching are changes that demonstrate not theological openness and malleability but only a willingness to change cosmetically.

Feminist Ecclesiology and the Emerging Church

A dominant and recurring theme of feminist ecclesiology is the conviction that the church is to represent a new model of social relations, one no longer bound by social hierarchies of ethnicity, class, or gender, but liberated to a new vision of community in which all, as an ekklesia of equals, have full citizenship with all the rights and duties that entails. Rosemary Radford Ruether explains that church as a spirit-filled community "suggests that all Christians are endowed with the spirit and should minister to one another. All have gifts that are needed to build up the whole body."[34] Elisabeth Schüssler Fiorenza points out that while Vatican II's Constitution on the Church confirms the Galatians vision that "there is neither Jew nor Greek, neither slave nor free, neither male nor female," such a vision has never

34. Ruether, *Women-Church*, 22.

been completely realized by the Christian church in all of its history.[35] She explains that in part this is due to the fact that the [Catholic] context which bore the conciliar statement reflects the "discriminatory praxis of the church, insofar as it maintains equality for all Christians only with respect to salvation, hope, and charity but not with respect to church structures and ecclesial office."[36]

Thus, the structure of church for which feminist theologians argued, one appropriate for the church as a community of liberation, was a direct challenge to the structures of church as they had existed for centuries. Their insistence that a liberated church was necessarily non-hierarchical and non-patriarchal undermined the authority of the structures of church leadership that depend on authorization from above, that function from within a system of hierarchy and domination. The new structure had to be one that affirmed the participation of all persons as equals and as no more and no less capable of reflecting the divinity of Christ than any other—as kin of mutual regard and status. Such a structure would explicitly seek to be non-patriarchal. Rosemary Radford Ruether defined patriarchy as "not only the subordination of females to males, but the whole structure of Father-ruled society: aristocracy over serfs, masters over slaves, king over subjects, racial overlords over colonized people."[37] She asserted that "the church in its essential nature is a community of liberation from patriarchy," and as such, "it should *most particularly* witness to an alternative pattern of relationship between its members based on a discipleship of equals and mutual empowerment."[38]

Another important framework of analysis raised by feminist theologians is the contrast between power-over-others and power-with-others. Kwok Pui-lan, for example, explains that in the struggle for equal partnership in the church it is necessary to conduct an analysis of the way in which power and authority are exercised.[39] Detailing the contrast between power-over-others and power-with-others, Kwok explains that in the first framework, "an individual or a group of persons assumes control and dominance

---

35. Schussler-Fiorenza, *Discipleship of Equals*, 69.

36. Ibid.

37. Ruether, *Sexism and God Talk*, 61.

38. Ruether, "Church as Liberation Community from Patriarchy"; my emphasis. This article is a keynote address given at the Women's Ordination WorldWide (WOW) Second International Ecumenical Conference, July 22–24, 2005.

39. Kwok, *Introducing Asian Feminist Theology*.

because of ethnic identity class privilege, education, status or gender," and continues, stating that "in a Christian context, this hierarchical pyramid is supported by the belief that God is at the top, followed by the male, then the female, and then other categories of creation."[40] In such a model of power, the exercise of power is non-reciprocal, often leading to "an imbalance or even abuse of dominant power."[41] Alternatively, the second model of power is one "based on the interconnection that exists between all who share in a community."[42] Such a framework of power has three primary characteristics: 1) it is not rooted in "a hierarchical model where authority is exercised from the top down, but in an egalitarian one where authority is communal and shared"; 2) it "respects the difference and diversity of each member, giving voice and support to each one who is 'the other,' who feels left out, silenced and abused"; and 3) power-with "seeks justice for all who belong to the community," which "implies accountability of those who use power to control," it challenges "authoritarian modes of leadership and unjust structures that create a power imbalance," and "it offers an opportunity to transform our image of God from one who is omnipotent and dominating to one who is the source of life-giving power."[43]

As with other feminist theologians in their respective contexts, Kwok Pui-lan noted that many churches, if not most, "operate according to a power-over model, with a top-down hierarchical structure" and lamented that there was still "a long way to go before the churches learn[e]d to exercise power-with so that all members can participate fully in the life of the church."[44] The dismantling of the ordained clergy, then, as it has historically functioned continues to be a concern of foremost importance for feminist theologians. The conviction being that in order to construct a church liberated from patriarchy, communities of faith have to form new patterns and structures of leadership, organization, and power-sharing that go beyond the current "interlocking structures of lordship" that continue to pose a fundamental structural problem for the church.[45]

---

40. Ibid., 106.

41. Ibid.

42. Ibid.

43. Ibid. Here Kwok Pui-lan is drawing on the work of Ranjini Rebera, "a consultant in communications and a feminist theologian originally from Sri Lamka, [who] has written on the nature of power and its impact on Asian women."

44. Ibid., 107.

45. Hunt, "Women-Church," 88–89.

PART 1: DEFINING BOUNDARIES

As with feminist ecclesiologies, the Emerging Church is likewise concerned with moving away from putative forms of church and of inherited theologies that its participants have experienced to be unchristian. In response, it seeks to form the church in ways that reflect being a living organism more than a static institution, continually transformed in response to and in relationship with its community, as a community of mutual trust and participation, and always open to change, based on encounters among those within the church as well as with those outside of it. Nonetheless, there has been concern from within the Emerging Church itself about the public face of its leadership, largely male and white, and about the structural direction Emerging Church congregations take institutionally and denominationally in the long run.

The organizational and leadership structures of a church that is "emerging," that seeks to reflect a new way of being and relating in the world, must not mimic the "father-ruled" structures of the world that exercise power from the top-down if it wants to give witness to a new way of being church. Such "father-ruled" structures imbue the few persons who are "higher up" with power that is exercised at the cost of the participation of the rest of the body. This power is expressed not only in economic terms, but is also theological and sacramental, and is often exercised unilaterally. For example, when at the (unnamed) church the financial situation became tight, the decision to cut the pastor's position from full-time to part-time, and thus his pay, was made without discussion with him or the rest of the body. Other concerns were taken to the whole community, such as whether to have one service or two, but regarding this matter—one with significant implications not only for the pastor but the life of the whole community—the wisdom of the community was not consulted.

At another congregation, which had recently voted to affiliate itself with a mainline denomination, the co-ministers expressed their ambivalence at how this would affect their practice of communion. Whereas up to that point the congregation practiced openness in terms of who could lead communion, be they ordained or not, once the congregation was mainline affiliated, the denomination designated that only an ordained person could preside over communion. What had been a communal practice of the whole body, in leadership and participation, would potentially now be threatened. Rosemary Radford Ruether makes two relevant points regarding this shift. The first is that:

> The Eucharist, above all, is the sacrament most rigidly guarded as a clerical power tool and defined as an act that no lay person can perform. Excommunication, or denial of the Eucharist, is the prime tool by which one punishes those who resist clerical control. Ordination is the hierarchially [sic] transmitted power to "confect" the Eucharist. Thus the simple act of blessing and distributing food and drink as a symbol of giving and nurturing life is turned into a power tool to control access to God and redeeming relation to God.[46]

The congregation's practice of having various persons lead communion, to hold the practice of the sacrament with openness and not with exclusivist control, would be undermined if the newly established relationship with the denomination required that an ordained person be the only one to bless and distribute communion. Here, the second of Ruether's points flowing directly from her comment regarding the Eucharist is particularly applicable, she observes: "we see a common pattern in church renewal movements by which initially laicizing and egalitarian movements are reclericalized as the movement becomes institutionalized."[47] Feminist Christians contend that a hierarchical division of labor within the church always thwarts the possibility of mutuality and the participation of all in the radical incarnation of a new creation.

Broadly speaking, Emerging Church congregations encompass a range of structures, both in terms of leadership and in terms of the division of labor. At some Emerging Church congregations, participants expressed the common concern that a small number of people do the majority of the work involved in carrying out the liturgical gatherings, which burdens the few, leading to stress and burn-out, while additionally creating a division within the church between those who are passive and those who are active participants. Other congregations, however, have very intentionally developed structures that facilitate the sharing and distribution of labor. Journey Church developed a model in which participants can self-nominate or be nominated for various roles and leadership structures, always with a term limit so as to allow others to use and share their gifts and talents too.

Keeping feminist ecclesiological contributions in mind, particularly its analysis of how sexism and misogyny are often entrenched in hierarchical church structures and Kwok Pui-lan's analysis of the different frameworks

---

46. Ruether, "The Church as Liberation Community from Patriarchy," 5.
47. Ibid.

of power, what is key for Emerging Church congregations is that they be willing to acknowledge explicitly the reality that power is always at play, exchanged and negotiated among all parties present, regardless of whether they are structured hierarchically or not and that these dynamics of power are always gendered. Nadia Bolz-Weber is clear that there is a certain power that is ascribed to her role as pastor; she is the theologian-in-residence who maintains the theological center for the rest of the congregation and is responsible for what people hear proclaimed from the pulpit. Her explicit acknowledgement of this fact provides an element of transparency that may serve to promote the church's critical self-reflection regarding its exercise of power and whether and how it embodies its expressed values. What avenues the church puts in place in order to share its collective wisdom and facilitate the participation of the whole body in its incarnation so that it does not fall into the well-worn patterns of church power as imposed from the top-down will be critical for a congregation that preserves a hierarchical church polity.

From a feminist perspective, one of patriarchy's greatest distortions in the body of Christ is its failure to value and facilitate the participation of all persons in the ekklesia, not simply as an abstract ideal of church, but as a concrete and practical requirement of being a new creation. Debbie Blue and Russell Rathbun, along with their third co-founder, Mark Stenberg, intentionally sought to found House of Mercy with an egalitarian leadership structure. Their conviction was that the church cannot emerge into something new or different if it starts with the same structures that have always been. The structure they sought to dismantle was one of hierarchy, maleness, set up by a solo founder. Attentive to the dominance of these characteristics embedded in typical church polity, they instead began as a mixed-gender team so as not to set up a structure that would have to be resisted from the start.

Conclusion

Both the Emerging Church and feminist ecclesiology have a concern for the wounds and negative experiences people have had with church and Christianity. In feminist ecclesiologies, women's experiences are made central in recognition that these have historically not been taken into account and that theology has largely been written in exclusion of women. A primary commitment of feminist ecclesiology is to contribute to forming egalitarian justice-seeking Christian communities that go beyond the patriarchal imaginations that have long dominated the church. To varying degrees, Emerging Church congregations are explicitly forming in response to the harm its participants have experienced in the past with church and Christianity and are seeking to form communities in new ways. Emerging Church congregations intentionally seek to form church in ways that do not replicate the rigid theologies and the damaging habits and patterns its participants have experienced in previous churches. In my data, it was clear that Emerging Church participants bring experiences both of woundedness and hope to their congregation. However, the degree to which their questions, doubts, and critiques cause the Emerging Church to reconsider its forms and practices and to rethink its theological presuppositions—the degree to which participants' negative experiences of church have a shaping effect on the church they help form—is a key consideration if Emerging Church congregations are to avoid replicating and perpetuating the harm its participants have experienced in the past. Reflection on the ways in which feminist theologies have noted women's experiences and the historical reality of their systemic exclusion and marginalization within church, serves as a model for how the church may transform itself in light of the harm it has caused.

What is largely missing in the Emerging Church at large is an *explicit* critique of patriarchy, and of the practices that are patriarchally infused but go undetected, and an intentional effort to draw from the work and resources of feminist liberation theologies, not only in order to prevent the erasure of women's voices and contributions, but in order actively to counter the patriarchal distortions that have become embedded in the body of Christ. It is not enough to seek the vision of an inclusive church without explicitly naming the concrete obstacles and privileging the voices of those who have been marginalized. To seek diversity and inclusion does not in itself enact the vision that is claimed. The enacting of a new way requires that the oppressions be explicitly named, that truth be spoken to power, and that those in power actually be decentered from their position of assumed privilege.

The work feminists do in terms of speaking back to the tradition and revealing the problematic substructures that helped institutionalize and perpetuate sexist oppressions in the first place continues to be of great relevance to the work of the Emerging Church as it structures and organizes itself in a variety of creative ways. Further, for the Emerging Church to draw on the contributions of feminist theology would represent an explicit resistance to the continued male-centeredness of its public witness and would disrupt the deeply rooted sexism and patriarchalism that continues within the church. An explicit feminist critique of church by those within the Emerging Church would reflect their willingness not only to decenter male voices and to subvert the pervasive pattern of its public representation but also to expand the kinds of voices to which it gives prominence, both in its public witness and in its own continued theological reflection.

To recognize the full humanity of *all* people and their equal participation in Christ, and to form structures that reflect that vision, undermines the authority of structures that depend on authorization from above, from within a system of hierarchy and domination, and calls for their dismantling. The *ekklesia* of equals affirms that participation in the divine through Christ's continuing incarnation is accessible to all. Such an *ekklesia* of equals supports that goal through a structure formed among equals—kin of mutual regard and status—often through the painstaking process of hearing one another into speech.[48] Optimistically, if those within the Emerging Church are willing to do the hard work of birthing new life despite the forces of resistance they may face, and if they are willing to maintain (or introduce) an explicitly feminist critique of its churches in order to disclose any latent patriarchal habits and patterns embedded within it, then the Emerging Church may well prove to be the organic, relational, and inclusive church it hopes to be. To do so the Emerging Church must be willing to raise questions of itself regarding the structures, both material and symbolic, and the unexamined theological assumptions that are left intact. Without that it cannot bring to light and actively dismantle the underlying

---

48. Morton, *The Journey is Home*, 127–28. Morton coined the feminist principle of "hearing to speech." Morton's particular understanding of hearing and speaking came to her while she was with a group of women who gathered to tell their stories. As one woman shared her story—a story that at times reached points of excruciating pain—no one moved or interrupted, everyone seemed to be holding their breath. At the end, when the woman finally finished, she said, "You heard me. You heard me all the way—I have the strange feeling you heard me before I started. You heard me to my own story." Morton recognized that hearing to speech, hearing all the way, was a "complete reversal of the going logic" in which a person speaks so that more accurate hearing may take place. What Morton was instead witnessing was a depth hearing, a kind of hearing that engages the whole self to the point of holding one's breath in order to allow the coherence of the story to form and come together. This kind of hearing evokes "a new speech—a new creation"—it enables one to be heard to one's own story, which then creates the possibility for new imagining, an imagining that contributes to the mutual empowerment and transformation of both hearer and speaker.

substructures that prevent the necessary material, relational, and structural changes needed to undo the embedded patriarchal patterns and habits of church and to thoughtfully, creatively, and communally create new radically organic, relational, and inclusive ones so that the living incarnation of Christ can be brought to fullness by the participation of all who are "drawn to the new thing" that may be emerging.

Bibliography

Hesse-Biber, Sharlene Nagy, and Patricia L. Leavy, eds. *Emergent Methods in Social Research*. Thousand Oaks, CA: Sage, 2006.

Hunt, Mary E. "Women-Church: Feminist Concept, Religious Commitment, Women's Movement." *Journal of Feminist Studies in Religion* 25, no. 1 (2009) 85–98.

Jones, Tony. *The Church is Flat: The Relational Ecclesiology of the Emerging Church Movement*. Minneapolis: JoPa Group, 2011.

Kimball, Dan. *The Emerging Church: Vintage Christianity for New Generations*. Grand Rapids: Zondervan, 2003.

Kwok, Pui-lan. *Introducing Asian Feminist Theology (Introductions in Feminist Theology)*. Sheffield, UK: Sheffield Academic, 2001.

Larson, Bruce, and Ralph Osborne. *The Emerging Church*. Waco, TX: Word, 1970.

Lohfink, Gerhard. *Does God Need the Church? Toward a Theology of the People of God*. Collegeville, MN: Liturgical, 1999.

Marti, Gerardo, and Gladys Ganiel. *The Deconstructed Church: Understanding Emerging Christianity*. New York: Oxford, 2014.

Morton, Nelle. *The Journey Is Home*. Boston: Beacon, 1986.

Rah, Soong-Chan, and Jason Mach. "Is the Emerging Church for Whites Only?" *Sojourners*, May 2010.

Ruether, Rosemary Radford. "The Church as Liberation Community from Patriarchy: The Praxis of Ministry as Discipleship of Equals." *Women-Church Convergence* (website), 7. Accessed March 1, 2015, http://women-churchconvergence.org/articles.htm.

———. *Sexism and God-Talk: Toward a Feminist Theology*. 10th anniv. ed. Boston: Beacon, 1993.

———. *Women-Church: Theology and Practice*. San Francisco: Harper & Row, 1985.

Schussler-Fiorenza, Elisabeth. *Discipleship of Equals: A Critical Feminist Ekklesia-ology of Liberation*. New York: Crossroad, 1994.

Snider, Phil. *The Hyphenateds: How Emergence Christianity is Re-Traditioning Mainline Practices*. St. Louis: Chalice, 2011.

Snider, Phil, and Emily Bowen. *Toward a Hopeful Future: Why the Emergent Church Is Good News for Mainline Congregations*. Cleveland: Pilgrim, 2010.

PART 1: DEFINING BOUNDARIES

Appendix—Congregational Information[49]

Revolution Church (aka Revolution NYC), Brooklyn, New York
Non-denominational
Co-pastors Jay Bakker and Vince Anderson

IkonNYC, Brooklyn, New York
Non-denominational
Founded by Peter Rollins, led and run by a team

The Gathering, Salem, Massachusetts
Inter-denominational; originally Four-Square Gospel
Pastor Phil Wyman

Journey Church, Dallas, Texas
Non-denominational; Baptist roots
Pastor Danielle Grubb Shroyer

Vintage Faith Church, Santa Cruz, California
Non-denominational
Staff leads [their term] Dan Kimball, Josh Fox and Kristen Jensen

Church of the Apostles (COTA), Seattle, Washington
Both Episcopal and Evangelical Lutheran Church of America (ELCA)
Pastor Ivar Hillesland

Church of the Beloved, Edmonds, Washington
Evangelical Lutheran Church of America (ELCA)
Pastor, "Beloved Architect," Ryan Marsh

House for All Sinners and Saints (HFASS), Denver, Colorado
Evangelical Lutheran Church of America
Pastor Nadia Bolz-Weber

House of Mercy, St. Paul, Minnesota
Evangelical Lutheran Church of America, originally American Baptist
Co-Pastors Debbie Blue and Russell Rathbun

---

49. The listed pastors were in these positions at the time of my research. Several congregations on this list have since experienced a change of leadership.

Mosaic, Hollywood, California
Non-denominational, originally Southern Baptist
Erwin McManus, "principal visionary and primary communicator"

Solomon's Porch, Minneapolis, Minnesota
Non-denominational
Pastor Doug Pagitt

Grace Commons, Chicago, Illinois
Presbyterian Church (USA)
Pastor Nanette Sawyer

5

The Possibility of Conflict

— Timothy K. Snyder —

In but a fragment of *Philosophical Investigations,* Ludwig Wittgenstein writes of the inescapable problem of the other. Despite our best attempts at self-assurance, often we are complete enigmas to one another. Writing of this obstacle to what lies between us, in the intersubjective *in between,* Wittgenstein remarks, "One learns this when one comes into a strange country with entirely strange traditions; and, what is more, even though one has mastered the country's language. One does not *understand* the people. (And not because of not knowing what they are saying to themselves). We can't find our feet with them."[1] Often this handicap limits our best efforts to manage the relationships of our everyday lives. If only our spouses, our colleagues, and our neighbors would see things as we do. Though we may be better off at least trying to listen and to relate to those who are different from us on their own terms, few ethnographers today would claim it is ever fully possible to "go native," to ever truly see things from the perspective of the other. This obstacle to understanding can also be viewed as a possibility, a creative breakthrough. The possibility, however, lies not in our best efforts to overcome the finitude of our abilities to understand each other, but in learning to confront the otherness we encounter, in our neighbors and ourselves. This essay is about the possibility of such confrontations and the unresolvable conflicts that they surface. It explores this idea through a particular possibility or proposal: that recent scholarship on the Emerging Church Movement (ECM) and other alternative ecclesial movements has understated the significance of the conflicts between these movements and more conventional forms of Christianity. Efforts to document these con-

---

1. Wittgenstein, *Philosophical Investigations,* 235.

flicts are common, especially in sociological research, but few theologians have been grounded in the concrete communities of Emerging Christianity themselves to reflect constructively on the *possibility* present in such conflicts. Such a shortcoming reflects a broader pattern in which contemporary theology has failed to see *pluralism* as the fundamental problem of otherness.[2] The ultimate significance of the Emerging Church Movement will be for historians to decide at a later date. For now, the most interesting reality of the movement is its otherness; its insistence on a way of being church beyond convention. Or, ecclesiologically put, the church is always more than you think it is. Otherness, however, must always be accounted for and it is to that account that I want to turn our attention. What follows is an exercise in ethnography, a growing scholarly commitment among theologians committed to the practice of fieldwork in an effort to expand one's attentiveness to "the social context of God's work in the world."[3] As such, the narratives of identity, culture and tradition in one of the oldest ECM communities of practice will often take center stage.

The Pregnancy

I first met Russell Rathbun and Debbie Blue in New Orleans at a conference hosted by Evangelical Lutheran Church in America (ELCA) on starting new churches. At the time, I was a lay pastor working with a small community of young adults in Austin, Texas, while Russell and Debbie were seasoned pastors. Their church, House of Mercy, had begun in the mid-1990s affiliated with a large, urban congregation of the American Baptist Convention in St. Paul, Minnesota. Surrounded by dozens of pastors planting new congregations in suburban America, the three of us banded together like outcasts with a leprosy of unconventionality. A few years later in the wake of the tragic demise of my own Emerging community, I moved to St. Paul to pursue graduate studies and there I reconnected with Russell and Debbie, first as a participant at House of Mercy and later as an ethnographer and theologian, trying to better understand the congregation's transition into the Lutheran tradition.[4] It was then, in a conversation with a long-time

---

2. For an extended discussion on pluralism and otherness, see Mathewes, "Life Together," in *A Theology of Public Life*.

3. See Scharen, *Fieldwork in Theology*.

4. This essay is based on research I completed between 2010 and 2011 while a student at Luther Seminary. Fieldwork for the project was approved by the seminary's

board member, that I first heard the story of how House of Mercy left their parent congregation:

> In the process of the move [out of the relationship with First Baptist], it was not neat and painless process at all. It was messy and painful. It had been getting clearer all the time that First Baptist was having terrible financial problems of their own and that House of Mercy—who had been getting significant financial support out of their century old endowment for a long time . . . the well started to run dry. So when it became really, really abundantly clear to us that we should not, could not and would not stay there, they still had incredibly ambivalent feelings about that. They were like, "No, no, no we own you, you owe us." And at the same time it was like, "Oh, we don't have any money" . . . very, very ambivalent feelings about that. It was not always handled in the kindest ways in dealing with Debbie and Russell or the Board. I remember well the meeting where it all sort of came out and various members of their Board tongue lashed [Debbie and Russell] in really pretty cruel ways. They were remarkably patient and they took it.

Meeting up with Debbie on a Sunday afternoon before an evening service, I asked her about the conflict that eventually led to House of Mercy affiliating with the ELCA. "Oh, I feel like I had to go to my parents and tell them I was pregnant," said Debbie. Her vivid description of that situation makes the emotional weight of their lack of understanding palpable. But she was right: House of Mercy *was* pregnant. The congregation was giving birth to new ways of being church together. They were giving birth to an "eclectic blend of high and low church," as they themselves described it, and they did so with a cast of characters American, mainline Protestant congregations rarely reach: young adults in their 20s and 30s, artistic folks and musicians, and agnostic skeptics too. Perhaps it's not surprising that their parent congregation experienced the disappointment and grief that settles in when parents must confront the reality that their children are not them and they will not make them immortal. Likewise, all children, like House of Mercy, must also come to terms with their aggrandizement of their parents. Both are merely the broken creatures they are. While it is

---

Institution Review Board and was conducted under the supervision of Dr. Christian B. Scharen. The names of most of my informants have been changed, the only exceptions here are those of Rev. Debbie Blue and Rev. Russell Rathbun. In the spring of 2011, I presented my research to the community and they had the opportunity to affirm or reject my interpretations. I am deeply grateful for their feedback and participation. For the full research report, see Snyder, "This Is the House of Mercy, and Welcome to It."

true that, in a sense, House of Mercy was in that moment a teenage pregnancy, it was hardly an unintended one. Congregations are traditions and as Alasdair MacIntyre writes in *After Virtue*, traditions are "an embodied argument, and an argument precisely about the goods which constitute that tradition."[5] House of Mercy, along with much of Emerging Christianity, is itself an embodied argument against the very modern forms of church that have been dominant in the mid-to-late twentieth century.

It's Not That Bad

On a bitter cold January night, as I prepared a small prayer chapel at my seminary for a group interview, I reviewed my list of questions in my field notes trying to come up with a way of getting at the very heart of this community I sought to better understand. As the group gathered, we exchanged the obligatory greetings and I passed out the consent forms. The group settled and after a round of introductions, I led with:

> "If you were to introduce House of Mercy to someone who had never heard of it, how would do that? What would you say?"

> "You should come, it's not that bad," replied one of the participants quoting an often used slogan in the community. *A long silence followed.*

Slowly one by one everyone in the group affirmed the slogan as the best introduction to House of Mercy. Later that week when I met with Russell for a follow up interview, I asked him about this episode from the group interview. I wanted his help understanding whether the group participants simply answered my question with what was most immediately available to them: an understated, though catchy description. Russell told me how regularly when checking the voicemails left on the office phone (the slogan is the last phrase of the pre-recorded greeting); a message would begin with laughter followed by comments of disbelief. The caller would inevitably have to call back a second time to leave the message they had actually called about. "Did you hear what it said? You should come, it's not *that bad!*"

I came to understand that these seven words provided a short hand way of getting at the heart of the place, the argument they sought to live out. It was a way of introducing House of Mercy: an ironic community whose life together embodies a counter-claim, an alternative testimony. It

5. MacIntyre, *After Virtue*, 207.

was a way of saying the church is not always honest about itself. The church has often been complicit in the creation of an exclusivist and discriminatory community; it has not always been a welcoming place. It has played a role in the suffering of others both in the past and today. In the allure of certitude, the church has often avoided difficult and honest questions of everyday people as they have sought "to know God truly" as David Kelsey might say.[6] Or in the grammar of confession, these words admit with an uncanny honesty and humility that churches have not lived up to their calling. Ignoring that failure is dishonest and it has been painful.

For many efforts at reimagining what it means to be the church, the conflict between House of Mercy and its parent congregation would have been the end. When I met Debbie and Russell in New Orleans they had just begun a relationship with the ELCA, a process that would eventually lead to House of Mercy becoming a full member of the largest Lutheran denomination in the US. Not often do congregations with roots in the Radical Reformation transplant into a denomination of Luther's reformation. While the ELCA has full communion and ecumenical agreements with several other mainline Protestant denominations, there was no such relationship between the ELCA and the American Baptist Convention, much less so with First Baptist Church in St. Paul. *Would this new relationship work? If so, how?*

Culture and Action

In their pioneering work, Gerardo Marti and Gladys Ganiel define the ECM by its characteristic practice of deconstruction by religious institutional entrepreneurs.[7] Implied in their definition is what I am calling "the possibility of conflict." Ann Swidler, in a seminal article in sociology, writes about the relationship between culture and action.[8] Against the prevailing social theories that inadequately capture the causal role of culture in social practice, Swidler suggests we need two different models for understanding how culture explains action. In settled lives, times in which people know how to act, "culture is intimately integrated with action; it is here that we are most tempted to see values as organizing and anchoring patterns of action; and here it is most difficult to disentangle what is uniquely 'cultural,' since

---

6. Kelsey, *To Know God Truly*, 31.
7. Marti and Ganiel, *The Deconstructed Church*, 25.
8. Swidler, "Culture in Action."

culture and structural circumstances seem to reinforce each other."[9] Here, one might think of European religious life before the disestablishment of state churches or American mainline Protestant religious life during its comfortable period of growth and cultural security in the 1950s. However, Swidler goes on to suggest that in unsettled lives, culture's role in sustaining traditional or assumed patterns of social practice—what Swidler often calls "strategies of action"—takes on a new role: that of constructing new ways of life.[10] In settled lives, culture can be thought of as inherited, assumed tradition or common sense. These cultural forms may shape action in indirect ways, but the overall effect is that of continuity of both style and form. During unsettled cultural periods, new highly coherent narratives emerge and make a more direct impact on action therefore producing new strategies of action. Few will wonder whether today we live in settled or unsettled lives. Western religious culture is in the midst of an extended unsettling and arguments abound concerning its future. With this framework in mind, we might say that Emerging Christianity embodies a new theological narrative about what it means to be Christian in this time and place. Swidler's insights here are helpful for understanding what the ECM offers to the church in its conventional forms: *conflict*. There is a conflict between church in unsettled lives versus the church in settled lives. And it is a conflict filled with possibility.

The Church in Unsettled Lives

In 2001, when the United States began its war on terror in the wake of the attacks in New York and Washington, DC, House of Mercy was, ironically, in the midst of a year-long theme of "war and peace" in the Christian tradition. Before that September, First Baptist Church had never placed an American flag inside its sanctuary. Caught up, as many congregations were, in an overwhelming sense of patriotism, an American flag and a Christian flag were placed at the front of the sanctuary. Rather than removing the flags, a politically possible response, House of Mercy commissioned some of its artists to make two additional flags. These flags were red and black, colors traditionally associated with revolutions. In the center of these two flags are gold stars, with a black peace sign superimposed over the star. The flags were intentionally made smaller than the full size American and

9. Swidler, 278.
10. Ibid.

PART 1: DEFINING BOUNDARIES

Christians flags they were made to cover. When displayed in worship, they are simply draped over the existing flags without removing them from their flagpoles. The result is a stunning eschatological image: flags of revolutionary peace only partially able to subvert the symbolic power of American and Christian flags in a sanctuary.

Though this ritual act was carried over into the new sanctuary at Immanuel Lutheran Church, House of Mercy's new home congregation in the ELCA, I did not notice them until I arrived early on a Sunday in January. Only the day before, a twenty-two year old Jared Lee Loughner emptied several firearms worth of gunfire at a public event hosted by U.S. Representative Gabrielle Giffords in Tucson, Arizona. It was a horrifically violent and senseless event that shook the country. During unsettled times, ritual takes on a heightened role in it's contribution towards shaping action in a community. Against the backdrop of that week's events I finally noticed the flags and peace—and they preached to me.

Ritual elements of House of Mercy's alternative narrative are reinforced by both the theology of their pastors and the experiences of its members. When I asked Russell about House of Mercy's theology of culture, he said to me:

> We are not culturally relevant; maybe we're culturally literate. We are aware and we are well versed in popular contemporary culture. We just don't think its necessarily an ideal model for how the church should function . . . We think the gospel is necessarily counter-cultural and we need to bear witness to culture, to popular culture and not completely embrace it. The gospel serves as a critique.

And when I asked Debbie about this:

> Because even in the Lutheran Church, its not morality so much there, but it's like you should be attending church, you should be conforming to something. It's the idea that we're creating this alternative narrative from the culture and that's what we're continuously focusing on.

This highly coherent cultural narrative from "the front," or in other words from the official voices of House of Mercy's pastors and ritual actions, also lives in the everyday lifeworld of its participants. I met Don early on in my time at House of Mercy. Don spent time as a social justice lawyer and he had graduate training at Union Theological Seminary in New York.

I ask him in one of our conversations, how House of Mercy showed up in his everyday life:

> I've been trying to align who I really feel as if I am with all the things I am in the world. And I feel like I am most myself at House of Mercy. I feel like when that part of my true self, when I'm most open about my despair or happiness, when I'm most vulnerable and when I'm most counter-cultural . . . that's when I feel closest to House of Mercy.

Don looks back on his life with a reflexivity common in mid-life, a life stage that mirrors the existential demands of an unsettled culture: What is all this for, anyways? But this sort of questioning of the status quo is common at House of Mercy across the lifespan. I met Courtney during my fieldwork and I was immediately inspired by her commitment to issues of gender equality on her conservative Evangelical college campus. She too used "counter-cultural" scripts in describing the role House of Mercy had come to play in her everyday life:

> In terms of the choices that I'm making, whether they're moral or more just what am I going to pursue as far as my interests or things like that. Especially now, graduating college, trying to figure out what job I'm going to have. What are my priorities? Is it money? Is it art? Is it giving back? As I've experienced with lots of my other friends who are also graduating, I think that House of Mercy really gives a validity to not choosing money as the ultimate kind of pursuit and I don't think there are really a lot of other communities—especially of adults who have lived that way—who will support that idea. That's been pretty influential.

Openness to despair, practices of vulnerability, and questioning economic norms are all concrete expressions of what Swidler has in mind with her notion of "strategies of action." They are patterned ways of connecting a cultural narrative to action, not by choosing actions one at a time, but through more flexible strategies of action or "repertoires." In this case these repertoires were learned through participation in a community of faith actively seeking to reimagine what it means to be church. From " . . . it's not that bad," to revolutionary ritual to narratives concerning the meaning of life, House of Mercy embodies a new way of being church.

PART 1: DEFINING BOUNDARIES

The Church in Settled Lives

The Evangelical Lutheran Church in America is the result of a 1988 merger between three smaller Lutheran denominations after a historic effort to unite the various divisions of the American Lutheran tradition under a single church body. The ELCA touts an impressive four million members worshipping locally in almost ten thousand congregations. The structure of the ELCA is three-fold beginning first with local congregations. Regionally, these congregations support and are supported by sixty-five geographic synods each with a regional (synodical) bishop administering the mission and ministries shared within the region. With a central headquarters in Chicago, Illinois, the national organization—called the Churchwide Organization—is led by a presiding bishop, hosts a biennial national assembly, governs standards for ministry, supports seminaries and sets Churchwide policy.

At the time of my fieldwork, the St. Paul Area Synod was served by the longest continually serving bishop in the ELCA. The son of a Lutheran pastor, the bishop was educated in Lutheran institutions of higher education with additional study at Union Theological Seminary in New York. Early on in his ministry he served as pastor of a predominantly African-American congregation in Milwaukee, Wisconsin. A district president in a predecessor denomination, he assumed the office of bishop in 1988 and in 2002 was elected bishop of the St. Paul Area synod.

On a Sunday evening in September, the bishop visited the congregation to preach and preside over a Rite of Reception for Debbie Blue as a pastor of the ELCA. The text for that day was from the gospel of Luke's "lost" parables. Yet, the symbolic presence of a bishop in a newly affiliating congregation, especially one as particular as House of Mercy, called a much more pressing demand than the gospel text: an opportunity to express the collective Christian identity of the ELCA. And so the bishop began his sermon with the following greeting: "Friends in Christ, grace and peace to you in the name of God, our Creator, and Jesus Christ our Lord and Savior, Amen. I start that way because that is that way most Lutherans start." With these words, an awkward laugh rippled through those gathered. They weren't accustomed to the apostolic greeting, but they were even less accustomed to such assumed deference to Lutheran identity.

This sort of assumed behavior is what Swidler is referring to when she suggests that in settled times, 'people know how to act.' Except in this moment, the people of House of Mercy, ironically, did not know this way of acting. After a brief reflection on the text for the day, the bishop spent the majority of his sermon reflecting on how congregations of the ELCA share a common life together. Within his reflection, the bishop took up the role of spokesperson-in-chief describing the range of ways in which congregations are engaged in shared ministry through the administration of the synod in which he leads. In his preaching and presiding, he performed the settled culture of the ELCA.

Culturally, the assumed identity of the ELCA is functional in the way it provides a stable, though somewhat ambiguous identity for what it means to be *Lutheran*. Theologically, this identity is complicated, often lacking the kind of coherence one finds in unsettled lives. This vague relationship between theology—itself a particular kind of cultural narrative and identity created a tension-filled process for Debbie as she was welcomed into the denomination:

> I was surprised at how much stake they have in being Lutheran. I think the idea that the Lutheran Church is what it has been and they want to keep it that way. In my final Candidacy Committee meeting, I had submitted my sermon and all that. But in the interview that final time there was all these responses like 'Well that's not very Lutheran . . . ' or 'Oh you're reading James Allison (a Catholic theologian), how can that be? That's not very Lutheran' I mean they said that almost exactly. I think I passed just perfectly well but I was surprised how often came up.

Certainly, this assumed identity is related to the theological tradition of the Reformation, with the life and writings of Martin Luther. Surely that is part of the story being told. Yet, clear distinctions between ethnic, ecclesial and theological commitments within a Lutheran identity, in the collective sense, are difficult to parse out. Often times what is "Lutheran" is a conflation of personal experience and assumed expectations concerning the role of tradition. For the ELCA, it would be, "difficult to disentangle what is uniquely 'cultural,' since culture and structural circumstance seem to reinforce each other."[11] The ambiguity of a tradition in settled lives creates a reliable stability that allows for a depth of roots. This ought not be underestimated or too easily dismissed. Yet, in the current American religious landscape where change and adaptation are becoming the new normal, the church may need to be less like a mighty cedar of Lebanon, and more like a mustard seed.

11. Swidler, "Culture in Action," 278.

PART 1: DEFINING BOUNDARIES

An Instance of Exclusion

Over six months had passed since Martin Luther had written his ninety-five theses. He now had the chance to articulate his views at the Heidelberg Disputation of 1518. There as a delegate of his Augustinian order, Luther laid out a *theology of the cross*, contrasting it with a *theology of glory*. "A theology of glory calls evil good and good evil," Luther argues. "A theology of the cross calls the thing what it actually is."[12] Calling a thing what it actually is, however, is not always plain to see, or immediately available. Dietrich Bonhoeffer rightly warns us that, "What matters is the 'right word' for any given circumstance. To discover this is a matter of a long, earnest, and continual effort that is based in experience and the perception of reality. In order to say how something is real—i.e., to speak truthfully—one's gaze and thought must be oriented toward how the real is in God, and through God and toward God."[13] This is the challenge of the theological ethnographer who stands at the intersection of her effort to immerse herself in such an advanced effort on the basis of experience and knowledge of the real, and another reality: God's.[14]

When I began my fieldwork at House of Mercy I sought out to learn from one of the oldest U.S. congregations in Emerging Christianity. Encouraged that my own tradition was taking a risk by adopting House of Mercy, I thought my theological work might bring forth practical insights for further experimentation. It was a glorious proposal I suppose, but I soon came to see the relationship between the ELCA and House of Mercy not as a triumph over divisions in the Body of Christ, but as a conflict between unsettled and settled cultures and an instance of exclusion. It's a mistake to think of exclusion only in the most extreme of terms: ethnic cleansing, Jim Crow laws, or gender discrimination. Exclusion is an often practiced with contradiction, ambiguity and subtlety. Often, it is less a result of strategic policy and more a result of a community's identity-forming *habitus*, the embodied "rules" of belonging. In *Exclusion and Embrace*, Miroslav Volf writes about the kind of exclusion that emerges from the refusal of differentiated identities, that is, the refusal to see another as *other*. The most startling insight from my interviews with denominational officials, leaders

---

12. Luther, *Luther's Works*, 31:40.

13. Bonhoeffer, *Conspiracy and Imprisonment*, 603.

14. Recently, theologians have turned to fieldwork to pioneer new forms of theological research. For an introduction to this development, see Scharen, *Fieldwork in Theology*; and for an exemplar, see Fulkerson, *Places of Redemption*.

and participants at House of Mercy, was that no one could meaningfully articulate the relationship between the congregation and the denomination. The relationship is not meaningful because neither had let each other into themselves *as other*. The ELCA's ambivalence is the result of profound misunderstandings of House of Mercy. The most problematic misunderstanding is one in which the bishop considered House of Mercy an instance of ascension to his version of orthodoxy—Lutheranism:

> A congregation and its leader in a course of living its life has discovered it has a natural affinity to this larger identity called Lutheran . . . The one time I was there, it was fun to hear from Debbie and Russell—more so Russell—and a few of the members there a kind of positive 'ah ha,' about this might be a good thing being a part of a larger church body.

In *Exclusion and Embrace*, Volf writes, "The more benign side of exclusion by elimination is exclusion by assimilation. You can survive, even thrive, among us, if you become like us; you can keep your life, if you give up your identity."[15] It became difficult to not see the relationship between the ELCA and House of Mercy in these terms. It was as Claude Levi-Strauss wrote in *Triste Tropiques*, that assimilation always rests on a deal: we will refrain from vomiting you out if you let us swallow you up. And so the deal is on.

The bishop's exclusionary idealism, however, was not the only narrative operating among denominational leaders. The bishop's associate for evangelism and mission spoke in more pragmatic terms:

> To be honest, I think one the main reasons they came in to the Lutheran tradition —certainly their theology fit better here— but they needed money and we had money and they were not getting anything from the Baptist church. And so we have been providing for them for the past two years $48,000.00. That is a significant chunk of change.

Though I have no doubt that such financial support was intended for goodwill, the actual impact is not without its symbolic violence. As Pierre Bourdieu writes in *Symbolic Power and Cultural Production*, a gift that cannot possibly be repaid or matched places the other in a state of indebtedness. It is a violently symbolic act creating dependence more than it is a gift of

---

15. Volf, *Exclusion and Embrace*, 75.

PART 1: DEFINING BOUNDARIES

grace or goodwill.[16] This symbolism was not lost on leaders at House of Mercy who described their sense of the relationship in soteriological terms:

> They saved us and we would not exist anymore (not like this). In a time of real desperation they came in with those funds and so we feel obligation to do whatever they want. That doesn't feel like there's a lot of mutuality in that. I don't know what they want from us.

And:

> We were able to leave a situation at First Baptist that we needed to leave at that point. That was made possible by the financial contribution of the ELCA and their facilitation of us finding a new location in an ELCA church. That was very important . . . it was such a long road and I am still very grateful for that.

Ordinary participants described the relationship in terms perhaps more unremarkable terms, if a bit naive concerning the significant investment the ELCA made:

> Not many in the ELCA like it—so I think it gives the denomination some more 'product' if you will. I've gone to a lot of Lutheran churches in the state. A lot of them are quite similar. So, from that standpoint . . .

And:

> If you've spent any time at House of Mercy . . . their involvement is an understanding of what House of Mercy is about: that the gospel is being preached and it is working. I would think their motive is that recognition in a way people are hearing and wanting. Why wouldn't you want to support that?

The relationship between the ELCA and House of Mercy is marked by the ELCA's inability to differentiate, a failed recognition of House of Mercy *as other*. In an over identification with the certainty of settled lives, the ELCA denies both House of Mercy's otherness and projects their own need for affirmation in the certainty of settledness. It is a denial of other and self, since the two belong together. Correspondingly, the narrative that dominates the relationship for House of Mercy is one of self-denial; one that suggests mutuality is an impossibility.

---

16. Bourdieu, *Language and Symbolic Power*, 23–24.

The Power of Not Understanding

Z.D. Gurevitch, an Israeli sociologist whose work centers on conflict resolution in the Palestinian-Israeli peace talks, has written compellingly about moving beyond conflict in his 1989 article: "The Power of Not Understanding: The Meeting of Conflicting Identities."[17] While most efforts at reconciliation stress a common ground as found in common understanding, Gurevitch argues, "Every attempt at understanding requires, therefore, not more explanations, but first the power not to understand . . . Only when the two parties grant each other the power of presenting themselves as other can origins of truth and justice dialogue begin."[18] If I have unduly been one-sided in my critique thus far, here my critique and judgment is meant equally for House of Mercy as it for the ELCA. The power to not understand critiques both parties and their perceptions of self and other. In Gurevitch's article, he refutes the typical pattern from " not understanding" to "understanding." In Gurevitch's circle of understanding a more complex process of understanding is modeled. First, the circle moves from an inability to understand to the ability to understand (As in the invitation: "You should come, it's not that bad"). Yet another set of moves is necessary. This is the inevitable and unavoidable move from the ability to understand to the inability to not understand. In this position, new understanding is not really new at all but merely a variation on the same old understanding (As in when the bishop claims House of Mercy has discovered "a natural affinity to this larger identity called Lutheran . . .). It is here that parties often find themselves at a loss to move the relationship towards reconciliation. Here old convictions and judgments concerning the other contribute to further inability to not understand and the genuine path to understanding has plateaued. The only way out, according to Gurevitch, is through the crucial point or breakthrough of an ability to not understand. The ability to *not* understand, or in relational term what others would call "differentiation," has two important implications.[19] The first is seeing the other in oneself and the second is seeing oneself in the other. Both of these require one to have the ability of *not* understanding in order to activate the process of making the familiar strange again. Ordinarily, a shift must be made: a shift from the

---

17. Gurevitch, "The Power of Not Understanding."

18. Ibid., 162.

19. For more on "differentiation," see Sandage and Harden, "Relational Spirituality," 819–38.

centered self to the perspective of the other, whereby one attains a separate perceptive center of consciousness enabling one to view the self as other. Shifting the center from the self toward the other and taking the other's role allows one to gain not only a new understanding of the other, but also a new understanding of the self. At the time of my fieldwork, this is as far as House of Mercy and its mainline denomination had come. This strategy based on the full circle of understanding ending with a new capacity—the ability to *not* understand—maintains a basic strangeness between the two parties. This basic strangeness is vital particularly when each party define themselves over and against the other. Only by maintaining this sense of strangeness between one another will each be able to not understand each other. The ability to not understand is a necessary, and often neglected step in the process, yet it is not the end. Still, the goal is to know one another in their differentiated otherness. Without such a move to know, mutuality can never be reestablished because old projections and misunderstandings dominate the relationship. From my ethnographic research, I want to suggest that the possibility of conflict between church in settled lives and the church in unsettled lives rests in the potential strangeness of the two, in each ecclesial form's capacity to not understand one another.

The Possibility of Conflict

The bishop's visit was an occasion for performing the ELCA's settled cultural identity. It was also an occasion for improvisational pastoral wisdom. Not only is there a possibility of conflict when established forms of church meet emerging forms, these conflicts also generate new possibilities in ritual, narrative and relationship.

After the bishop's sermon, the sermon that began with the "Lutheran way," he moved into a Rite of Reception—a liturgical rite welcoming a pastor of one tradition onto the official roster of ordained ministers in the ELCA. Typically, such rites are developed alongside ecumenical agreements, but in this case no such arrangement existed. There was no precedence for a Baptist congregation becoming Lutheran. Officially, the bishop would need to ordain Debbie whose ordination in the Baptist tradition couldn't be formally recognized by the ELCA. Leaders in the ELCA struggled to discern what this situation called for. "Well, Debbie has been a pastor at House of Mercy for fourteen or fifteen years, you re-ordain her?" an associate of the bishop told me. "You basically call into question every baptism she has ever done. All the sudden people start saying, 'Well, what do you mean she wasn't a pastor before? But she was our pastor? How can this be?'"

Officially, Debbie was ordained on that day. Liturgically, however, she was welcomed through the Rite of Reception. In times of unsettled lives, rituals take heightened significance. The pastoral wisdom shown in this ritual performance illuminates an impulse to make room for the uniqueness of House of Mercy to shape the relationship. The rules were broken out of faithful sensitivity to the experiences of the community. Pastoral wisdom here called for new strategies of action for new situations.

Theologians and scholars of religion studying the Emerging Church Movement have often focused their inquiries on what is particular and novel among in the movement's conversations and communities. Seeing the movement through this lens has, at times, caused scholars to miss out on the conflicts present in Emerging Christianity. My hope is that in this new wave of research, scholars will pay more attention to the conflicts and the possibilities that emerge from them. Such inquiries will require new approaches to our "earnest and ever more advanced effort of the basis of experience and knowledge of the real" as Bonhoeffer writes. To that end, I propose scholars paying attention to this movement begin immersing themselves not only in the writings and ideas of the movement's thought leaders, but in the actual concrete communities in which everyday Christians are improvising new ways of being church.

Bibliography

Bonhoeffer, Dietrich. *Conspiracy and Imprisonment 1940–1945*, Edited by Mark S. Brocker. Translated by Lisa E. Dahill. Dietrich Bonhoeffer Works 16. Minneapolis: Fortress, 2006.

Bourdieu, Pierre. *Language and Symbolic Power*. Edited by John B. Thompson. Malden, MA: Polity, 1991.

Fulkerson, Mary McClintock. *Places of Redemption: Theology for a Worldly Church*. Malden, MA: Oxford University Press, 2010.

Gurevitch, Z. D. "The Power of Not Understanding: The Meeting of Conflicting Identities." *The Journal of Applied Behavioral Science* 25, no. 2 (1989) 161–73.

Kelsey, David H. *To Understand God Truly: What's Theological about a Theological School*. Louisville: Westminster John Knox, 1992.

Luther, Martin. *Career of the Reformer I*. Vol. 31 of *Luther's Works*, edited by Hardold J. Grimm. Philadelphia: Fortress, 1957.

MacIntyre, Alasdair C. *After Virtue: A Study in Moral Theory*. Nortre Dame: University of Notre Dame Press, 1981.

PART 1: DEFINING BOUNDARIES

Marti, Gerardo, and Gladys Ganiel. *The Deconstructed Church: Understanding Emerging Christianity.* Malden, MA: Oxford University Press, 2014.

Mathewes, Charles. *A Theology of Public Life.* New York: Cambridge University Press, 2008.

Sandage, Steven J., and Mark G. Harden, "Relational Spirituality, Differentiation of Self, and Virtue as Predictors of Intercultural Development." *Mental Health, Religion, and Culture* 14 (2011) 819–38.

Scharen, Christian. *Fieldwork in Theology: Exploring the Social Context of God's Work in the World.* Grand Rapids: Baker Academic, 2015.

Snyder, Timothy K. "'This Is the House of Mercy and Welcome to It': An Ethnographic Exploration of Concrete Ecclesiology and Theological Otherness." MA thesis, Luther Seminary, St. Paul, MN, 2011.

Swidler, Ann. "Culture in Action: Symbols and Strategies." *American Sociological Review* 51, no. 2 (1986) 273–86.

Wittgenstein, Ludwig. *Philosophical Investigations.* 4th ed. Malden, MA: Oxford University Press, 2007.

Volf, Miroslav. *Exclusion and Embrace: A Theological Exploration of Identity, Otherness and Reconciliation.* Nashville: Abingdon, 1996.

Part 2: Crossing Boundaries

6

From Boundaries to Borderlands: The Emerging Church's Imaginative Work of Fostering Relationships across Difference

Lloyd Chia

Introduction: How the Emerging Church Draws Maps

WHEN I FIRST STARTED my research on the Emerging Church, one of the first things that struck me was its attempts to be inclusive. This inclusiveness extended to atheists and other religions. My contribution to this volume explores how the Emerging Church thinks about its relationships to others through "mapping." This paper will explore how the Emerging Church goes about drawing maps, as it imagines its relationships with others, whether they are other Christian groups or other religions. As the title of my contribution suggests, this work of drawing maps enables them to foster relationships with diverse groups. Instead of erecting boundaries to keep people out, I will show how the Emerging Church tries to forge borderlands, or safe spaces for groups to come together despite their differences.

My contribution to this volume is a sociological analysis that employs insights from social cognition theories to make sense of the Emerging Church. I will discuss how the Emerging Church uses maps to practice reflexivity: thinking self-critically about themselves and their relationships with others. I will also show how the movement engages in offensive and defensive mapping to define "who's in and who's out." Next, I explain how the Emerging Church tries to be a borderland, or an encounter space to bring people from different perspectives together, rather than a harsh boundary that divides people. Lastly, I shed light on the "navigational affinity" that the Emerging Church uses to map religious others who are on a similar journey of rethinking their faith.

Making Sense of the Map Metaphor

My paper takes maps and mapping as a revealing metaphor for how the Emerging Church thinks about its relationships with others. Mental maps structure our perception of reality.[1] At times the maps we carry in our heads are more real than what the world actually looks like. Maps also enable us to mentally "discover" previously unchartered territories.[2]

We can also think of maps as cognitive schemas that help make the world coherent for us under conditions of incomplete information. We rely on approximations and representations of "how things are" in the world. Schemas are essentially a kind of "map" in our mind, since schemas are "knowledge structures that represent objects or events and provide default assumptions about their characteristics, relationships, and entailments."[3] Hence, we carry around in our heads all sorts of mental maps about things in the world, despite our lack of complete information. But these mental approximations of the social world do not come out of nothing. It's our human condition that we share with likeminded others a common vision of how things in the world are. This then, is a "mental cartography" of our fundamental social categories, which is indispensable for understanding the underlying structure of the world.[4]

Social cognition theorists establish the complex way we map our world, and construct distinct and tightly bounded identities for ourselves based on these maps. We create boundaries for a reason. For groups to establish a distinct "who we are," to perceive fundamental differences between "us" and "them," we exaggerate in our minds the mental divides that separate us from other people.[5] In other words, in the mental maps that

---

1. Zerubavel, *The Fine Line: Making Distinctions in Everyday Life*.

2. Smith, *Map Is Not Territory: Studies in the History of Religions*; Zerubavel, *Terra Cognita: the Mental Discovery of America*.

3. DiMaggio, "Culture and Cognition," 269.

4. Foster, "Menstrual Time: The Socio-Cognitive Mappings of the 'Menstrual Cycle'"; Zerubavel, "Lumping and Splitting: Notes on Social Classification."

5. Zerubavel, "Lumping and Splitting: Notes on Social Classification."

we make of the social world, we lump and split people according to our perception of where they fit in relation to us: whether they are similar and hence "closer" to us, or whether they are different and should hence be considered "distinct," separate or "cut off" from us.

I'm asking that we think of mapping as a *verb* or something that people are actively doing. In sociological parlance the term would be *cultural practice*, here instead of focusing on what is on the object "map," our focus is rather on "mapping" as an action word. In these terms, mapping is an ongoing collaborative process of figuring out who is out there and how to relate to them.

Sociologists look at how religious groups act in ways that cohere with a group's imagined map, and strategize their actions and affiliations to stay as much as possible on the "good" side of the map.[6] Through mapping, religious groups can resolve conflicts and work across difference with other groups by redrawing identities and relationships.[7]

During my research, I tried to "listen to mapping as it happens"[8] at Emerging Church events, through books and publications coming from the movement, as well as online environments like blogs and websites. I looked specifically for "mapping talk" expressed through ideas, language and concepts. I operationalized mapping by tuning in to where the Emerging Church talked about themselves in relation to other groups. I describe this as discourses that talk about "where we are" in relation to "others." I focused on reflexive talk of how people from the movement saw how they "fit into the bigger picture," or the larger scheme of things. In looking for mapping practices, I was able to find data where individuals in the movement were diagrammatically "mapping" itself in relation to others symbolically through Venn diagrams and other types of diagrammatical drawings.

Types of Maps

The three broad categories of mapping I identified from my data are, 1) the Christianity in America map, 2) the interfaith map, and 3) the global Christianity map. As all these types of mapping will feature in my subsequent analysis, here I would like to just briefly describe these three types of mapping and how they relate to the Emerging Church.

6. Eliasoph and Lichterman, "Culture in Interaction," 763.
7. Lichterman, "Religion and the Construction of Civic Identity," 85.
8. Ibid., 86.

PART 2: CROSSING BOUNDARIES

Type 1: The Christianity in America Map

The Emerging Church attempts to situate itself in relation to the broader religious landscape of established institutions and denominations. Due to the history of divisiveness between denominations that defines Protestant Christianity, The Emerging Church does not want to be "another slice of the Christian pie." It also has no aspirations to become another denomination. Polarizing maps that divide "liberals" against "conservatives" and "mainliners" versus "evangelicals," need to give way to an alternative basis of mapping that is not couched in binaries or dualisms. The Emerging Church also seeks to map how other groups have tended to be marginalized by institutional Christianity, like minorities along race, gender and sexual orientation.

Type 2: The Interfaith Map

At the heart of interfaith mapping, the Emerging Church is concerned with how Christians "otherize" people of non-Christian faiths, including atheists and agnostics. They see that Christians have traditionally mapped the religious other as either being in alien/ enemy territory, which 1) then is a no-go danger zone for fear that Christians will be "taken," or 2) is an area on the map that must be conquered and colonized, so that the religious "other" will either disappear off the map (conquest) or be assimilated into Christianity (colonized). The Emerging Church seeks to draw an interfaith map, where Christians perhaps can see religious others as friendly territory, as "neighbors" of a different faith that Christians can get along with, and perhaps even learn from.

Type 3: The Global Christianity Map

The Emerging Church is sensitive to the ways that Christianity in the West, and particularly in the United States, has tended to perceive that it occupies the center in the map of global Christianity. For the Emerging Church, the Western Church needs to be "decentered." The Eurocentric version of Christianity needs to be replaced with a global view of Christianity. Translating this to the Emerging Church, the movement highlights how Christians (and the Emerging Church) need to pay attention to non-Western, non-white voices of Christians from other parts of the world. Global mapping sensitizes the Emerging Church to how they think that the landscape of global Christianity has changed.

Reflexive Mapping: Being Self-critical and Pondering Relationships

As stated earlier, one of the primary functions of mapping is for the Emerging Church to turn a critical lens on itself and ponder its relationships with others. Here, I raise two examples of how the movement engages in reflexivity through mapping. The first example centers on an article posted on the Emergent Village website, in it, the author asks: Where does the Emerging Church fit into the Christian tribes? What followed was a robust discussion that elicited a robust dialogue. The second example centers on Emergent author Tony Jones reflecting on an event he organized. In his reflection, he was assessing whether the people they invited to speak at the conference were "representative" of a broad spectrum of Christian groups in America.

Who are we engaging?

This first example of mapping is typified in the question: *Who are we engaging in the Emerging Church conversation and who are we not?* The Emergent Village article entitled "Where Does Emergence Fit in the Christian Tribes?" was authored by an Emergent-identifier named Gideon Addington. The editor introducing the post notes that it "addresses a fundamental question that we've been wrestling with . . . who is 'in' and who is 'out'? Why do some feel like 'outsiders' to the emergent church movement (and to Emergent Village, specifically), while others don't?"[9]

The author draws a big "circle" that represents the Emerging Church and maps the location of different "tribes of Christianity" outside or partially located within the big circle that represented the Emerging Church. Altogether, there are eight different "tribes of Christianity": 1) Missional and Social Justice; 2) Revolutionaries; 3) Fundamentalists; 4) Mystics and Monastics; 5) Institutionalists; 6) Unifiers; 7) Politicos; and 8) Closet Secularist. In the article itself, the author does not provide any definition of these eight tribes, but, for my purposes, this omission does not hinder the analysis.

9. Gideon Addington, "Where Does Emergence Fit in the Christian Tribes?" August 25, 2009, http://www.emergentvillage.com/weblog/where-does-emergence-fit-in-the-ch ristian-tribes (accessed 07/30/2010).

PART 2: CROSSING BOUNDARIES

In the first diagram (below) he depicts what he thinks is the "ideal" scenario. He notes in the post that while ideally all the stated groups should be located within the circle to denote an engagement with the Emerging Church, he notes that "the mark of the ideal is almost always missed" and in reality many of these groups stand outside the circle that represents the Emerging Church.

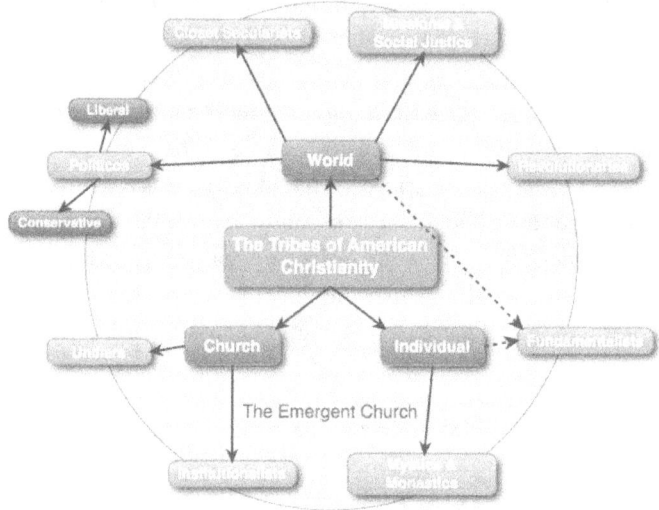

Figure 1: The Ideal

In the second diagram below, he shows which groups in particular are "outside" of the circle that depicts the Emerging Church. In particular he notes four groups that are either outside of the circle, or are just barely in it. These four groups are 1) Closet Secularists, 2) Fundamentalists, 3) Institutionalists, and 4) Conservative Politicos.

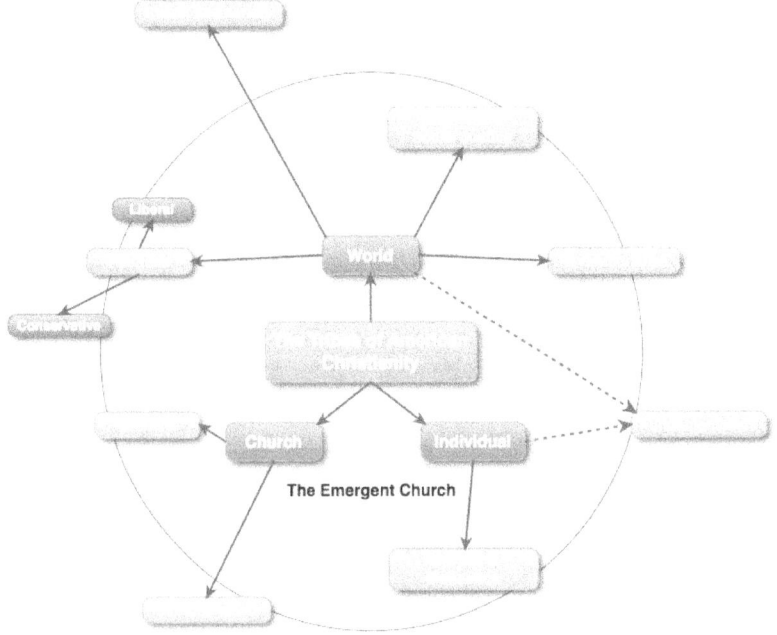

Figure 2: The Reality

The author notes at the end of the post that the whole purpose of these diagrams was to help facilitate the Emerging Church to be reflexive: *"I think we need to take a long look at who is being left out of our conversation, and how we might better invite them in if it is at all possible."* What followed the post was a robust discussion by different voices (both supporters and critics) that raised questions about the way the map was drawn, what terms were used and why some groups were located where they were.

The discussion that ensued saw the author interacting with identifiers and critics, as they discussed why some groups were more engaged with the Emerging Church than others. Some critics criticized the movement for not being inclusive enough. Simultaneously "identifiers" made efforts to incorporate the opinions of its critics into the mapping exercise. Identifiers thanked critics for their perspective, and affirmed that their voices were needed. For instance, one Emergent identifier replied to a critic saying,

> Your critiques are very helpful, because they help us to see our "blind spots" . . . when our desire for "radical inclusiveness" comes

off as hyperbole and superiority, then we need to pay attention and humbly thank you for pointing out our weaknesses.[10]

To which the critic replied,

> I was so encouraged by Steve's generous response. Any person who serves the Savior is a friend of mine and the fact soooo transcends any of our differences.[11]

Through the discussion, and through dealing with criticism, the author says all the input, both positive and negative, is useful feedback. The author notes, that "any typology will be faulty: prone to leaving things out, and touching upon the biases inherent in the person that made such a thing." The author further says, "I actually asked for response regarding what biases I might be demonstrating in the original post," showing personal expressions of reflexivity in this example of group reflexivity.

In all, this mapping exercise is a prime example of how the movement attempts to locate itself in relation to other Christian groups in America. The diagrams appropriately represent how the movement seeks to engage, and be relevant to as many of the Christian tribes in America as possible, and the interactional dimension illustrates their seriousness about including critics in the conversation.

Who did we give a voice to?

I saw the practice of another kind of reflexivity, asking: *Who did we give a voice to?* We got a hint of it in the previous example, where the identifier apologized to the critic for the movement failing to live up to its ideals of being "radically inclusive."

The event in question was a Christianity 21 conference that was organized by Emerging Church key voices Tony Jones and Doug Pagitt. The data being analyzed here is a post-event reflection by Tony Jones on his blog, as to whether the people invited to speak at the conference were sufficiently diverse and sufficiently representative of *both* liberals and conservatives. The Christianity 21 conference, which consisted of all women speakers, was held in Minneapolis, Minnesota. Jones describes how he, Doug Pagitt and two other people involved with organizing the event attempted to "map" the speakers who had already been invited:

10. Ibid., response 10.
11. Ibid., response 19.

We made a chart with two axes on a large piece of paper, thus dividing the paper into four quadrants. One axis was "practitioner—theorist" and the other was "liberal—conservative." We then took our best guess on all 21 of the presenters, and placed them along the axes. *We were pleased to see that we had representation in all four quadrants.*[12]

In this example, mapping was done with a vertical and horizontal axis. It was an exercise to see where the already-invited speakers might fit within the four quadrants produced by the two axes. Jones went on to reflect on how untypical it was to find both conservatives and liberals sharing the same stage. This comparison provided the basis for Tony Jones to conclude that the conference had created a "convergence space" not typically found on American Christianities polarizing maps that divide liberals and conservatives. Jones further notes, "and this got me thinking about how rare it is that among the most liberal Christian leaders (think GLBTQ supporters) and the conservative evangelicals (think Willow Creek) share the stage. In fact, it got me to wondering if there are 21 men out there who would even accept an invitation like this.[13] While in the blog post, Jones did not provide the actual chart, from his description, I thought the chart he described might look something like this:

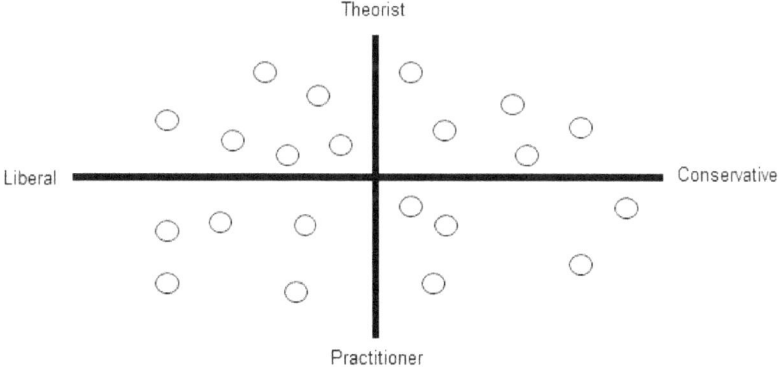

Figure 3: Hypothetical Diagram of "who spoke at Christianity 21"

12. Tony Jones, "Looking Back on Christianity," October 16, 2009. http://blog.beliefnet.com/tonyjones/2009/10/looking-back-on-christianity21.html (accessed 07/04/2015).

13. Ibid.

This exercise in reflexivity, however, sought to assess whether the event featured speakers, both theorists and practitioners, who were along the liberal conservative continuum. This instance of reflexivity showed the Emerging Church's attempt to reflect on whether it was skewed one way or another.

Mapping activities in the Emerging Church take on various forms. Some reflexive mapping activity is retrospective and seeks to evaluate the degree of inclusiveness based on the amount of diversity in Emergent gatherings, or whether they can identify people who belong to a wide spectrum of locations. The core concern of this kind of mapping is to establish: does the reality match our ideals? The first instance of mapping showed the Emerging Church attempting to map itself in relation to other Christian "tribes" with the purpose of better engaging them. From these two mapping examples, we can see how maps are important to the movement in aiding reflexivity.

Offensive and Defensive Mapping

The Emerging Church engages with observers and critics over *how* to map and *who* to map. This can be contentious. This plays out in broadly two styles of mapping: offensive and defensive. I'll firstly explore offensive mapping, which seeks to critique and deconstruct existing maps, while defensive mapping defends new maps and new ways of mapping.

Offensive mapping: critiquing and deconstructing existing maps

The Emerging Church critiques the polarizing and dichotomizing maps that are often drawn by Christian groups. They take issue with the conservative impulse to draw clear-cut and dichotomous maps, to carve "distinct islands of meaning"[14] around labels like "saved" and "unsaved." The Emerging Church also points to the kinds of ethnocentric drawing of maps that where Christians think that they are ostensibly the "center" of the world. In my previous section, I looked at how the movement deals with a type 1 map: the Christianity in America map. To raise a concrete example of

---

14. Zerubavel, "Lumping and Splitting: Notes on Social Classification," 54.

offensive mapping in this section, I look at it with reference to a type 2 map: the interreligious map.

What interfaith maps do the Emerging Church Movement critique and deconstruct? In their article on "Atheist as Other," Edgell, Gerteis and Hartmann give us a flavor of how people of faith draw "maps" in relation to atheists.[15] Their findings tell us, for many Christians in America, atheists are perceived as less trustworthy and less moral than themselves or any other religious adherents. Many Christians do not perceive atheists to be on the same map as people of faith. Even if they are, "on the map," there are distinct and unbridgeable divides between people of faith and atheists.

Although the authors do not use the language of mapping, we can interpret their findings through the mapping metaphor. Essentially, Christians cannot see themselves sharing the same "location" on their map as atheists, because this threatens the boundedness of the Christian identity. The proximate location of religious "others" like atheists and Muslims then becomes untenable to those who draw maps that are absolute and dichotomous, to those who map out the territories distinctly and unequivocally.

The Emerging Church perceives the construction of absolute boundaries and distinctions between Christian groups and other religions, as a deterministic impulse to place people into neat boxes. To sustain a well-ordered reality, "ins" and "outs" are well-defined, and "orthodoxy" and "heresy" are clearly identified.[16] When such clear-cut maps are drawn, it creates a virtual "safe-space" where religious others are categorically placed "outside" the boundary-line. The language and concepts from the movement seek to subvert this whole basis of mapping "insider" from "outsider." Emergent thinker Samir Selmanovic demonstrates one telling example of how this "insider" and "outsider" is subverted. He writes,

> For God to create human beings to die in order to show the consequences of life outside Judaism, Christianity, or Islam is incompatible with the core teachings of Judaism, Christianity, and Islam. To think of God as favoring any human group would be simply un-Jewish, un-Christian, un-Muslim. A god would take a place of One God. *If God is not on the outside of our religions, whatever is inside is meaningless. Without God on the outside, the inside crumbles.*[17]

15. Edgell, Gerteis, and andHartmann, "Atheist as 'Other': Moral Boundaries and Cultural Membership in American Society."

16. McLaren, *A New Kind of Christian: A Tale of Two Friends on a Spiritual Journey.*

17. Selmanovic, *It's Really All about God: How Islam, Atheism, and Judaism Made*

Selmanovic's quote represents how the Emerging Church subverts the binary of inside and outside. In addition to deconstructing the division, Emergents further critique the "safe-zone" of the "inside," with Christians not seeing the need to engage or commune with religious others since they stand completely "outside" the one true faith.

Selmanovic is arguing that *both* other religions and atheists should not be mapped "outside" of Christianity. In fact, he maps both other religions, and atheists as integral to broader map of Christianity and other faiths. He writes,

> Other religions can challenge (or at least help us to see) the idols we create because they expand the whole territory of knowing. They post difficult questions we don't want to ask, make assumptions we don't want to acknowledge or examine, create meaningful arguments against us we don't want to consider, and expose harmful practices we don't want to stop. Where we have created a vacuum of knowledge and virtue through our own religions, God enters that space through the religions of others—through strangers. When we let them come close and embrace them as our neighbors, they can help us see God's presence, grace, and care where we cannot see it on our own.[18]

In similar fashion, for atheists, he writes,

> Thus for me atheism is not an enemy of religion but another "rabbi of life." Atheists are our brothers and sisters, our partners and teachers, necessary and good, in a circle with Jews, Christians, Muslims and people of other religions. They are not to be thought of as guests; they are part of the human household to which we all belong and without whom we would be worse off.[19]

From this example, we can see how this kind of mapping is "offensive" in another sense of the word, where it is deeply offensive to the boundary sensibilities of the kinds of Christians who are adamant that no good can come out of other faiths, and even less so, atheists. This offensive mapping also takes place in face-to-face encounters. For instance, in a Chicago Emergent gathering an Atheist author was invited to speak about his view of Christians and Christianity.[20]

Me a Better Christian, 11.

18. Ibid., 146.

19. Ibid., 176.

20. "Reflections on the Midwest Gathering," August 03,2007. http://www.

In offensive mapping, the Emerging Church seeks to subvert dualisms. They want to transcend saved/ unsaved, insider/ outsider, even liberal/ conservative dualisms. "Bad" maps entrench people in binaries, and hence they see a need to formulate new ways of mapping, or to look "outside" of existing maps. The Emerging Church breaches such either/ or clear-cut distinctions by themselves taking up many of these labels. For instance, in the prominent use of the term "heretic" or "heretical" in some Emergent authors' books, they make the paradoxical point that one has to be a "heretic" to the establish encrusted Christian religion, in order to be faithful followers of the way of Jesus.[21]

Defensive mapping: defending new maps and new ways of mapping

The Emerging Church has also had to defend themselves from critics in how they construct maps. For instance, in the post I analyzed previously: "where does emergence fit in the Christian tribes?" the author faced criticism by one commenter for being "presumptuous by making charts of 'who's in and who's out,'"[22] another chimed in, calling the author "presumptuous, and a bit arrogant," and that "using broad brush to describe any group . . . grossly simplifies the discussion." [23]

The author responded by clarifying his intention for the diagram to "facilitate contemplation and hopefully conversation," while a more sympathetic commenter labeled the attempt as "a brain storm session thrown up on the wall."[24] This situation seemed to boil down to the critics perceiving that the map was *prescriptive* as opposed to *descriptive*, while the author expressed his intent to do the latter. The author further clarifies that "what I'm saying is 'if this is so, if this is what we imagine it to be . . . we have to figure out who is being left out, why, and how to change that." Hence the author

---

emergentvillage.com/weblog/reflections-on-the-midwest-gathering (accessed August 7, 2010).

21. Rollins, *The Fidelity of Betrayal: Towards a Church Beyond Belief*; Burke, *A Heretic's Guide to Eternity*.

22. "Where Does Emergence Fit in the Christian Tribes?," response 1, August 29, 2009. http://www.emergentvillage.com/weblog/where-does-emergence-fit-in-the-christian-tribes, ("where does emergence fit in the Christian tribes?" response 1, posted 08/29/2009, accessed 08/August 06/, 2010).

23. Ibid., response 2.

24. Ibid., response 6.

argues that this mapping exercise was to provide a tool for the movement to be more inclusive rather than as a statement of exclusion.

Critics, like those found on the Website apologeticsindex.org, have called into account various maps the Emerging Church has drawn up in relation to other faiths. For instance, a quote from Brian McLaren that has been much criticized, by apologeticsindex.org, and other "online discernment" websites, he expresses:

> I don't believe making disciples must equal making adherents to the Christian religion. It may be advisable in many (not all!) circumstances to help people become followers of Jesus and remain within their Buddhist, Hindu or Jewish contexts . . . rather than resolving the paradox via pronouncements on the eternal destiny of people more convinced by or loyal to other religions than ours, we simply move on . . . To help Buddhists, Muslims, Christians, and everyone else experience life to the full in the way of Jesus.[25]

The paradox that Brian McLaren speaks of that is not to be resolved, essentially addresses the impulse for clear-cut maps that pronounce the "eternal" status of people. He marks a distance between "disciples" and "adherents to the Christian religion," saying that one does not necessarily need to equate to the other. McLaren is arguing for a map where "disciple" does not preclude Buddhists, Hindus or Jews. There is a level of cartographic dissonance that does not sit well with critics as clear boundaries (that should be) have been breached. In addition, instead of seeing Christianity, Islam and Judaism as completely different religions with nothing in common, The Emerging Church emphasizes the shared traditions of monotheistic religions. In their mapping practices, they bridge the divide between what are perceived as "distinct islands of meaning," i.e., other religions. Emerging Church conferences have been held with Catholic groups, Jewish groups and have also included atheists as speakers. They espouse the idea that, while yes, there are fundamental differences between us and atheists, or Jews, none-the-less they are not so "alien" to our context that they belong on another stratosphere. For Emergents, these "others" have a place on their map. People from other religions, as well as atheists are mapped as "fellow journeyers of a different path."

---

25. McLaren, *A Generous Orthodoxy*, 260–64.

Turning Boundaries into Borderlands

Another way that the Emerging Church seeks to "do things" with maps in practical ways, is to subvert boundaries and instead, recast borderlands.[26] Boundaries, or "borders" often brings to mind conflict and tension where "lines in the sand" are drawn. As Jeffrey Sacks notes in the award-winning book *The Dignity of Difference*, this is nowhere more apparent than with religious identities, where "the very process of creating an 'Us' involves creating a 'Them'—the people not like us. In the very process of creating community within their borders, religions can create conflict across borders.[27] Eliasoph and Lichterman also note that mapping borders is crucial to a group's definition of itself, and does not come *after* identity is constructed, but that borders are part of the fabric that *make* identity.[28] However, Anzaldúa's idea of "borderlands" modifies border to become more than just a boundary-line. With an addition of the modifier "land," the "borderland" becomes a place for encounter rather than just a line that one either crosses or stays on one's "own side."

"Borderlands" is an important concept for understanding what groups are doing with boundaries, since "it acknowledges the boundaries, but shifts the analysis to look for ways that boundaries are neither static nor unbridgeable."[29] Borderlands are places where different people encounter each other, and where something new can come out of that *encounter*. A "borderland," a place where "us" and "them" come together, creates an "opening for productive confusion."[30] Borderlands are "a place of possibility, or new creation" and denote a "shifting landscape of changing possibilities . . . where boundaries are unstable, and identities and relationships are in flux."[31]

---

26. Anzaldúa, *Borderlands = La Frontera*.

27. Sacks, *The Dignity of Difference*, 10.

28. Eliasoph and Lichterman, "Culture in Interaction."

29. Neitz, "2008 Association for the Sociology of Religion Presidential Address. Encounter in the Heartland: What Studying Rural Churches Taught Me about Working across Differences," 358.

30. Tsing, *Friction*, 247.

31. Neitz, "2008 Association for the Sociology of Religion Presidential Address. Encounter in the Heartland: What Studying Rural Churches Taught Me about Working across Differences," 358.

Below, I illustrate the difference between a "border" and a "borderland," and how the latter is a "space" for productive encounters between "us" and "them."

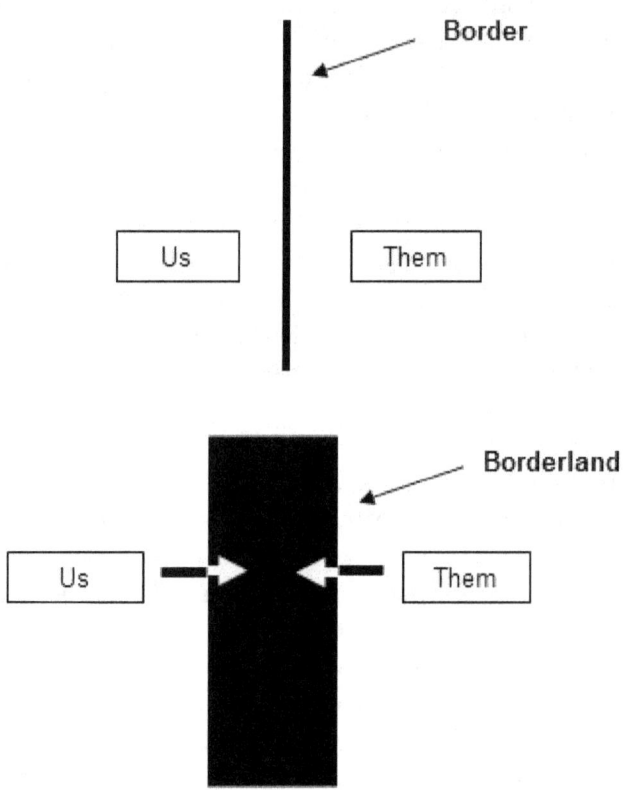

Figure 4: Borders versus Borderlands

For the Emerging Church, borderlands are important places of "encounter" with religious others, where taken-for-granted boundaries of separation are suspended for the sake of mutual encounter. In similar fashion to how Neitz describes the centrality of boundaries to borderlands, for the Emerging Church boundaries *are* still necessary, since to not respect or to gloss over boundaries does not respect "the dignity of difference."[32] Hence for the Emerging Church, to locate borderlands, is not a desire to find places where difference can be collapsed into sameness (assimilation.)

32. Sacks, *The Dignity of Difference*, 2002.

Rather, the intention is to locate places where proximity is possible, while holding the tension of differences, be it in identity or in particular theological beliefs. Borderlands are hence locations where the delicate tension of *difference + closeness* is possible. An excerpt of my interview with Brian McLaren explains what he thinks are the necessary ingredients that engender a borderland of encounter:

> Jesus invites us to love our enemies. To treat everyone, including our enemies, like neighbors. That idea to me is very powerful because he doesn't say "everyone is your friend" or "you have no enemies." To do that is a kind of colonization. But allowing the other to define himself as my enemy, in a sense allows the other to keep his dignity and differentness. But for me to include the person in my circle of concern preserves both otherness and some sense of unity and connectedness. *To me this is what the message of the Kingdom of God does. It invites us into some kind of embrace where you have the distinction of otherness, but also have the connection of relatedness.*

Looking at this quote through the framework of the mapping metaphor, McLaren conceptualizes a potential borderland when an individual maps a religious other "in [their] circle of concern," preserving both the identity and distinctiveness of the other (difference) while also accomplishing "unity and connectedness." In my survey of the literature from the movement, as well as my data from blogs, this "talk" of relational borderlands appears very prominently in various forms.

Emergent thinker and author of *Thy Kingdom Connected*, Dwight J. Friesen notes in a contributing article to a multi-author edited work called *An Emergent Manifesto of Hope*, envisions this "borderland" in the concept "Orthoparadox," or "holding difference rightly."[33] He asks: What would a borderland look like? What would happen there? And what are the rules of engagement in the borderland? He asserts:

> Orthoparadox seeks to hold difference, tensions, otherness, and paradoxes with grace, humility, respect, and curiosity, while simultaneously bringing the fullness of self to the "other" in conversation, not to convert or to convince but with the hope of mutual transformation through interpersonal relationships.[34]

---

33. Eisenhower, *An Emergent Manifesto of Hope*.
34. Friesen, *Thy Kingdom Connected*, 205.

PART 2: CROSSING BOUNDARIES

In a relational borderland, the goal of engagement and interaction is not to "conquer" through assimilation, which characterizes much of what we think of as "proselytizing" or "evangelism," where the goal of establishing *closeness*, is inadvertently to work toward *sameness*: an exercise to enact transformation in the "other." Instead of assimilation, Friesen proposes the concept of "differentiation," which according to him is "our ability to live separately from others, without being separated."[35] In the borderlands, instead of seeking to instrumentally, "defeat, debate, condemn or even convert the other,"[36] or to insist that someone crosses over the line in the sand and comes over to "your side," relationships in the borderlands are marked by "mutual exploration, humble submission, deference, and wonder."[37] We can interpret this as a commitment for religious others to mutually engage one another in the borderland with sustained and honest contact, instead of merely making forays across the border with the offensive mindset of wanting to "win people over" to one side or the other.

Emergent thinker Samir Selmanovic says in concert with borderlands metaphor, that Christians need to entertain the possibility of "finding our god in the other."[38] Samir is also founder and Pastor of Faith House Manhattan, which is a faith collective that houses Christians, Muslims and Jews who worship together as a community. Samir's own collective embodies this idea of a borderland of encounter where difference meets closeness. Elsewhere in his writings, Samir has elucidated how borderlands can produce a "productive tension" when groups enter into disagreement. Selmanovic writes,

> When we take a stand and pull the argument in our own direction, *we create an empty space between us, a possibility for the emergence of a truly new idea, an unexpected solution, a way forward.* When we disagree, we pit ourselves against one another. But seeing that all of us humans are in this together, we can learn to disagree for one another. When we disagree against one another destruction or even death results; when we disagree for one another, life happens.[39]

35. Ibid.,206.
36. Ibid.
37. Ibid.,209.
38. Friesen, "Orthoparadoxy: Emerging Hope for Embracing Difference," 189.
39. Friesen, *Thy Kingdom Connected: What the Church can Learn from Facebook, the Internet, and Other Networks*, 175.

According to Selmanovic, in the borderland of encounter, when groups pull in different directions, then they engender "space" for "something new" to emerge where both will benefit. This is embodied by the paradoxical notion of groups disagreeing *for* one another. Where Tsing notes "encounter" as a "productive confusion"[40] Selmanovic voices encounter as "productive disagreement." Both occur in the borderland.

The Emerging Church as Borderland

The Emerging Church envisions itself as a "borderland": a safe place for people of different persuasions to encounter each other. My research brought me to an Emerging Church panel in a seminar at Calvin College in Grand Rapids, Michigan. It was here that I was first introduced to the idea of "suspended space" by author Pete Rollins. I would later encounter this concept in Rollins' writings. Rollins is also the founder of an Emerging Church collective in Belfast, Ireland, called Ikon. He is a prominent Emergent writer and sought-after speaker, influential in the movement in America. During the Seminar, Rollins explained how he adopted the term "suspended space" from philosopher Emmanuel Levinas to think about the kind of worship collective that he wanted to form. He described how Ikon meetings are a "suspended space" because individuals symbolically "empty themselves of their identities" and suspend their positionalities when they come for the service. Rollins explains in an interview that Ikon tries to,

> . . . create a place in our week, a liturgical hour where there is neither Jew nor Greek, slave nor free, male nor female, republican nor democrat, employed nor unemployed, liberal nor conservative, where we can encounter each other at a deeper level.[41]

Rollins expresses the Ikon meetings are purposed to create a participation space where labels do not matter and where people come to converse and decompartmentalized instead of being compartmentalized as labels, hence being perceived through the stereotype of any one identity (e.g. gay, conservative, atheist, etc). In comparison to what Brian McLaren and Dwight Friesen say in the previous section, where a borderland denotes

---

40. Selmanovic , *It's Really All About God*, 247.

41. "Part 1—Phyllis Tickle and Peter Rollins discuss Emergence Christianity," February 9, 2009. http://www.youtube.com/watch?v=9sRsOhy_WWAandfeature=PlayLista ndp=B9E3E8FF329EB156andplaynext=1andplaynext_from=PLandindex=7 (,"accessed July 3, 2015).

bringing the "fullness" of the other to all interactions, *Ikon* practices suspending identities and positionalities as a way of creating this convergence space. The means and the conceptualizations differ but the intended goal is the same: to promote true encounters across difference, between diverse people.

In *How (not) to Speak of God* Rollins underscores how in the borderland of an Ikon service, conversion is not one that is offered "by 'us' to 'them,'" but rather, that everyone in attendance "is a potential implement of our (collective) further conversion. Consequently, the evangelical nature of the community does not resemble a one-way diatribe leading from 'us' to 'them' but rather embodies a multiple dialogue that moves from one to another."[42]

Rollins' description of Ikon's attempt to engender "suspended space" here fits the conceptualization of borderlands, since the linear and singular direction "us to them" in conversion encounters is exchanged for a dynamically engaged "multiple dialogue" *conservation* encounter where the intention is that all experience and receive "conversion" from all others in attendance. This example gives us a flavor of how Emergents approach thinking about difference, where The Emerging Church and their meeting spaces seek to be the "borderland" of encounter they envision.

Other data from my research also indicates that people engaging the movement from their existing faith traditions, see The Emerging Church Movement as a borderland, where regardless of their denominational affiliation, or specific theological/ doctrinal orientation, they feel both the desire and the safety to "draw near" to others involved with the conversation because they are potentially going to hear something different, and encounter something unexpected, but in a spirit of mutual discovery and learning from what denominational "others" bring to the table.

One prime example comes from an interview I conducted with a pastor of a Lutheran Church located in the Chicago area. I first met Pastor Fred Nelson at a Chicago area Emergent gathering in 2007. I later interviewed him in early 2010. Pastor Nelson is a white male in his mid 40s, who received a doctorate prior to entering into ministry. When asked about his involvement with the Emerging Church, he expressed that he saw in the Emerging Church a "convergence" space for Mainliners and Evangelicals to bring the strong points of their traditions together and learn from each other. Pastor Nelson expressed a concern that Evangelicals and Mainliners,

42. Rollins, *How (Not) to Speak of God*, 79.

while "moving toward each other," might be in danger of "bypassing" each other by adopting each others' "extremes." Pastor Nelson mapped the Emerging Church as a borderland of encounter where those who partake stand to mutually benefit through the encounter.

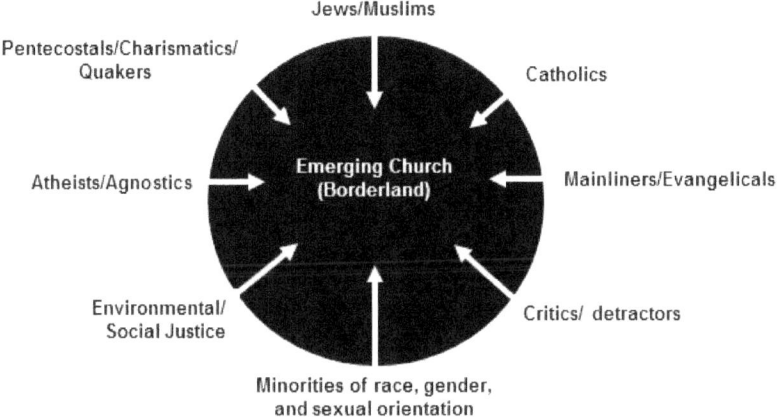

Figure 5: The Emerging Church as Borderland

My research also revealed how Borderlands was expressed through different, but parallel concepts. As my diagram demonstrates above, the Emerging Church envisions itself as a location for a variety of groups to come together across their differences, not just between mainline and evangelical Christians. In fact, the diagram above represents different groups that the Emerging Church has engaged. One individual, writing on an Emergent Village article posting, expresses this borderlands concept this way,

> One thing I've been thinking about recently is the idea of Emergent Village as a "liminal space" or, to use Peter Rollins terminology, a "suspended space," where some personal theological positionality is "suspended" or held as "transitional"/"in-between" in order to really listen and engage "the other" in dialogue. We are fully who we are (e.g., evangelical/post-evangelical, Presbyterian, Anglican, etc.), and we allow others to be fully who they are (e.g., Catholic, Lutheran, Baptist, etc.). We are all followers of Jesus Christ, part of his body, the Church. And there's an epistemic humility in being willing to enter that "liminal space" and do so in community together—because it's an admission that we each could be wrong,

and, even more than that, that we ARE wrong, we just don't know what we're wrong about (yet).[43]

Hence the Emerging Church locates itself as a "borderland" where different groups of people can converge on to encounter each other. I have also heard the idea of "borderlands" being expressed as "temporary autonomous zones," by Brian McLaren, and as "Liberated Spaces" by former Emergent Village board member Eliacin Rosario-Cruz. Hence, there are many ways that people from the Emerging Church attempt to articulate a relational borderland of encounter.

Navigational Affinity: Learning from Other Faiths

The "mapping" metaphor can also be extended to understand how the Emerging Church thinks about itself, in tandem with other religions, each navigating their respective journey of faith. Instead of drawing dichotomous maps, where religious "others" are perceived as residing in completely alien territory, with nothing in common, the Emerging Church maps religious "others" as different, but still sees them as having common experiences worth learning from.

Where previously I have discussed mapping in terms of cartography, or "map making," in this section, I discuss the map metaphor in a somewhat different dimension, in terms of navigation, which connotes travelling and "getting" to places. The Emerging Church imagines themselves in relation to diverse others, not just in terms of "encounters" in borderlands, as I discuss in the previous section. In this section, I analyze how *religious others are mapped in terms of being on a similar journey, though on different paths*. And in the dynamic of different faiths being on similar journeys, Emergents think that there is much to learn from the religious "other."

Emerging Church discourses often seek to map signs of emergence that are occurring in other faiths. For instance, on emergentvillage.com, there have been several blog postings identifying and discussing an "Emergent Islam." One particular Emergent Village blog entry picked up on a blog by a Muslim writer, Andrea Useem, who writes of "The Emergent

---

43. "The Circle of Inclusion," response 51, June 6, 2009. http://www.emergentvillage.com/weblog/the-circle-of-inclusion (accessed August 6, 2010).

Islam I Want."[44] Part of the blog post was reproduced, where the author states, "I have also begun to hope for the emergence of a post-modern, post-9/11 Muslim faith life." The Emerging Church pays attention to this, not as a concern for territory in the way of saying "they are lifting a page from us," but rather as a way of establishing that people from other faiths are experiencing similar conditions of existence, and are coming face-to-face with the same set of potentially paradigm-shifting questions Emergent Christians are asking.

The same dynamic of navigational affinity can be seen through how the Emerging Church imagines its engagement with Jewish groups. Leaders from Emergent Village had a well-documented and much-publicized meeting with a progressive Jewish group called Synagogue 3000 (or S3K), in 2006. A joint press release expressed the purpose of the meeting for participants to, "share experiences and exchange ideas about reinventing the meaning and practice of community in their respective faith traditions, *especially for unaffiliated Christians and Jews who are not attracted to conventional congregations.*" This statement voices the navigational affinity based on a shared concern with the future of each faith, particularly toward those who are falling off at the margins. Brian McLaren, who was part of this meeting, noted that, "we (Christians and Jews) face similar problems in the present; we have common hopes for the future, and we draw from shared resources in our heritage."[45]

By focusing on how other faiths are attempting to "get there" in their own journey, The Emerging Church Movement asks: What questions are people from other faiths asking? What are the common struggles that different faiths share? What contextual and theological issues are other faiths similarly dealing with? How are people of other religions being reflexive about their faith in the same way that we are? The Emerging Church Movement locates Christianity on a map, which considers what religious others are dealing with as an indication of broader cultural shifts that are not exclusive to what Christian Emergents are facing. As one Emergent blogger, commenting on the Jewish Emergent meeting as an exciting development, attempts to broaden the map by asking:

44. Andrea Useem, "The Emergent Islam I Want," July 23, 2008. http://newsweek.washingtonpost.com/onfaith/guestvoices/2008/07/the_emergent_islam_i_want.html (accessed July 3, 2015).

45. Shawn Landres and Tony Jones, "Emergent Jewish and Christian Leaders to Meet," January 3, 2006. http://www.wnrf.org/cms/emergent_jewish_christian.shtml (accessed July 3, 2015).

> I am really interested in whether there are Emergent Muslims too ... Anyone out there want to fill us in on some emerging mosques? It's clear that "emergent" is not just a Christian-fad—but is a much wider and greater phenomenon.[46]

Emergent Christians adopt the "similar journey" metaphor to map how Muslims and Jews are experiencing the same conditions of existence. The descriptive "postmodern" has been used in talk of both Emergent-style Islam and Judaism. This allows them to say, "We are experiencing very similar cross currents," and without saying "we are the same." Hence they identify the *navigational affinity* between Muslims, Christians and Jews, while preserving the distinctive route, path or journey that each faith is attempting to navigate.

Conclusion

It is my hope that the chapter has given the reader and understanding of how the Emerging Church engages in mapping as both a cognitive and practical activity that can be done as an exercise in reflexivity, and also as collaborative activity through diverse interactions. In line with my training, my analysis has been sociological rather than theological. I hope I have demonstrated how the Emerging Church imagines itself in relation to others, and fosters diverse relationships through seeking Borderlands, or encounter spaces, as well as identifying common experiences with fellow religionists with whom they share a navigational affinity.

Bibliography

Anzaldúa, Gloria. *Borderlands = La Frontera*. San Francisco: Aunt Lute, 1999.
Burke, Spencer. *A Heretic's Guide to Eternity*. San Francisco: Jossey-Bass, 2006.
DiMaggio, Paul. "Culture and Cognition" in *Annual Review of Sociology* 27, no. 1 (1997) 263–88.
Edgell, Penny, et al. "Atheist as 'Other': Moral Boundaries and Cultural Membership in American Society." *American Sociological Review* 71, no. 2 (2006) 211–34.
Eliasoph, Nina, and Paul Lichterman. "Culture in Interaction" in *American Journal of Sociology* 108, no. 4 (2003) 735–94.
Foster, Johanna. "Menstrual Time: The Socio-Cognitive Mappings of the 'Menstrual Cycle.'" *Sociological Forum* 11 (1996) 523–48.

46. "Christians and Jews Discuss Emergent Sacred Communities," January 19, 2006. http://pomomusings.com/2006/01/19/christians-jews-discuss-emergent-sacred-communities (accessed July 3, 2015).

Friesen, Dwight. *Thy Kingdom Connected: What the Church Can Learn from Facebook, the Internet, and Other Networks*. Grand Rapids: Baker, 2009.

———. "Orthoparadoxy: Emerging Hope for Embracing Difference." In *An Emergent Manifesto of Hope*, edited by Doug Pagitt and Tony Jones, 201–12. Grand Rapids: Baker, 2007.

Lichterman, Paul. "Religion and the Construction of Civic Identity." *American Sociological Review* 73 (2008) 83–104.

McLaren, Brian D. *A Generous Orthodoxy*. Grand Rapids: Zondervan, 2004.

———. *A New Kind of Christian: A Tale of Two Friends on a Spiritual Journey*. San Francisco: Jossey-Bass, 2001.

Neitz, Mary Jo. "2008 Association for the Sociology of Religion Presidential Address. Encounter in the Heartland: What Studying Rural Churches Taught Me about Working across Differences." *Sociology of Religion* 70, no. 4 (2009) 343–61.

Rollins, Peter. *The Fidelity of Betrayal: Towards a Church Beyond Belief*. Brewster, MA: Paraclete, 2008.

———. *How (Not) to Speak of God*. Brewster, MA: Paraclete, 2006.

Sacks, Jonathan. *The Dignity of Difference: How to Avoid the Clash of Civilizations*. London: Continuum, 2002.

Selmanovic, Samir. *It's Really All about God: Reflections of a Muslim Atheist Jewish Christian*. San Francisco: Jossey-Bass, 2009.

Smith, Jonathan Z. *Map Is Not Territory: Studies in the History of Religions*. Leiden: Brill, 1978.

Tsing, Anna Lowenhaupt. *Friction: An Ethnography of Global Connection*. Princeton: Princeton University Press, 2005.

Zerubavel, Eviatar. *The Fine Line: Making Distinctions in Everyday Life*. New York: Free, 1991.

———. "Lumping and Splitting: Notes on Social Classification." *Sociological Forum* 11, no. 3 (1996) 421–33.

———. *Terra Cognita: The Mental Discovery of America*. New Brunswick, NJ: Rutgers University Press, 1992.

7

"There Are Not Two Worlds": Transcending the "Modern" Categories of Sacred and Secular in the Emerging Church Movement

Jason Wollschleger

"I HAVE A BIG view of God . . . I also don't see the sacred/secular divide . . . *there are not two worlds.*"[1]

Introduction

The Emerging Church Movement (ECM) has been hailed as both the future of Christianity as well as an indication of Christian decline. The ECM is known for its young congregants (20s–30s), its innovative worship practices, effective incorporation of technology, irreverence, and ease with popular culture.[2] The roots of the ECM in the US can be traced back to Gen-X churches of the late 1980s and the "church within a church" model used by megachurches in the early 1990s to reach youth and young adults.[3] There is broad agreement that the ECM grew out of the efforts of existing Evangelical churches and denominations to reach out to younger populations[4] through either special youth ministries or generational churches, it was not until the late 1990s that the Emerging Church as a movement coalesced as a result of a conference of young church leaders hosted by the Leadership

---

1. Personal interview; emphasis added.
2. Wollschleger, *Off the Map*, 69–70.
3. Gibbs and Bolger, *Emerging Churches*, 30–34. Wollschleger and Killian, *Emerging Church*, www.has.vcu/wrs/profiles/EmergingChurch.htm.
4. Jones, *The New Christians*, 67–68.

Network.⁵ This conference created the "conversation" that has evolved into the Emerging Church Movement.

There has been a recent upsurge in the scholarship on the ECM and its significance for the religious landscape. Bielo sees the ECM as a response to modernity and focuses on three essential practices/defining features of the ECM; he argues they are missional, ancient-future oriented in their worship, and driven by narratives of deconversion from mainstream evangelicalism.⁶ Packard focuses on the ECM from the perspective of organizational sociology.⁷ He argues that the ECM is intentionally an anti-institutional organization, i.e., the DNA of the movement is resistance to institutionalizing forces. Marti and Ganiel view Emerging Christianity as a religious orientation built on a continual process of deconstruction, and the ECM as "the institutionalizing structure, made up of a package of beliefs, practices, and identities that are continually deconstructed and reframed by the religious institutional entrepreneurs."⁸ Wollschleger discovered that, while the ECM is often thought to be a monolithic movement, really it is best described along a spectrum that contains distinct types of congregations. On one end of the spectrum are the "emerging" congregations, those congregations that seek to embody a new way of doing church in a postmodern context. On the other end of the spectrum are "relevant" congregations: young conservative evangelical congregations that have adopted practices associated with the ECM but not the movement's unique ideals and beliefs.⁹

In their review of the literature Wollschleger and Killian have identified a set of five values that scholars have identified in their research that characterize the Emerging Church: "(1) being missional (Bielo 2011; Packard 2012; Wollschleger 2012), (2) emphasis on place (Bielo 2011; Packard 2012; Wollschleger 2012), (3) egalitarianism (Packard 2012; Wollschleger 2012), (4) ancient-future worship (Bielo 2011; Wollschleger 2012), and (5) authenticity (Bielo 2011; Wollschleger 2012)."¹⁰ They are not arguing that all Emerging Churches embrace these five values as doctrine but rather that

---

5. Driscoll, *A Pastoral Perspective*, 87–88. Jones, *The New Christians*, 41–43. Bielo, *Emerging Evangelicals*, 8.

6. Bielo, *Emerging Evangelicals*, 10–16.

7. Packard, *The Emerging Church*, 29–31.

8. Marti and Ganiel, *The Deconstructed Church*, 8.

9. Wollschleger, *Off the Map*, 88–90.

10. Wollschleger and Killian, *Emerging Church*, www.has.vcu/wrs/profiles/Emerging Church.htm.

these are themes that different scholars working on different projects in different places have identified as central to the Emerging Church Movement. For the purposes of this chapter I want to focus on two of these crucial aspects of the ECM: the ECM as a reactionary movement to the forces of modernity and radical authenticity as the core value of the ECM.

The ECM as Reactionary Movement Committed to Radical Authenticity

Bielo identifies the ECM as primarily a cultural critique—a critique of modernity and its consequences for Christianity, especially conservative Evangelicalism. He argues that Evangelicalism, both in terms of its congregational structure (ecclesiology) and its theology, was formed within the context of modernity and as such has deeply flawed assumptions and is disconnected from the holistic expression of Christianity as well as the lived experiences of younger evangelicals.[11] Additionally, he identifies authenticity as the "organizing trope"[12] of the ECM: Emerging Christians want "to have authentic lives, faith, community, relationships, experience, worship, tradition, and spirituality."[13] Marti and Ganiel echo this twofold reaction against mainstream religious institutions and their embeddedness in modernity as well as a drive for authenticity: "Emerging Christians see themselves as rescuing core aspects of Christianity from the entanglement of modernity, bureaucracy, and right wing politics. Emerging Christians are also rescuing their own selves from the shallowness, hypocrisy, and rigidity of their religious past."[14]

Thus, if the ECM is a reactionary movement as Bielo as well as Marti and Ganiel argue and if the search for radical authenticity is at the movement's core, as both Bielo and Wollschleger argue,[15] then one is left with the question of what aspect of modern culture the movement is reacting against. The answer, I think, is the differentiation of social spheres into sacred and secular.

---

11. Bielo, *Emerging Evangelicals*, 16–21.
12. Ibid., 16.
13. Bielo, *Emerging Evangelicals*. 16.
14. Marti and Ganiel, *The Deconstructed Church*, 29.
15. Wollschleger, *Off the Map*, 76–82.

Differentiation of Social Spheres

One of the hallmarks of the religious landscape in the "modern" world is the separation of the sacred and the secular, i.e., the differentiation of social spheres.[16] Drawing on theoretical work that goes as far back as Durkheim and his argument that increased social differentiation as a result of the expansion of the division of labor would lead to the separation of the sacred and secular realms, Berger and other secularization theorists argued that the forces of modernity led to increased social differentiation and the separation of the sacred and secular. They argued that as a result of rationalization and other modernizing forces social institutions and culture were "removed from the domination of religious institutions and symbols."[17] This social differentiation led to the modern reality of a separation of the sacred or religious spheres from all other secular spheres of social life. The influence of religious institutions was drained from the other sectors of society and confined to a single social space—the church.

Thus, modernization has led to both the secularization of the world and sacralization of the church, and individuals who move between both of these spaces can feel as if they are two different people. Or maybe a better way to say it is that they are not fully, authentically themselves in either space, in each social sphere they must compartmentalize aspects of their identity. It makes sense then that religious individuals who grew up in this socio-religious environment and believe that their religion is meant to be holistic with implications for all aspects of life would view the church, its leaders, and followers as inauthentic and/or hypocritical. If this is the case then what we would expect from this generation of believers would be a reactionary, religious movement. In fact, Wollschleger and Beach argue that one of the likely consequences of having a large number of religious people who still belong to and identify with a religious group but no longer hold the same beliefs as the majority will be a religious revolt—a reactionary, religious movement. [18] This is especially the case if these individuals have the ability to identify one another and organize. This is what we see in the ECM—a generation of people who grew up within Protestant churches had a belief/preference that their religion be holistic but who experienced a divide between their religious lives and secular lives. They organized, through

---

16. Berger, *The Sacred Canopy*, 107; Packard, *The Emerging Church*, 64–66.
17. Ibid., 107.
18. Wollschleger and Beach, "Religious Chameleons," 187–91.

conferences and the internet, in response to this social and religious reality and sought to create an alternative expression of their religion that was more holistic and therefore more "authentic."

Methods

I attended an Emerging Church, Church of the Apostles, as a participant observer for a period of about a year, from the early spring of 2009 to the fall of 2010. This attendance included worship services, small group meetings, meals and parties at congregants' homes, theology pub nights, and church government and annual meetings. I conducted a one-on-one interview with the senior pastor, as well as group interviews/focus groups with four to six congregants, I spent a good deal of time interacting with congregants in and after worship services and group meetings, and I performed content analyses of the church websites, written materials, and sermons. In the hope of future comparability and replicability, the field research was structured around Pitchford, Bader and Stark's agenda for field research on religious organizations.[19] Data was gathered on the groups' organizational history and context, mobilization, organization, governance, and outcomes. Pitchford, Bader, and Stark provided a structure to shape observations in the field as well as the questions included in the pastor interview and focus group (although in both of these there was room to follow new topics as introduced by the research participants.) The pastor interview schedule focused on background details of both the pastor and the congregation, definition of the Emerging Church and an explanation of how their congregation was "emerging," questions on what makes their congregation different, why they decided to become an Emerging Church, the vision and mission of their congregations, plans for the future, a description of their relationship with and to the community, and a question concerning politics and how political issues were handled in the congregation. The focus group schedules focused more on why congregants chose the congregation, their past religious involvement, their perception of what made the congregations different from others, what they understood the term Emerging Church to mean, how political issues were handled in congregational life, and the level of involvement of members in the running of the congregation. Although the observations were framed by theoretical concerns and by the Pitchford, Bader, and Stark framework all the data was analyzed systematically using

19. Pitchford, et al., *Doing Field Studies of Religious Movements*, 380–89.

principles from grounded theory: data analysis started with open coding, in which data elements were labeled and categorized, followed by selective coding focusing on key concepts.

An Emerging Congregation: Apostles

Church of the Apostles, as a congregation, has been featured in nearly every major study of the ECM, both by scholars[20] and by movement leaders.[21] The pastor of Apostles has been in the core group of movement leaders since early in the movement's history and additionally one of the board members of Emergent Village (an important ECM organization and website) is a regular-attending member.[22] While I was there Apostles was regularly hosting visitors from all over the country—researchers, seminarians and congregational leaders—all of whom were there to learn how church was "done" at Apostles. Apostles is as close to the core of the movement as possible and while generalization may not be possible from this case, it is fair to say that by studying Apostles I have had my finger on the pulse of the ECM movement.

Located in the city of Seattle, WA, Apostles has been an Emerging church since its founding. The pastor of Apostles moved to Seattle from Chicago specifically to plant an Emerging church. As a denominational researcher, she had noticed a change in how people were "doing church," and was involved in some of the earliest conversations among Emerging leaders. The congregation views itself as a contemporary urban abbey. It has four community houses in which a handful of members live and practice their own distinct spirituality. The pastor is referred to as the Abbess, and the assistant pastor is the Community Architect. The congregation has about 150 members who attend about twice a month on average; although on any given Saturday night there are only fifty to sixty in attendance at the main worship service.

The congregation meets in an old church building it had renovated to meet its unique needs, mainly to reduce the barriers between the congregation and the community. Thus, it removed the slanted floor and pews and

---

20. Gibbs and Bolger, *Emerging Churches*, 33; Wollschleger, *Off the Map*, 73; Wollschleger, *Disengaged and Indistinct*, 116; Marti and Ganiel, *The Deconstructed Church*, 35–37, 202.

21. Jones, *The New Christians*, 203–8; Jones, *The Church Is Flat*, 69–72.

22. Gibbs and Bolger, *Emerging Churches*, 33; Wollschleger, *Off the Map*, 76.

turned the recessed altar area into a giant closet. There is now a hard level floor, ideal for multiple uses. The sanctuary of the Abbey is a central component of its outreach to the community; all the items used during services can be readily collapsed, wheeled, folded, and shifted into another massive closet at the far end of the sanctuary. The aesthetic principles of the Apostles can be described as local and practical. The layout of the sanctuary changes by liturgical season and even sometimes by the week, adapting to meet the needs and highlight the themes of each unique liturgy. There are icons, with buckets of sand in front of each to place candles in. Notably, the icons were painted by members and built out of old doors or cobbled together with recycled lumber. The music used for worship is global, including ancient hymns, contemporary praise, and songs from contemporary secular artists, almost all of which is rearranged by congregation's musicians. At Apostles, there is no consistent preaching; here, the sermon is called "Reverb," and as it is more of a response to the Scripture reading, tends to be "abductive" rather than inductive or deductive.[23] These are stories that arrest you, and echo the Scripture. The work of thinking, connecting, and applying is left to the listener. I have heard poems and spoken word Reverb, stories told from personal experience, and readings from other contemporary authors like Annie Dillard. When there is a sermon it tends to be short and personal, yet full of metaphor.

Transcending Sacred and Secular

One of the hallmarks of Apostles is their consistent effort to reduce the barriers between the congregation and the community. This was noticeable on my first visit to the congregation as a participant observer—the worship space was dominated by a large blue steel trapeze. On one end was the altar and facing it at the other end was the blue trapeze, the seating was arranged so that half the chairs were on either side of the worship space facing in towards each other. Everyone in attendance thus had the altar on one side of their peripheral vision and the trapeze on the other. The Reverb that day focused on shared space with the community and included journal readings by leaders reflecting on the process of developing community, focusing on the messiness of shared space, and the idea of being part of the neighborhood—not just the congregation. They read these entries while seated on the base of the trapeze, which was set up for a Masquerade

---

23. Sweet, et al., *A is for Abductive*, 31–33.

Ball being put on by—and for—an arts group in the neighborhood. As the worship service ended, congregants mingled in an almost surreal scene of men and women dressed in risqué masquerade outfits while food caterers and servers made their way into the sanctuary carrying cases of wine and hard liquor.

Apostles is focused, missionaly, upon being a good neighbor, i.e., as an organization being a responsible member of the community. Located in an artistic neighborhood, they've created an arts program that offers low-cost/high-quality programming, with space available for local events. Apostles literally shares its space with the community: it has studios for visual arts, recording, and even dance. The arts program was created as a separate organization headed by a member of the congregation. Congregational sponsorship of this program is never mentioned nor advertised. There is no bait-and-switch, and most people in the community are under the impression that an arts center inhabits the old church building and the congregation just rents space from them on Saturday evenings. And the congregation wants it this way. Individual congregants and the abbess informed me that they wanted the community to use their space, without seeking to transform the community. They want to provide the community with a service without proselytizing. They want to blur the boundaries between congregation and community. Ultimately, they just want to be good neighbors.

This blurring of the boundaries between congregation and community is an important part of the group's collective story. In both formal congregation meetings and informal discussions amongst themselves congregants often recalled with fondness their previous worship setting—the coffee shop across the street. This collective memory was usually referred to in the context of future renovation plans for the Abbey building and in discussions concerning the congregation's vision for the future. Often told with a sense of wistfulness, members invoke the memory of when the congregation rented a retail space and ran a tea and coffee house. This shop was in business every day and it was also where the congregation held all of their meetings—worship, group, and congregational government meetings. The shop remained open throughout all of these, thus allowing community residents and customers to come and go, interact, and participate as they liked. This participation included giving input during congregational government meetings, asking questions during worship services, or just observing over a cup of coffee and a newspaper. This blurring of the boundary between congregation and community is the part of the story that is recalled wistfully and is used to frame how the group plans to use their abbey—they hope one day to run a full service, pay-as-you-can restaurant with a glass wall on the street level. This is an intentional effort to blur the boundaries between the congregation and the community, between the church and the world, between sacred spaces and secular spaces.

This blurring of the boundaries between sacred and secular in order to remain consistent with identity did not just happen at the organizational or congregational level. Rather this was a persistent feature of the congregational culture and was manifest at the individual level as well as the congregational. One way that this was manifest was through clothing. Typically in a congregational worship setting people "dress up" to go to church, at Apostles this was not the case. Worship service was scheduled for early evening on Saturday and participants were encouraged to come to service from their weekend daytime activities or prior to hanging out for the night with fellow congregants. Thus people came to worship dressed in attire related to either where they had come from prior to church or where they were going after. There was no intentional effort to put on a special appearance to attend church, but rather one was encouraged "to come as you are" as well as to be who you are at worship.

Two examples of a rather common occurrence illustrate this nicely. One week one of the actively involved congregants was doing one of the scripture readings for the liturgy. He had spent the afternoon on an extended bike ride and had finished his ride at church. He was dressed completely in form-fitting, spandex bike wear and only had his clip-in bike shoes. Yet, he was perfectly comfortable getting up and reading the day's scripture. Another week the president of the congregation stood up one Sunday to address the congregation. He gave a brief overview of the church's finances, as well as what would be discussed in an upcoming annual meeting. It was business as usual, except he was barefoot. Both of these examples might appear to be random occurrences however they were not. No one commented on either of occurrence nor did anyone seem uncomfortable, because this was a normal part of congregational life and people in the congregation were dressed similarly. This relaxed approach to dress was a logical and even verbalized implication of their congregational commitment to authenticity, and another example of the blurring of the boundary between the sacred and secular spheres.

In addition to dressing as they wished, congregants also acted in a manner consistent with how they were feeling and their expression of emotion. On two separate occasions during the Eucharist spontaneous outbursts of laughter erupted amongst the congregation—pastor included—when something unexpectedly comical arose. In both cases, all enjoyed the moment, and no one felt the need to hold back or appeared uncomfortable with laughing in the midst of a "holy" moment. Once the laughter subsided, however, there was a seamless transition back to quiet reverence. The first trigger occurred when the pastor accidentally banged the chalice on the microphone while raising it and the second took place during the thanksgiving, when all gathered around the table offered up what they were thankful for. One member mentioned bobble heads, followed by "Chocolate Rain," then quantum physics. In this case, each additional item added to the collective laughter, but once the moment was over, the congregation turned its attention back to the Eucharist.

This culture of authentic self-expression was also embodied in the church's worship service. On a typical Saturday night following the Reverb, there is time for small group discussions, and following the discussion time is Open Space:

> Open space happens after the discussion. There are multiple choices for open space activities. There is a well-attended, hands-on workshop on using prayer beads i.e., a rosary; the icons of the risen Jesus, prayer and anointing near the altar, quiet devotional prayer upstairs in the chapel (more icons); or tea in the back. I am surprised with how involved individuals are in this process: people are really paying attention to the leader of the prayer bead workshop, the chapel which is small is full of people quietly praying, and there are people lighting candles, meditating, and praying in front of the icon; including one young woman who appears to be very emotionally integrating yoga poses (nothing dramatic) into her meditation and prayer.[24]

Thus, while Apostles follows a set liturgy, it is always fresh and changes by season or topic, and there is plenty of room for each individual to have a unique and personalized worship experience—including the incorporation of yoga and prayer/meditation. This moment almost perfectly captures both the focus on authenticity and the blurring of the boundaries between what is considered sacred and secular. Multiple congregants reflected on

---

24. Field Notes.

previous church experience and how there was an expectation to be a different person in church from the outside world, and that one of the things that drew them to Apostles was the emphasis on authenticity and the ability to be the same person both inside and outside of the congregational setting.

The blurring of the boundaries between sacred and secular was not limited to individual spiritual practices but also occurred in the liturgical worship of the congregation. While I was there the congregation put on a Bjorkarist for the service on the Feast of the Ascension (a Christian holy day celebrating the ascension of the post-crucifixion, risen Jesus into heaven). A Bjorkarist, as I discovered, is a worship service that combines the Eucharist liturgy from the Book of Common Prayer with the music of Bjork. Upon entering the building I was handed a piece of red yarn, about four inches in length by a greeter. There were yellow, orange, and red pieces of yarn of varying sizes. Once in the sanctuary I noticed a large ball of yarn—about a foot and a half in diameter—dominating the altar. It is in the center with four strands stringing down the front of the altar and onto the floor. The strands were not individual strings but rather bits and pieces tied together. On the far wall, over the altar there was a projected image, a likeness of Jesus in the style of an icon, a pink icon.

The service itself was a series of movements comprised of readings and songs that culminated in a Eucharist. The whole liturgy was built around a Bjork song that played in the background prior to service and then bits and pieces of it were played throughout, the lines creating the headings for the movements. There were three movements with readings. The themes of the readings for the movements tied into the titles and they were from a fictional account of an unnamed, post-resurrection disciple's journal (written by an Apostle's member), and the songs for the movements i.e., the congregations responses to the readings (which were sung), were Bjork songs that also fit the theme.

The pivotal point in the service was the singing of *Unravel*, a haunting, Bjork song about lost love and the need to reconnect and renew it. After the singing of *Unravel* it was time for Open Space. This week the congregants were invited to tie their piece of yarn to the strands hanging from the ball on the altar. The ball of yarn is the heart that comes undone when Christ is gone, as an act of faith in the unseen God we were invited to reconnect our piece. People trickled up to the altar unselfconsciously, tying their yarn to the ball. Everyone in attendance participated, quietly, reverently. There was no mingling or chatting as usual during this open space, although there are a few people praying fervently before the icon of the risen Christ. Throughout Open Space a track of Bjork singing "light, Jesus Christ Son of God, have mercy on me a sinner" plays. It was, as the rest of the service, haunting and moving.

Apostles does a pop-music service like this each year. The year before I visited they had an U2charist. Their playful creativity and incorporation of material from the "secular" world is not limited to a once-a-year service however; the services regularly vary from week to week, although often they are organized along a seasonal theme. For instance, services for the season of Advent were organized around science and discovery and the services were created and led by the members of the congregation who were PhDs and grad students in the "hard" sciences. Regularly throughout the year the week's "sacred" readings were from sources other than the sacred scriptures. While I was there they included congregants' personal diary entries, original spoken word pieces, and passage of prose from authors such as Annie Dillard.

Thus, from the formal, organizational efforts like the content of the liturgy and the organizational presence of the congregation in the community to the informal norms and expectation of authenticity including clothing style of the congregants and emotional expression, Apostles seeks to overcome the modern boundaries between the sacred and the secular realms.

Discussion

While it is not really possible to generalize from a single case to the whole population of Emerging congregations it is worth noting that this case, Apostles, has been held up by movement insiders as an ideal type, as typical of the movement.[25] Apostles is close to the center of the movement as a congregation, both in terms of its creative use of liturgy and in terms of the connectedness and centrality of the pastor to the network of Emerging pastors. Thus, there is reason to believe that Apostles is in some way indicative of the movement as a whole. Additionally, Gerring, in his discussion of types of case studies, their uses, and generalizability says that this type of case study, a "typical" case, is one of the types of case studies that can be

---

25. Gibbs and Bolger, *Emerging Churches*, 33. Jones, *The New Christians*, 203–8. Jones, *The Church Is Flat*, 69–72. Marti and Ganiel, *The Deconstructed* Church, 35–37, 202. Wollschleger, *Off the Map*, 76. Wollschleger, *Disengaged and Indistinct*, 116.

used for generalization to the whole.[26] Thus while I recognize that generalizability is not perfectly possible, in the following discussion I will act as if Apostles is a synecdoche of the Emerging Church Movement.[27]

The findings from my research suggest that the ECM is a reactionary movement with a core value of radical authenticity reacting against the compartmentalization of the sacred as part of the differentiation of social spheres that is manifest through three themes: be who you are, God is the God of all or the secular is sacred, and the sacred isn't as holy as it used to be.

Be Who You Are

Emerging Christians seek to overcome the sacred/secular divide through their presentation of self. They seek to present who they really are or at least what they define as their authentic self without having to modify or hide who they are as they enter the church for worship. This is manifest in their clothing, language, interaction, and expression of emotional states. Emerging Christians don't see the need to put on a separate persona or face for their worship, in fact, doing so would be hypocritical.

God is the God of All . . . or the Secular is Sacred

Emerging Christians also seek to overcome the sacred/secular divide through the use or incorporation of non-religious cultural material into their corporate worship and spiritual practices. This is done through the use of pop music; non-religious but meaningful prose; pop-culture ideas and images; science, nature and the scientific process; and, the incorporation of non-Christian practices such as yoga into the church calendar, liturgical worship, and pietistic practices. This use of "secular" material for worship demonstrates a clear attempt to transcend the differentiation of social spheres into sacred or secular, and is exactly the type of behavior that has earned the ECM censure from more traditional religious groups.

The Sacred Isn't as Holy as It Used to Be

Whether it's the presence of a trapeze in the middle of the sanctuary, yoga poses in open space, cursing in the sanctuary, laughter in the Eucharist, laid back clothing and the occasional bad attitude that's inevitable in a come-as-you-are culture, the evidence suggests that for Emerging

---

26. Gerring, *Case Study Research*, 91–93.
27. Becker, *Tricks of the Trade*, 67.

Christians the sacred just isn't as holy as it used to be. The congregations are seeking lower barriers between themselves and the community, and the individual participants are seeking integrity and authenticity across their institutional contexts. They don't view their religious spaces as holy or as sacred as people in other traditions within Christianity. In both their institutional culture and polity as well as individual attitudes and behaviors the ECM is seeking to transcend the modern categories of sacred and secular.

These efforts to transcend the categories or blur the lines between sacred and secular are not accidental, in fact they represent an intentional, thoughtful strategy laid out by the pastor and leadership and are indicative of the orientation of the ECM as a whole. In my interview with the lead pastor, or Abbess, at Apostles, the Abbess spoke about this topic specifically. She said that she started the congregation as an Emerging church that was an embodied response in part to what she saw as the failings of the "modern" church that had allowed modernity to impose it's categories upon the world. She saw these dichotomous categories as misleading and harmful for the church—categories such as liberal/conservative and sacred/secular. The quote at the beginning of this chapter is from this interview. She said "I have a big picture of God . . . I also don't see the sacred/secular divide . . . there are not two worlds . . . everything belongs to God."[28]

Conclusion

Thus the ECM can be understood as a reactionary movement to both Evangelicalism and its dominant organizational forms as well as to the cultural and social conditions of late modernity. In this paper I have focused on Apostles (as a synecdoche of the ECM) and their reactionary efforts to the intersection of dominant church forms and modernity—namely the division of the world into the categories of sacred and secular. Viewing this division of the world into sacred/secular as a "modern" imposition on congregational life and identifying themselves as a post-modern religious movement, the members and leaders of this congregation seek out ways to effectively transcend this divide. These efforts are embodied in both intentional, formal efforts at the organizational level as well as in their informal, congregational cultural norms and expectations.

---

28. Personal interview.

PART 2: CROSSING BOUNDARIES

Bibliography

Becker, Howard S. *Tricks of the Trade: How to Think about Your Research While You're Doing It*. Chicago: University of Chicago Press, 1998.

Berger, Peter. *The Sacred Canopy: Elements of a Sociological Theory of Religion*. New York: Anchor, 1967.

Bielo, James S. *Emerging Evangelicals: Faith, Modernity, and the Desire for Authenticity*. New York: NYU Press, 2011.

DeYoung, Kevin, and Ted Kluck. *Why We're Not Emergent: By Two Guys Who Should Be*. Chicago: Moody, 2008.

Driscoll, Mark. "A Pastoral Perspective on the Emergent Church." *Criswell Theological Review* 3 (2006) 87–93.

Gerring, John. *Case Study Research: Principles and Practices*. New York: Cambridge University Press, 2007.

Gibbs, Eddie, and Ryan K. Bolger. *Emerging Churches: Creating Christian Community in Postmodern Cultures*. Grand Rapids: Baker Academic, 2005.

Jones, Tony. *The Church Is Flat: The Relational Ecclesiology of the Emerging Church Movement*. Minneapolis: JoPa, 2011.

———. *The New Christians: Dispatches from the Emergent Frontier*. San Francisco: Jossey-Bass, 2008.

Marti, Gerardo, and Gladys Ganiel. *The Deconstructed Church: Understanding Emerging Christianity*. New York: Oxford University Press, 2014.

McLaren, Brian. *A Generous Orthodoxy*. Grand Rapids: Zondervan, 2006.

Pitchford, Susan, et al. "Doing Field Studies of Religious Movements: An Agenda." *Journal for the Scientific Study of Religion* 40 (2001) 379–92.

Samson, William. "The New Monastics and the Changing Face of American Evangelicalism." Paper presented during the Society for the Scientific Study of Religion Conference, Milwaukee, 2011.

Suddaby, Roy. "From the Editors: What Grounded Theory is Not." *Academy of Management Journal* 49 (2006) 633–42.

Sweet, Leonard, et al. *A is for Abductive: The Language of the Emerging Church*. Grand Rapids: Zondervan, 2003.

Wellman, James K., Jr. *Evangelical vs. Liberal: The Clash of Christian Cultures in the Pacific Northwest*. New York: Oxford University Press, 2008.

Wollschleger, Jason. "*Disengaged* and *Indistinct*: The Sub-Cultural Identity of the Emerging Church Movement." *Social Compass* 62 (2015) 105–21.

———. "Off the Map? Locating the Emerging Church." *Review of Religious Research* 54 (2012) 69–91.

Wollschleger, Jason, and Mark Killian. "Emerging Church." *World Religions and Spirituality Project, VCU*, 2014. http://www.has.vcu.edu/wrs/profiles/EmergingChurch.htm.

Wollschleger, Jason, and Lindsey R. Beach. "Religious Chameleons: Exploring the Social Context for Belonging without Believing." *Rationality and Society* 25 (2013) 178–97.

8

The Kingdom of Heaven Is Within You: Emerging Churches and (Un)Secular Music

April Stace

I had to drive around the block a few times on the morning I visited Community Church.[1] *The building is located just off a busy intersection outside of Washington, D.C., and street parking is limited. I eventually glimpsed the small parking lot behind the church building. There were eight spaces, and only one was taken. I was early. I walked up to the traditional Baptist church and opened big blue doors, stepping into a hallway with the sanctuary on one side and the fellowship hall on the other.*

A recording of ethereal instrumental music, reminiscent of music one might hear on a movie soundtrack, filled the room. A large screen was set above the baptistery, and stained-glass windows lined the walls. Wooden pews ran the length of the room, with small tables and chairs in the back of the room, obviously a space meant for children to color and play during the service. In the front of the sanctuary, the Communion table was covered with colored cloths, candles, flowers, and other flora appropriate to late summer. Traditional icons were displayed around the front of the church, many with small tables and candles nearby. Three kneelers were placed strategically around the sanctuary, and two large crosses were placed in the corner with various images, writings, and post-it notes on them.

As I sat alone in the sanctuary, I began to hear people gathering in the hall behind me. A woman came in and invited me to come into the fellowship hall to have some tea and snacks before service. The service began informally, as about twenty-five people gathered in the sanctuary. The pastor came to the front and said, "Good morning, everyone. We begin our time of worship with

[1] All names of individuals and churches have been changed to protect anonymity.

a prayer." The prayer of St. Columba was read aloud, and a short responsive reading of a Psalm followed.

Throughout the service, dialogue was encouraged. During the sermon, questions were asked; during the Prayers of the People (which was the last element of the service) people shared their concerns and joys. During the "time of response," which began with the sharing of Communion, people left their seats and made use of the kneelers, the icons, the candles, and various other items throughout the sanctuary. This time seemed to end spontaneously once most people had returned to their seats.

Music was used in this service in a variety of ways. During the sermon, the pastor referred to the work of Lenny Kravitz as an example of how God could speak through various popular media, although he did not play the music. The same instrumental music that was played before the service was also played while people were engaged in the "time of response," during which members walked around the sanctuary, kneeling before the crosses, lighting candles, and other tactile practices. After ten minutes of this time, the congregation gathered in the pews again and sang three songs together, all from the contemporary worship music genre. The songs were led by a singer, a pianist, and a recorder player. Although a drum set and amplifiers were set up nearby, they were not used on the Sunday I visited.

This excerpt from my field notes provides an example of how Emerging churches utilize resources from a variety of liturgical and musical sources in their worship services. In this volume, Heather Josselyn Cranson describes the musical practices of an Emerging congregation in the Pacific Northwest as creating a pastiche of musical genres and styles specific to the needs and tastes of that particular congregation, and suggests that the musical practices of Emerging congregations should be viewed through the lens of postmodern musical sensibilities. My fieldwork with Emerging congregations corroborates hers; the Emerging congregations in my study also borrowed freely from a variety of musical sources.

In this chapter, however, I explore one particular element of this pastiche: the use of music often termed "popular" or "secular" within the context of a worship service. Both terms that will be briefly interrogated in this chapter. I suggest that Emerging congregations ascribe two inter-related meanings to this music; first, that popular-secular music functions as a contemporary psalmody for Emerging congregations; second, that using popular-secular music is an expression of an ecclesiology and worldview in which there is no boundary between the sacred and the secular.

The data for this study was gathered over the course of two years, during which I regularly visited five congregations that identified in varying degrees with the Emerging church movement in the Baltimore/Washington suburbs. I was a participant-observer in each of the congregations and also conducted several interviews with music leaders at each church. In some cases this was a paid person on staff, although in some congregations, the music was led completely by volunteers. I also interviewed the pastoral staff in congregations where there was such a position.

Key Terms: "Popular" and "Secular"

The music that this chapter focuses on is what I term "popular-secular." The terminology I employ to describe this music is meant to specify as accurately as possible the kind of music that will be studied. However, both "popular" and "secular" are terms that require some clarification.

Many scholars trace the roots of the Emerging Church Movement to American evangelicals.[2] Therefore, it is worth noting that the term "popular music" has frequently been employed in the scholarly treatment of the contemporary worship music of American evangelicals.[3] Many studies of contemporary evangelical music refer to the genesis of the music as coming from an impetus to use the styles of "popular music" in church settings. The use of "popular" styles of music combined with religiously themed lyrics was initially cause for discord within American evangelicals circles with ecclesiological models at the heart of the conflict, namely, the relationship between the church and the "culture." The use of such music in religious settings challenged American evangelicals to negotiate their understanding of the role and meaning of liturgical music and the expression of particular ecclesiologies.

However, the term "popular" has also been used in problematic ways in the academy. Many studies have shown that the category of the "popular" in culture often functions to designate subjects as somehow inauthentic—particularly because of the mass-production that is often at the heart of any

---

2. See, for example, Michael Clawson's excellent chapter in this volume.

3. Most historical treatments of contemporary worship music describe it as music that has come about from the combination of popular music styles with religious lyrics. See, for example, Howard and Streck, *Apostles of Rock: The Splintered World of Contemporary Christian Music*; and Stowe, *No Sympathy for the Devil*.

definition of the "popular—and, therefore, unworthy of study.[4] At the heart of this interpretation of the word is an assumption that cultural productions that are readily available for mass consumption are somehow inherently inferior, shallow, or corrupt. Such definitions assume that there is some kind of "pure" culture. We must remember, however, that popular culture and all forms of culture are both manipulative and dependent on monetary profit while at the same time expressive of experiences which people recognize to be their own and to which they are responding.[5] "Popular" is a discursive term, shorthand for a set of specific interests.[6] To determine that it is somehow authentically "of the people"—*or* to claim that it is somehow inferior because it is popular—is an oversimplification.

A working definition of "popular music" was necessary in this study because even as I searched for churches using popular-secular music in their services, I was aware that there are competing definitions of "popular music" even within congregations today and that each music leader would have a specific view of what constitutes "popular" music. The way this term was defined by each interviewee, in fact, shed light on differing attitudes regarding ecclesiology. Thus, a working definition of popular music for this study is derived from the following three inter-related characteristics: first, it is popular because it has a wide audience.[7] Its presence in the culture makes it popular. Second, it is popular because it is produced for wide audiences. Third, it is popular because it is, in fact, one of the few options available from the culture industry.[8] By holding all three of these characteristics in tension, I affirm the complexity of defining such a term.

The music I considered for this study also needed to satisfy the designation "secular," another contested term. Its conventional usage is an issue at the heart of this study. Just as "religious" has come to mean something related to institutional expressions of faith, "secular" may be understood to be something that is free *from* those religious institutions. Secular might also be contrasted with "profane." Something that is secular is not quite "profane"—it is, perhaps, simply ordinary.[9] As with the term "popular,"

---

4. See Stuart Hall, "Notes on Deconstructing the 'Popular,'" in *People's History and Socialist Theory*; or Frith, *Performing Rites: On the Value of Popular Music*.

5. Hall, "Notes on Deconstructing the 'Popular,'" 233–35.

6. McCutcheon, "'They Licked the Platter Clean,'" 180.

7. Pinn, "Rap Music and Its Message," 293.

8. Chidester, *Authentic Fakes*, 19–20.

9. Baily, "The Implicit Religiosity of the Secular," 63–66.

each music leader used slightly different criteria set "secular" apart from "sacred" music. Many reported relying on lyrical content to determine a songs status, and questioned the very premise of dividing music into such categories based on theological concerns.

The descriptor "popular-secular," in the light of these challenges, may at first seem to cloud an already murky definitional area by combining two contested terms, but it provided a useful term to communicate clearly with my interviewees and also provided a way to specify the type of music referred to in this study.

Psalmody: The Full Human Experience

The psalms of the Hebrew Bible are known for the wide variety of emotions expressed therein: joy, sadness, anger, the sense of having been betrayed, alienation from others and from God, even doubt of God's existence. The historic centrality of the psalms in Christian worship speaks to the importance of accepting and embracing the full spectrum of human emotion in liturgical settings, and the insistence by many in my study that worship needs to give voice to both the positive and negative human emotions speaks to the oft-cited interest of Emerging congregations in recovering the practices of the "ancient church." The "sacred" music from which most music leaders in my study drew from—contemporary Christian music and traditional Euro-American hymnody—were found to be lacking in emotional "depth" and "authenticity." Certain music from outside the realm of "sacred" music, however, was seen to address a more complete range of human emotion in culturally familiar terms. In other words, popular-secular music was used to affirm the darker side of faith: doubt, fear, and even feelings of God's absence—exactly the expression found in imprecatory and lamenting psalms.

All of the churches in this study primarily used music from the contemporary worship music genre for congregational singing, although traditional hymns were used as well, along with other styles such as Taize and even an occasional piece from the classical music genre. Popular-secular music was employed to varying degrees, but the vast majority of liturgical music was what is typically regarded as "sacred," that is, from hymns of contemporary Christian music, with overt references to God. The popular-secular music is used somewhat sparingly, then, to fill very specific emotional "holes" that many of the music leaders believe could be addressed as successfully by "sacred" music, whether hymns or contemporary worship music.

Jeff Hays, a pastor at Keystone Baptist, described how and why he used popular-secular music to evoke certain emotions in his congregation.

> The music evokes something in students or in myself or other people that helps to acknowledge heartbreak, or feelings of longing in relationships, or with God, or which express some kind of connection to something happening in life that might be happening. So the table for people to be honest about what is happening in life, so that we enter in worship with people actually feeling this stuff. Church is where you bring who you are, not the best version not the fake version. I want those songs, even if they're just in the background. Every week I select three or four, some on radio, some are not, that say something to hopefully get people to think and are sitting there before the service if they want that time.

Hays clarified his critique of contemporary music as follows.

> I think there is plenty that is lacking. I think you could take out many of the personal pronouns and insert "baby," and the songs would work [as love songs.] They lack theological substance, and are emotional train wrecks pointed at God. It's not that sometimes singing "na na na" can't be helpful, but a lot of contemporary music sounds like love songs to God, in a way you'd speak to another human—not that that isn't there in Scripture.

Martin Frank at New Life Church suggested that, in fact, contemporary worship music was in many ways inferior to traditional hymns, and explained why popular-secular music was necessary to address the deficits in both genres.

> I feel like there's a more of a void [in contemporary worship music] than in hymns, on multiple levels. Musically, it can be very boring. I think lyrically it lacks kind of theological depth or emotional depth that you even get in hymns. The range of experience that people go through, in experiencing god, is lacking. We turn to secular music to fill those gaps. We do use contemporary praise music, but it helps to draw from different pools.

Hays explained why popular-secular music addressed the deficit of emotional depth in sacred music.

> We use it to address a deficit. In some ways there are "Christian artists" who aren't making art that is engaging to the questions that

people are asking. They are mimicking bad Christian subculture, not saying things that anyone who isn't a Christian would care about. And so, if I use it in a sermon illustration, I think they are more accurately or authentically speaking to a human or human-divine relationship situation that some Christian music isn't getting to.

While much of the critique of sacred music compared popular-secular music to contemporary worship music, some expressed a similar frustration with traditional American hymnody, explaining that while hymnody had a "depth" that contemporary worship music lacked, the hymns were still wanting in addressing legitimate needs of his congregation. Martin Frank explained his assessment as follows:

> Yeah, I mean, I think in terms of hymnody, on the one side, it's musical. It's just because, people in our congregation like hymns, but if we sang them all the time, people would get bored. They don't quite meet the musical palette people have today. Lyrically and theologically they are very rich, but maybe there's kind of a grittiness missing.

However, traditional hymns generally faced a slightly different critique than Frank's. A worship leader at a church named "Patchwork" described his ambivalence about hymn-based worship as follows.

> I felt like the traditional hymn-based music, there's a lot there that we miss out on. A lot of them are sermons that are compacted in 4 or 5 stanzas. But, a lot of the language is hard to decipher. I'm still not sure what an "Ebenezer" is.[10] We've used hymns in a rock band format, more than we do now. Part of that is feeling like, these are the things that say it best, trying to reach out to people who have that kind of church background. But we've leaned away from that, maybe not intentionally. But we're going to be able to relate to people who have a church background without having to use hymns, and we try really hard to avoid using language that doesn't translate. And a lot of hymns kind of break those rules.

Several other music leaders reported that the language was too antiquated to relate to contemporary concerns. A majority of the leaders admitted, however, that they still used hymns on occasion in service, albeit in a rock style, and often amended with a repeated chorus. Most acknowledged, like Alistair, that hymns had a theological "depth" to their lyrics that

---

10. The term "Ebenezer" is found in the hymn "Come Thou Fount."

contemporary worship music could not compete with. However, the ability of contemporary worship music to provide a relatable style of sacred music often trumped the deeper theology of hymns. Alistair continued:

> Lyrically and musically, the hymns are the deep end of the pool. These [contemporary worship music] are not deep-end kinds of lyrics. They don't cause you to rethink your theology unless you're just forming it for the first time. You aren't going away thinking, "That was masterfully done." You might think, "I like the energy or the feel," or hopefully people will say "I relate to that." That is where the hymn-based services lack, being able to relate to people in normal situations.

The dissatisfaction voiced by several of these music leaders with hymns and contemporary worship music, then, can be classified as follows: First, lack of accessibility of style and/or lyrics that are also theologically meaningful; Second, lack of diversity of style; and third, inability to speak to "real feeling" or "human experience." In these ways, popular-secular music has become, in part, a new psalmody in Emerging congregations. The variety of musical styles in popular-secular music are believed to serve the lyrical expressions of lament, anger, and doubt and address this perceived deficit in sacred music.

The Secular Is Sacred

All of the music leaders in this study expressed that in their contexts, "secular" was a meaningless category. While they often still acknowledged that "worship" songs were often treated differently than popular-secular songs (namely because the congregation often did not sing popular-secular songs), they emphasized that whether a song was from popular culture or not had no bearing on whether or not it was chosen to be in the service. The secular "status" was simply non-functional. The emphasis was not on choosing music outside of a sacred canon but instead on the meaning of the lyrics or the ambiance provided by the music. Martin Frank at New Life Church described how he and his music team approached music planning.

> I guess the only thing is that, honestly, when we're picking songs, or someone suggests a song—I mean—I know, I was thinking about secular songs, but we don't talk about, "Is this secular or Christian?" No one is even asking, "Is this a secular song? Is he a Christian?" It doesn't come up. Even when we're selecting songs,

we're not saying, "Oh, we haven't used a secular song in awhile, we need to use one . . ." They're songs that are just part of our canon. They're interesting. Do they fulfill a need? Do they work? That's what drives the music. I think because I'm a team leader, I'm thinking of some of these larger issues. But we don't think in terms of secular and sacred. It's more in terms of how we serve the congregation.

Perhaps because of this focus on how the song "serves" the congregation, not by way of being secular and therefore appealing to their preferences and/or experiences outside of church services, the popular-secular songs used in these Emerging churches tended to be songs with subtle spiritual undertones. The example of "Blackbird" by the Beatles, used at Oakview Community Church during an Easter service, serves as a good example of this: the image of a Blackbird, in the dead of night, waiting for the moment to "arise," has metaphorical meaning when sung with the Christian Easter narrative in mind.

The leaders in these churches also reported using popular-secular music that did not have any words at all. Examples came from artists such as Thievery Corporation, a band based in Washington, D.C. who uses a mixture of live instruments with sequenced electronic tracks, and world-music inspired cellist Rufus Cappadocia. While not "popular" in the sense that these musicians have never been on the top ten downloads list on iTunes, their music has been used in motion pictures and is widely known among the "indie" music scene. Beth Mitchell described the various styles of music they have incorporated at Oakview.

> It's important to use good music that does what we want it to do. For us, using all kinds of music, including good, popular, secular music, reinforces theology, helps different kinds of people feel included, and creates moods we want to have. In my time, though the bulk of our congregational singing has been contemporary, commercial worship music and hymns, we have used jazz, classical, contemporary orchestral music, film soundtracks, pop songs, Black gospel, Celtic and Celtic-influenced, folk, bluegrass and whatever else: Arcade Fire, Talking Heads, Kanye West. I don't recall ever using opera in Sunday service, though I did play some at a funeral once.

Mitchell's response highlights two key motivations in Emerging churches that use popular-secular music: to create a "mood" or ambiance, and for the meaning of the lyrics.

This example stands in contrast with what I experienced at Community Church, in which pastor Ted Todd referenced the work of Lenny Kravtiz as music that, to him, seemed to be music in which "God is active."

The music leaders emphasized that music was chosen for worship services with disregard for any sacred/secular binary. However, this did not mean that songs were chosen without discernment. There were explicit criteria mentioned for song choices, and a song selection process that went beyond simply matching song lyrics with the day's Bible verse. Ted Todd at Community Church described it this way.

> It needs to be accomplishing something. Musically it's helping us frame space, lyrically it's supporting something that I view or the congregation views as the movement of God in the world.

Martin Frank (New Life) expressed a similar perspective on music planning.

> I think the criteria are, does it express some kind of part of the faith journey well that people can relate to and sing? So sometimes we have conversations about, can this be sung communally, publicly? Some songs express issues of faith that we think they aren't appropriate for communal, public expression. Faith experience, and also we try to go with the liturgical calendar. We always think how it is in that larger scheme.

Music leaders at these churches are not selecting music for congregation members whom they perceive to be living highly secularized lives. To clarify, they are choosing music for people they perceive, through their experience and discussions with them, have abandoned a secular/sacred binary in life, basing song choices on the current state of the congregation itself, with some regard also to the traditional Christian liturgical calendar. In short, they are selecting music for people who, they believe, already see a "sacralized" world. While they expressed a general concern that the music be "relatable" for people in attendance, including non-Christians, they do not perceive their congregations as residing in a highly secularized outside world. Therefore, they find little purpose in using songs that cannot be tied to the "faith journey" of the community or an individual, although the lyrics may be understood metaphorically or reinterpreted in a sacralized way. The music leaders take for granted that their congregations already have the ability and the agency to do so.

Conclusion

One may argue that the use of popular-secular music in a worship service represents a kind of "secularizing from within." This is the argument that Justin Wilford attempts to subvert in his treatment of the architecture of Saddleback Church and other post-denominational evangelical churches like it. Wilford suggests

> The performances of Saddleback and churches like it work, in part, because they seamlessly incorporate everyday places into larger evangelical narratives, fusing them with deep religious themes and thereby transforming everyday places into religiously meaningful places . . . Saddleback members recast places in their lives as sites of spiritual self-transformation.[11]

Wilford argues that the "secular" architecture of post-denominational evangelical churches functions not to "secularize" the worship service or the church, but serves to reimagine sacred space for the congregation members. If one can have a spiritual experience in a church that looks like an office building, then one can interpret one's own workplace as a potential site of sacred action.

A similar interpretation can be applied to the use of popular-secular music even outside of traditional evangelical circles, such as in the Emerging congregations in this study. In other words, if one can have a spiritual experience in popular-secular music within a worship service, then one can interpret popular-secular music *outside* the worship service as a sacred space—a space where God is speaking.

Music leaders and pastors in this study did not view themselves as capitulating to or accommodating an increasingly secularized society. Indeed, such a conviction would not have been tenable in these congregations, as the functioning ecclesiological models do not support the view that the "church" is set apart from the "culture." The boundary is a fluid and porous one with the "culture" understood to simply be another source to draw upon; in fact, there is no boundary because there is no binary. Instead, the "potential for the sacred" is everywhere.[12] The key term for these congregations, then, is not "secularization" of the church but "sacralization" of all life experiences. This worldview is at the heart of both the construction

---

11. Wilford, *Sacred Subdivisions*, 4.
12. Ibid., 5.

of an alternative psalmody based in popular-secular music genres and the construction of an ecclesiology that rejects a secular/sacred division.

In fact, the use of popular-secular music (or other media) in such congregations might be *necessary* to construct an alternative, modern-day, localized psalmody and to maintain a non-binary ecclesiology. Tia Denora, an ethonomusicologist, suggests that recorded music—a category in which all of the popular-secular music falls—is used by people to interpret and understand social situations, and to locate themselves in their environment.[13] That is to say, recorded music is constitutive of our identity, both reflecting and forming our perception of ourselves in relation to our environment. In a congregational setting, it follows that popular-secular music in congregational settings is a constitutive element of reflecting and forming the attitudes of the congregation in regards to ecclesiology.

Mary McGann, whose work focuses on the interpretation of music within congregational settings, corroborates Denora's work and goes a step further by situating music within a liturgical context. McGann suggests that liturgy, as a mix of faith and culture, *is* embedded theology. Therefore, the postures fostered by a community articulate, reflect, and encode attitudes, and in turn give rise to perceptions of both self and Church.[14] The role of music is central in ritual, as the choice of music in ritual can "situate a community's ritual experience *vis-à-vis* its everyday life."[15]

The popular-secular music in the Emerging congregations in this study embody and express something of the hopes and ideals of the music leaders for their churches' identity and ecclesiology in American culture. Maintaining such an ecclesiology requires the use of media in worship—whether musical or otherwise—from sources outside of what is traditionally perceived as "religious." In incorporating popular-secular music in their worship services and relying on this music in the construction of a modern-day psalmody, these Emerging congregations implicitly affirm a non-dual worldview and the "sacralization" of everyday life.

---

13. Denora, *Music in Everyday Life*, 13.
14. McGann, *Exploring Music*, 14–18.
15. Ibid., 35–36.

Bibliography

Baily, Edward. "The Implicit Religiosity of the Secular." In *Defining Religion: Investigating the Boundaries between the Sacred and Secular*, edited by Arthur L. Greil and David G. Bromley, 58–64. Oxford: JAI, 2003.

Chidester, David. *Authentic Fakes*. Berkeley: University of California Press, 2005.

Denora, Tia. *Music in Everyday Life*. Cambridge: Cambridge University Press, 2000.

Frith, Simon. *Performing Rites: On the Value of Popular Music*. Cambridge: Harvard University Press, 1996.

Hall, Stuart. "Notes on Deconstructing the 'Popular.'" In *People's History and Socialist Theory*, edited by Raphael Samuel, 227–41. Boston: Routledge, 1981.

Howard, J. R., and John M. Streck, *Apostles of Rock: The Splintered World of Contemporary Christian Music*. Lexington: University Press of Kentucky, 1999

McCutcheon, Russel T. "'They Licked the Platter Clean': On the Co-Dependency of the Religious and the Secular." *Method and Theory in the Study of Religion* 19, nos. 3–4 (2007) 176–90.

McGann, Mary Ann. *Exploring Music as Worship and Theology: Research in Liturgical Practice*. Collegeville, MN: Liturgical, 2002.

Pinn, Anthony. "Rap Music and Its Message: On Interpreting the Contact Between Religion and Popular Culture." In *Religion and Popular Culture in America*, edited by Bruce David Forbes and Jeffrey H. Mahan, 145–60. Berkeley: University of California Press, 2000.

Stowe, David. *No Sympathy for the Devil*. Chapel Hill: University of North Carolina Press, 2011.

Wilford, Justin G. *Sacred Subdivisions: The Postsuburban Transformation of American Evangelicalism*. New York: New York University Press, 2012.

9

"Messy Vitality":
The Diverse Musical Canon of a West-Coast Emerging Congregation

— Heather Josselyn-Cranson —

This volume seeks to shed light on worship within the Emerging Church, in the many manifestations that it presents across geographic, political, and religious spectra. While the Emerging Church movement encompasses enough breadth to make forming strict parameters for belonging difficult, most scholars assume a connection between the Emerging Church and postmodernism. Tenets of a postmodern worldview, therefore, ought to affect particular choices made by Emerging congregations, including decisions concerning congregational worship. A brief survey of some of the primary assumptions of postmodernism will provide context in understanding one postmodern value in particular—the importance of diversity. This chapter will then investigate the music of a single congregation within the Emerging Church movement in order to learn how one community enacts a musical practice of variety.

Hallmarks of Postmodernism

Scholars offer a multitude of perspectives on postmodernism, embodying as much as describing the subject upon which they treat. We read variously that postmodernism is a continuation of modernism or a reaction against it; is growing in influence or is fading in importance; it is pervasive throughout all disciplines or it is best evidenced in literature or the visual arts. A survey of various descriptions provides some consistent elements, however. One of these is found in the denial of reason, an undergirding feature of rational modernity. Whether this denial is labeled "the undercutting of an all-encompassing rationality,"[1] a "loss of faith . . . in the power of reason to resolve differences and deliver solutions,"[2] or a looking "beyond reason to nonrational ways of knowing, conferring heightened status on the emotions and intuition,"[3] a lack of trust in human intellectual processes seems central to a postmodern mindset.

Given this loss of faith in human reason, postmodernism consequently dismisses a typically modern confidence in the future. Whereas modernism looked to scientific discovery and technological innovation as proof of human improvement, postmodernism sees the atrocities of the twentieth and twenty-first centuries as confirmation that things are not getting better. Having suffered this "loss of hope . . . in progress based on human knowledge,"[4] postmodernism largely abandoned all-encompassing theories of progress throughout history. Indeed, all global theories that seek to explain the world largely receive suspicion and disdain from postmodernism. According to theologian Stanley Grenz, a "postmodern outlook entails the end of the appeal to any central legitimating myth whatsoever . . . [it] demands an attack on any claimant to universality."[5] Instead, it "seeks local or provisional, rather than universal and absolute, forms of legitimation."[6]

Having withdrawn faith in human reason and in our ability to formulate a global theory, or narrative, to explain the world around us, postmodernism must identify new ground upon which to stand. One locus for this is found in the community. Postmodernism favors communal processes rather than individual decisions, being "keenly conscious of the importance of community, of the social dimension of existence."[7] Rather than maintaining a modernist stance that "the life of reason becomes a solitary task performed by an individual person,"[8] postmodernism finds that all

---

1. Woods, *Beginning Postmodernism*, 10.
2. White, *Postmodernism 101*, 49.
3. Grenz, *A Primer on Postmodernism*, 14.
4. White, *Postmodernism 101*, 49.
5. Grenz, *A Primer on Postmodernism*, 45.
6. Woods, *Beginning Postmodernism*, 11.
7. Grenz, *A Primer on Postmodernism*, 14.
8. Penner, "Introduction," 23.

important work, and even truth itself, must come to fruition within a particular community.

Postmodernism and Eclecticism

Given postmodernism's recognition of the local community and disdain for unified theories, it is unsurprising that respect for variety forms an important part of the postmodern worldview. The current generation has greater access to such variety, including the ideas and cultural artifacts of many times and places, than people of earlier times, due in part to the effects of colonialism, economic integration of the world, media and communication, and growing rates of immigration.[9] But rather than subjecting such variety to judgment or classification through the lens of a modernist hierarchical system, postmodernism largely embraces this diversity of style, thought, and ways of being. Grenz calls this the "central hallmark" of postmodernist expression, and by "[juxtaposing] seemingly contradictory styles derived from immensely different sources . . . [postmodernism] not only serves to celebrate diversity but also offers a means to express a subtle rejection of the dominance of rationality in a playful or ironic manner."[10]

Such an emphasis on variety and juxtaposition can be found within postmodern approaches to a variety of fields. In architecture, the clean, box-like structures of the modernist International Style first came under postmodern scrutiny in Robert Venturi's book *Complexity and Contradiction in Architecture*, the very title of which makes evident his preference for "messy vitality over obvious unity."[11] Postmodernism within architecture implies "buildings which self-reflexively 'quote' historical characteristics and make ironic use of local content; which utilize a certain metaphorical quality in their design; which encapsulate a pluralism or hybridity of style; and which construct a new ambiguous space."[12] Such pluralism has been explained as "*purposefully* disunified . . . not a covert 'remaking' of the past of the modernists, but a blatant co-opting of the past for [the architects'] own ends and their own use."[13]

9. White, *Postmodernism 101*, 125.
10. Grenz, *A Primer on Postmodernism*, 20.
11. Clendinning, "Postmodern Architecture/Postmodern Music," 121–23. The quotation comes from Venturi's book itself, written in 1962 and published in 1966.
12. Woods, *Beginning Postmodernism* 117.
13. Clendinning, "Postmodern Architecture/Postmodern Music," 127.

Postmodernism has led to similar results in the world of visual and plastic arts. As in architecture, artists working in painting, printmaking, and sculpture sought to offer alternatives to the "clinical purity of form and autonomous abstraction" of the modern visual palette.[14] In finding this alternate visual language, artists "exhibit a nonchalance in dealing with seemingly incompatible styles, practice an aesthetic pluralism, and combine a number of different styles of art in one work, rather than keeping to the purity of form desired by modernists."[15]

While literature differs greatly from visual art and architecture as an art form, it, too, developed a postmodern strain that values variety and juxtaposition. This can be seen in postmodern literary texts that eradicate "the cultural divide between high and popular forms of culture, embracing all in a mélange."[16] Literary critic Alan Wilde posits that the substance or content of postmodern literature, as well as its approach or style, should reflect this "mélange," striving to accept the world "in all its fragmentation and incoherence, without seeking to control its tensions by aesthetic means."[17]

Musical Diversity in Postmodernism

Before turning to music as a forum for postmodern ideas and practices, we should note that postmodern scholarship on music reflects interest in the community as well as the "solitary task" of individual composers or performers. Scholars view musical activity broadly, exploring listening as well as composing and domestic as well as public music-making. Thus, it is appropriate in our consideration of postmodern musical practices to consider how music is understood by those who hear it as well as those who create it.

We should expect postmodern music, as another artistic medium, to embrace the same pluralistic and juxtaposing way of interpreting and making that obtains in literature, visual art, and architecture. According to those who have studied the music of postmodernity, this expectation holds true. As traditional or modernist concepts of "high" and "low" art forms dissipate, composers and listeners alike incorporate a broader range of sounds and genres.[18] Facilitating this inclusiveness, advanced technol-

---

14. Woods, *Beginning Postmodernism* 152.
15. Ibid., 165.
16. Ibid, 82.
17. Bertens, *The Idea of the Postmodern*, 77.
18. In fact, the equation between postmodernism and the inclusion of popular

ogy throughout more of the globe and greater connectivity through social media have brought the sounds and rhythms of even isolated cultures into the ear buds of people the Western world—and vice versa.[19]

While access to more music has become both possible and permissible, priorities among composers, scholars, critics, and listeners have also changed. Creating and recognizing the structural unity of various pieces of music has been a primary goal of musicians throughout the last several hundred years of music-making in the Western tradition. Now, however, some "postmodern composers have . . . embraced conflict and contradiction and have at times eschewed consistency and unity. Similarly, postmodern audiences do not necessarily search for or find unity in the listening experience."[20]

Disjunction features in most, if not all, descriptions of what postmodern music entails. In Jonathan D. Kramer's "The Nature and Origins of Musical Postmodernism," the author lists sixteen characteristics of postmodern music, more than half of which point to musical variety or disjunction:

> [postmodern music] (3) does not respect boundaries between sonorities and procedures of the past and the present;
>
> (4) challenges barriers between "high" and "low" styles;
>
> (5) shows disdain for the often unquestioned value of structural unity;
>
> (6) questions the mutual exclusivity of elitist and populist values;
>
> (7) avoids totalizing forms (e.g., does not want entire pieces to be tonal or serial or cast in a prescribed formal mold) . . .
>
> (9) includes quotations of or references to music of many traditions and cultures . . .
>
> (11) embraces contradictions . . .

---

musical genres is so complete that it is becoming easier to find scholarship on postmodern music relating to pop music than to art, or "classical," music. For example, in *Beginning Postmodernism*, chapters on postmodernism as it pertains to literature, architecture, and visual art are followed by a chapter entitled "Postmodernism, Popular Culture, and Music," a title that communicates preference for contemporary music relating to popular culture.

19. Lochhead, "Introduction," 1–9.
20. Kramer, "The Nature and Origins of Musical Postmodernism," 14–15.

(13) includes fragmentations and discontinuities;

(14) encompasses pluralism and eclecticism;

(15) presents multiple meanings and multiple temporalities.[21]

Other authors support Kramer's identification of postmodern music as that which includes sounds and influences from many times, locations, cultures, styles, points of view, and intentions. Anne LeBaron finds that collage, a technique of surrealism, provides evidence that surrealist music should be considered as a form of postmodernism.[22] Musicologist Timothy D. Taylor assembled lists of postmodern stylistic traits from multiple authors; each of the lists he included refers to the musical pluralism mentioned above.[23] In his description of postmodern pop music, Tim Woods both mentions and explains particular forms of creating variety in recorded music. He writes that "the techniques of 'sampling,' 'theft,' and appropriation of other records constitute some form of satirical or self-reflexive pastiche of past styles."[24]

Woods's comments raise the question of the purpose of variety and appropriation in postmodern music. As noted above, such an inclusive stance becomes possible as a greater variety of music becomes accessible through recording technology and social media sharing. Postmodern philosophical positions, such as the eradication of musical hierarchies that belittle music outside of the "classical" Western European tradition, encourage listeners and musicians to take advantage of the incredible variety of styles and pieces now available. But what do composers seek to communicate through their use of eclectic musical juxtaposition?

Woods finds that postmodern musical appropriation is employed for the purpose of satire or "ironic humour" [*sic*].[25] Some musicians might make use of "features of older styles specifically in order to reject or ridicule certain aspects of modernity."[26] Other scholars find that postmodern

---

21. Ibid., 16–17.

22. LeBaron, "Reflections of Surrealism in Postmodern Musics," 27–73.

23. Taylor, "Music and Musical Practices in Postmodernity," 94–97. Taylor includes lists from Ihab Hassan (which refers to "combination" as a postmodern way of making), David Harvey (which cites "reproduction/pastiche/eclecticism" as postmodern tendencies), and a chart from Charles Jencks, which describes postmodern tastes as "pluralist," "eclectic," and "inclusive."

24. Woods, *Beginning Postmodernism*, 205.

25. Ibid., 206.

26. Grenz, *A Primer on Postmodernism*, 20.

musicians employ juxtaposition to protest or speak against the modernist favoring of unity, as referenced above. By creating music which moves abruptly from one style or sound to another, musicians demonstrate independence from the modern assumption that music must be continuous and teleological.

Postmoderns might also turn to sampling, imitation, and appropriation in their music-making to raise questions about communal versus individual creation, questions at the heart of the difference between modernism and postmodernism. According to Grenz, "postmoderns often seek to undermine the concept of the powerful originating author. They attempt to destroy what they see as the modernist ideology of style, replacing it with a culture of multiple styles. To achieve this end, many postmodern artists confront their audience with a multiplicity of styles, a seemingly discordant polyphony of decontextualized voices."[27] By so doing, these artists declare that their creation was not individual but communal, upholding the postmodern preference for community over isolation.

Finally, many postmodern musicians may create music that is disjunct, heterogeneous, and varied in order to reflect their understanding of their own lives. According to Heath White, "the postmodern picture of the self is more like a jumbled, flickering movie collage, a screen on which society projects all kinds of changing, ultimately meaningless images."[28] A postmodern worldview sees objects and even people as collections of varied constituent parts, and creates artwork in a similar fashion.

Musical Eclecticism within the Emerging Church: A Case Study

For musicians and pastors who plan and lead worship, the chief artistic medium is not a sermon or a particular piece of music but the service itself. The worship service or liturgy, as a collection of prayers, songs, silence, sermon, sacrament, and other elements, becomes an artistic and theological whole. One would expect Emerging churches that acknowledge postmodern leanings to reflect the inclusive and juxtaposed musical approach described above in creating their liturgical structures. In a previous study of three Midwest Emerging congregations, however, this author found a

---

27. Ibid., 21.
28. White, *Postmodernism 101*, 76.

surprising lack of variety in musical style.[29] While not explicitly dealt with in the earlier article, it is possible that the geographical location of the three congregations—the Midwest—in some way affected the musical choices of congregational leaders. Given that earlier study, it seemed appropriate to conduct another investigation, specifically searching for musical variety within Emerging worship. In contrast to the earlier study, this inquiry would focus on just one congregation, over the course of several months, and the congregation chosen would be outside of the American Midwest.

The Abbey Church of St. Andrew and All Souls came about through a merger of St. Andrew Episcopal Church, founded in Portland, Oregon in 1895, and All Souls, an "emerging Episcopal mission" founded in 2012.[30] The congregations merged in 2013, and the community worships in the Portland Abbey. This location also houses Abbey Arts, a "nonprofit community development initiative, fostering . . . collaborative arts education, performances, and cross-cultural community building,"[31] as well as a food and clothing pantry for those in need. Through 2014, St. Andrew and All Souls (SAAS) maintained two worship services on most Sundays: a 9:15 "Traditional Mass" according to the 1979 Book of Common Prayer, and an 11:15 "Emerging Mass" described as "Anglican liturgy creatively expressed."[32] On the last Sunday of the month, one joint service, or "All Community Mass" alternated in style between the musical and liturgical choices of the two separate services. Since 2015, the church has moved to holding one service each Sunday.

According to Matthew Morris, a musician involved with worship at SAAS, the congregation is

> diverse in a number of ways—ethnically, culturally, religiously. Some members have been attending this church for decades, a few of them for their entire lives. Others are younger, and new to the Episcopal church; some post-evangelical, and a few former-Catholics. There are people in the congregation who lean more toward traditional forms of worship, including the choice of song and instrumentation. Others grew up in churches that utilized modern

---

29. Josselyn-Cranson, "Local and Authentic," 429–30.

30. Some historical information can be found at the church website: www.portlandabbey.org/about/faq.

31. See abbeyarts.org/about-abbey-arts-pdx.php.

32. www.portlandabbey.org/about/faq/.

forms of Christian worship music, and they tend to gravitate to those kinds of Praise and Worship songs.[33]

Before diving into musical choices, it may be helpful to explain how "Anglican liturgy creatively expressed" works out in practice at SAAS. The 11:15 mass begins with a "Pre Liturgy MP3": music from a variety of sources to which the congregation can listen as it gathers.[34] Then people may be called to liturgical participation by the sounding of a bell; poetry; or a call to worship (often featuring scripture) that might be read by the congregation, a leader, or by both in alternation. This is followed by a congregational song, the text of which usually reflects the scripture readings to be used that day or themes of invocation and coming to worship.

After the song, the congregation enters into a time of hearing scripture. At its briefest, this time includes the reading of the Gospel for the day according to the Revised Common Lectionary. Often, however, the psalm, epistle, and/or Old Testament reading are included as well. Rather than mentioning a sermon, the bulletin lists "Reverb" after the final scripture reading. "Reverb" is explained in the church's bulletins as a "reflection on the scriptures to help deepen our trust [in] God and guide our practice of faith in the way of Jesus Christ." This time of communal reflection, by way of a homily or discussion, is then complimented by "Open Space": "a time for personal reflection on the theme of the liturgy and how God is speaking to you so far," also described in the bulletins as "a five minute oasis of silence for reflection and meditation on the theme of today's liturgy, aided by prayer stations and accompanied by thematic vocal or contemplative music." Congregants may attend to the quiet music playing, serve themselves coffee and tea, record thoughts in a journal, or meditate.

When the congregation gathers again after "open space" time, they join together in prayer usually called "Prayers of the People," or occasionally "Intercessions." These times of prayer frequently borrow from the Book of Common Prayer's forms of intercession,[35] though they also feature prayers of St. Francis and St. Clement of Rome, among others. Congregational singing may also play a role in the congregation's communal prayer, in the form of a Taizé chant repeated after each intercession or petition. After the

---

33. Matthew Morris, email interview with the author, May 28, 2015.

34. Dido, Helios, Rivertribe, Moby, Switchfoot, and Handel have all featured as sources of "Pre-Liturgy mp3" music. Many of these artists will be discussed later in the chapter.

35. See *The Book of Common Prayer*, 385–89, Forms II and IV.

prayers, the congregation passes the peace and contributes to an offering taken to support the church. On occasional Sundays these liturgical actions are supplemented by singing a song that reflects on passing the peace itself or on the Nicene Creed.

A eucharistic prayer, called "Table Talk," follows the offering. This prayer can take many forms, but nearly always contains dialogic material, spoken by both pastor and congregation. In addition, the congregation frequently sings verses, choruses, or stanzas of songs or hymns throughout the Eucharistic prayer. These musical excerpts rarely link explicitly to the action of sharing bread and wine, but rather connect the "Table Talk" to the day's scripture and themes or the liturgical season. Once the congregation has been invited to commune, the community observes silence for contemplation during a period of time set apart by the ringing of a bell. Following the sound of the bell, the congregation turns its attention to "Community Matters," or announcements, before a charge to the assembly. This charge usually comes from a previously unread scripture for the day from the Revised Common Lectionary. The congregation responds to the charge by singing a final song together, and then receiving the dismissal, which is frequently followed by a "Post-Liturgy MP3."

The Emerging mass at SAAS, as described above, largely follows the structure of the traditional Christian pattern of Word and Table. The headings of "Gathering," "Word," "Table," and "Sending" present in the bulletins for this service give evidence to the importance of historic liturgical roots in constructing the mass. In large part, the way that the service has been "creatively expressed" comes from the music included in the service, and it is to that music that we now turn.

Music at the Church of St. Andrew and All Souls

The musical discussion that follows draws from fourteen bulletins for the Emerging Mass at SAAS, taken from June 1 through December 7. That number is nearly two-thirds of the number of Sundays between the two dates, excepting the last Sunday of each month, which is given to the joint services that are exempt from this study.

In the services for which bulletins are available, between two and eight pieces of music appear in each of the services, with half of all the services studied containing seven pieces of music. The service with two pieces of music, on October 5, was atypical in that it included pet blessings in honor of Saint Francis, whose feast day is celebrated on October 4. The extra time allocated to this activity, and the absence of the usual MP3 musical selections, may account for this discrepancy.

Music for Listening

In almost every other instance, three of the pieces of music used in each service were not intended for congregational music-making. The "Pre Liturgy MP3," the "Open Space MP3," and the "Post Liturgy MP3" all featured recordings, intended for use as "reflection music," as stated in the instructions in the worship bulletin for Open Space time each week. While the Post Liturgy MP3 often repeats the closing song sung by the congregation, the Open Space and Pre Liturgy recordings tend to offer spacious, synth-heavy, ambient sounds. The recordings used come from a variety of sources, favoring groups of the first decade of the twenty-first century, though a few pieces come from the late 1980s and early 1990s. One instance uses a melody from George Frederick Handel, an eighteenth-century composer, although both the recording and the meandering accompaniment style date to 2010. The music of the three most frequently featured artists during these times (The Album Leaf, Helios, and Moby) offers a representative aural snapshot of the sounds featured during these contemplative times.

Musician Jimmy LaValle took the name "The Album Leaf" for his solo recording project, producing music "inspired by a number of genres—classical, jazz, and post-rock[36] among them . . . [and] utilizing everything from ambient noise to field recordings to radio transmissions."[37] SAAS has made use of "Seal Beach" and "The Light," two recordings by LaValle that evidence great attention paid to timbre: bright, reverberant synth tones, soft washes of muted, breathy chords, and dark, muffled, almost nasal instrumental "voices" layer upon each other. Both recordings are firmly tonal

---

36. The term "post-rock" refers to music from the 1990s and 2000s that employs instruments associated with rock music (electric guitars, percussion tracks, synthesizers) in ways that break free of the constraints usually placed on rock music due to the expected structure of verses, chorus, and bridge. Post-rock songs evolve over time, adding layers and shifting timbres, much as the minimalist music of Steve Reich and Philip Glass does. Most post-rock pieces do not include voices, and they tend to be atmospheric, sweeping, and evocative rather than explicit in their sonic references.

37. Taken from the web page for the project: http://www.thealbumleaf.com/index.php?textNum=2 (accessed June 10, 2015).

and simple in their melodic and harmonic motion, yet compelling due to the juxtaposition of different timbres and melodic lines against each other.

Helios is one of many names employed by musician Keith Kenniff.[38] As Helios, Kenniff creates music that incorporates field recordings and synthetic timbres, as does the music of The Album Leaf. But Helios' tracks tend to employ more acoustic instruments, including guitar, snare drums played with brushes, cello, and piano. The juxtaposition of scratchy field-recorded sounds, plucked guitar strings (including the sounds of fingers sliding along the strings), and spacious synth chords (often with added seconds or sevenths for a richer texture) creates music that can feel both distant and intimate.

Of the three most frequently used artists for MP3 listening at SAAS, Moby is undoubtedly the best known. While the music of Keith Kenniff and Jimmy LaValle has gained some following and has appeared in advertising or in documentary soundtracks, Moby receives frequent airtime on radio stations and has sold millions of albums across the globe. The four Moby tracks that have been used as music for reflection at SAAS include "ISS," "Snowball," "One of These Mornings," and "In My Heart." These pieces employ far more regular and prominent rhythmic patterns, generally created out of synthetic sounds, than the music previously described. Like The Album Leaf and Helios, Moby incorporates slowly evolving textures, layered over simple and repeating harmonic progressions ("ISS," for example, alternates between minor i and major IV chords throughout the duration of the almost nine minute recording). Unlike the other artists, however, Moby frequently uses recorded vocal tracks in his music. One can hear the voice of Dianne McCaulley in Moby's "One of These Mornings," and that of a singer from The Shining Light Gospel Choir on "In My Heart."

Curiously enough, Moby is not known as a Christian artist, yet he chose to incorporate samples from specifically Christian songs: "In My Heart" comes from the spiritual "Lord, I Want to Be a Christian," while "One of These Mornings" comes from the gospel song "Walk around Heaven All Day." His editing of the vocal samples, and their brevity, obscures to an extent the Christian origin of the songs. In contrast, the music of Helios and The Album Leaf seems to have no explicit spiritual connection. Each of these pieces receives meaning connected to the Christian faith from its

38. Kenniff also produces music under the names Goldmund and Mint Julep: Goldmund features solo piano work, while Mint Julep's mix of indie rock and ambient music comes from a collaboration between Kenniff and his wife Hollie. See www.unseen-music.com for more information on Helios and Kenniff's other projects.

use within the liturgy at SAAS, but it is clear that Karen Ward and her congregation are able to find and use "secular" music to contemplate the workings of God.

While the function of these MP3 recordings is to provide a meditative space within the liturgy, several of them also have clear connections to the lectionary readings for the day. Both "One of These Mornings" and "In My Heart," for example, were used on Ascension Sunday, when scripture readings show Jesus being lifted up on a cloud and leaving his disciples, who stand looking after him. The Pre Liturgy MP3 for the day included the lyrics "One of these mornings . . . they will look for me and I'll be gone," clearly resonating with the themes of the ascension. The Post Liturgy MP3 pointed to the ascension with the phrase "I want to be *up* in my heart" (italics added). Another Pre Liturgy MP3, this time for December 7, reflected God's mercy and care-taking of all of creation, as found in the day's psalm and epistle reading (Ps 85:1–2, 8–13; 2 Pet 3:8–15a). This track, Tara Ward's creative mix of Handel's "He Shall Feed His Flock" with an ambient, slow, synth-driven accompaniment, speaks of God's care using the metaphor of shepherd. The recording also brings to mind Advent and Christmas connotations, as Handel's *Messiah* is frequently performed during December. Thus we see that recordings are chosen to fit their particular spot in the Emerging Mass, but also to contribute to the understanding and message of the day's liturgy and season within the church year.

Music for Singing

In addition to music for listening during the Pre Liturgy, Open Space, and Post Liturgy MP3 times, SAAS employs music for congregational singing. Most Sundays, the congregation sings four pieces of music, the first one shortly after the call to worship, greeting, or other opening words. A second congregational song frequently appears as part of the prayers of the people, or in between the prayers of the people and the offering. Portions of a third song feature as part of the Eucharistic prayer, interspersed between prayers by the pastor or by the whole congregation. Finally, the congregation sings a closing song in between the charge and the dismissal.

These four locations for congregational song make room for great variety of musical style, instrumental accompaniment, and focus or function within the service. Over the course of the 14 Sundays for which bulletins were available, the congregation sang thirty-eight songs or hymns a total of fifty-one times (eight songs were sung twice, one was sung three times, and one was sung four times). While the great majority of the music sung at SAAS comes from the 2000's, the congregation has sung a translation of a prayer dating back to the fifth century, giving its repertoire a span of six hundred years.

Among the thirty-eight songs from these services, one can find two Taizé chants from 1984; two songs by the punk-influenced Mars Hill band Team Strike Force; four hymns (including St. Patrick's Breastplate mentioned above as well as "Holy, Holy, Holy" from the nineteenth century, "All Creatures of Our God and King" from the thirteenth century, and "Comfort, Comfort Ye My People" from the seventeenth century); one song from the 1980s by the secular post-punk British band The Cure; and numerous others from Christian artists of the late 1990s and 2000s. Roughly one-fourth (ten out of thirty-eight) of the congregation's repertoire comes from artists related to Enter the Worship Circle, so we will turn to an examination of those songs in order to present a sonic image of the music sung by the people of SAAS.

Enter the Worship Circle formed at the juncture of two musical couples: Ben Pasley and Robin Weisinger, who perform and write music as 100 Portraits; and Don and Lori Chaffer, who create music as Waterdeep. In 1999, these two couples collaborated on an album of psalm-inspired songs that would be simple to learn and free of churchy language. The album featured acoustic instruments and raw, unprocessed singing of songs designed to be used and imitated by Christians at worship.[39] The group, with a changing line-up of musicians, has gone on to produce four albums under the name Enter the Worship Circle as well as four solo recordings by different singer-songwriters, under the name *Chair and Microphone Volumes 1–4*.

The mellow tracks of these albums feature folky and repetitive melodies, sung in harmony and accompanied by acoustic guitar and hand drum. The straightforward performance and recording techniques seem to come from a coffeehouse set in an intimate setting, in contrast to the carefully produced and thickly layered ambient music played on MP3 during worship. These rougher recording values can be found on all the Enter the Worship Circle albums, as described by Ben Pasley:

> It does not take a lot of gear to record music that sounds like *Enter the Worship Circle*. It does take some musicians who are skilled

---

39. See www.entertheworshipcircle.com/our-story/ for a more complete retelling of the beginnings of the group from the perspective of Ben Pasley.

in their craft enough, however, to play from their strengths and submit to one another. All great rhythm sections have this in common. Each person plays their [sic] strength whether on bass, or drums, or percussion, or rhythm instruments, and in that confidence they lean into one another to find what magic happens when they lose themselves in the song. This cannot be accomplished in a multi-tracking environment where everyone plays one instrument at a time . . . On the "group" Worship Circle albums we would first run through the songs, picking up ideas, dropping certain instincts, and work to find a musical fit with one another. When we thought we had an overall energy we would turn on the recording machines and track it all down at one time . . . Worship Circle recordings were done in a "live" room with no separation booths, click tracks . . . and we could hear one another in the room, and in our headphones, during the taping.[40]

This straightforward and immediate approach reflects Pasley's goals for Enter the Worship Circle music. On his cross-country tours with *100 Portraits*, he noticed small fellowship groups of students, accompanied by a very few instruments, singing songs intended for performance in large worship settings by carefully rehearsed and amplified rock groups. Pasley and his fellow musicians wished to provide songs, based closely on the psalms, which would fit the scale of these smaller college gatherings. Indeed, this attempt betrays a postmodern distrust of the large-scale and desire to locate meaning and authority within the small community.

The congregation at SAAS has sung five songs from *First Circle,* the first of the Enter the Worship Circle recordings, released in 1999. These include the saucy minor blues "Those Who Trust" (derived from Psalm 125), the confident, folky "Whatever Thing" (a declaration of intention to remove all obstacles to an encounter with God), the shaggy folk rock "Come Fall On Us" (borrowing from Psalm 50), "I Will Not Forget You" (which continues the gratitude of Psalm 50, only in the major mode), and the contemplative, gentle "You Are So Good to Me" (which reflects themes of Psalms 34 and 147).

While subsequent Enter the Worship Circle albums featured changing rosters of musicians, the acoustic, folk-influenced sound of the music continued. This approach is magnified on the *Chair and Microphone* albums, each of which features only one artist, singing and playing his or her own songs. The congregation at SAAS has sung two songs from these

---

40. www.entertheworshipcircle.com/making-the-music/ (accessed June 12, 2015).

recordings: "Centuries" by Aaron Strumpel on the second volume of this series, and "Lord's Prayer" by Tim Coon on the fourth volume.

Such simplicity makes sense for St. Andrew and All Souls. The congregation tends to follow only one musical leader, who often sings while playing acoustic guitar or keyboard.[41] The intention of Enter the Worship Circle to provide songs appropriate for smaller, more intimate worship settings may explain their usefulness and popularity at SAAS. Yet not all of the music chosen by the congregation's leaders comes from bands intent on working with simplicity and minimalism. Among the congregation's repertoire, songs from The Restoration Project ("Arise") and Sufjan Stevens ("Vito's Ordination") participate in the simple, folky flavor of the Enter the Worship Circle repertoire. Songs from Soul Junk, Team Strike Force, and Sixpence None the Richer, however, make use of larger, more layered, and often louder musical forces. In these cases, the lead musician at SAAS must adapt the music from its original recording to the more intimate and musically restrained context of worship at the Emerging Mass.

As mentioned above, this folk-rock musical core is supplemented with a wide variety of other musical styles, including larger rock sounds, more contemplative and quieter contemporary pieces, Taizé chants, hymns from several different centuries within the Western European Christian tradition, and music from non-Christian sources. This last category deserves exploration, as it is an unusual feature even in congregations that pride themselves on an inclusive canon of congregational music.

During the time of the study, the congregation at SAAS sang a number of songs by bands that many would consider secular. "Chariot," by Page France, includes several phrases that bear Christian resonance: "the heart of God," "the wedding feast," "breaks the bread," and "like a chariot, swing it low." Yet the band Page France dismisses the label "Christian." In a September 2007 interview, songwriter and band creator Michael Nau responded to questions about the interpretation of his songs by saying "I try not to think about it. For the most part, we're just making records, and it happens so quickly that I don't have time to think about these things . . . records are trains of thought, and I don't have an agenda, and I'm not trying to say anything more than what's there."[42]

Musician Sufjan Stevens, whose song "Vito's Ordination" appears among the congregational repertoire at SAAS, feels similarly about

---

41. Matthew Morris, email interview with the author, May 28, 2015.
42. Nau, "Page France: Interview."

references to his faith within his music. After narrating his childhood activities at a Methodist church to an interviewer, Stevens says

> I still describe myself as a Christian, and my love of God and my relationship with God is fundamental, but its manifestations in my life and the practices of it are constantly changing. I find incredible freedom in my faith. Yes, the kingdom of Christianity and the Church has been one of the most destructive forces in history, and there are levels of bastardization of religious beliefs. But the unique thing about Christianity is that it is so amorphous . . . We live in a post-God society anyway—embrace it![43]

Elsewhere, Stevens elaborated on the relationship between his faith and his music:

> I suppose my process of making art is driven less by abstractions of faith or politics and more by practical theory: composition and balance and color . . . it's not so much that faith influences us as it lives in us. In every circumstance . . . I am living and loving and being. This absolves me from ever making the embarrassing effort to gratify God (and the church) by imposing religious content on anything I do.[44]

We find a similar attitude toward religion on the part of the British group Mumford and Sons, whose song "I Will Wait" has been used by SAAS. While Marcus Mumford grew up the son of Vineyard Church leaders John and Eleanor Mumford, and while ideas connected with the Christian faith appear in Mumford and Sons songs (such as the phrases "I'll kneel down," "You forgave, and I won't forget," "tame my flesh and fix my eyes" in "I Will Wait," sung at SAAS on December 7), he has publically denied his own Christianity while maintaining his ongoing faith journey.[45]

The congregation of SAAS does not limit itself to singing music by "secular" bands that flirt with the label "Christian," however. During the time of the study, the congregation sang "Lovesong" by The Cure, a British band known for Gothic sensibilities and punk and New Wave-influenced sounds. Karen Ward, vicar of SAAS, explains her congregation's inclusive stance as an embodiment of a carefully articulated theological position.

---

43. Stevens, "True Myth: A Conversation with Sufjan Stevens."

44. Stevens, "How Sufjan Stevens Subverts the Stigma of Christian Music."

45. In an interview with *Rolling Stone*, Marcus Mumford claimed that he was not a Christian, but that his faith was a "work in progress." Mumford, "Mumford and Sons: Rattle and Strum."

> We hold a high view of God. Anything or any music or cultural component that we discern to be good (and we do discernment on anything and everything before use) and is not antithetical to the teachings of Christ can be considered for use, as the Spirit of God blows where it will and is not controlled by or domesticated by the church or the label "Christian." We seek to use "good music" that inspires us and brings resonance with the Good News.[46]

The sung repertoire of the congregation at SAAS encompasses a wide variety of musical styles and genres, as we have seen. Like the selection of MP3 music for listening, the selection of music for congregational singing takes place with regard to the scripture readings for each Sunday, as given in the Revised Common Lectionary. A few examples will serve to demonstrate the connection between music and scriptural themes. On June 15, Trinity Sunday, the congregation sang St. Patrick's Breastplate, a nineteenth-century adaptation of an ancient prayer ascribed to Saint Patrick in the fifth century. The prayer begins and ends with the Trinitarian words

> I bind unto myself today the strong name of the Trinity,
>
> by invocation of the same, the Three in One, and One in Three.

The song by The Cure, mentioned above, featured in the Emerging Mass at SAAS on July 6, when the congregation heard scriptural accounts of God who offers rest to the weary (Matthew 11:28–30) and who is praised by all creation for God's steadfast love and compassion for those who have fallen (Psalm 145:8–14). This witness is echoed in "Lovesong," which declares "I will always love you" to the One who makes us "whole," "young," "free," "clean," and "home."

On August 10, the congregation heard several passages relating to trust, faith, and doubt, including Romans 10:5–15 ("if you confess with your lips that Jesus is Lord and believe in your heart that God raised him from the dead . . .") and Matthew 14:22–33 (in which Jesus asks Peter "You of little faith, why did you doubt?" when he begins to sink into the water). During the eucharistic prayer on this day, the congregation sang "Those who trust in the Lord are as Mount Zion/ they will not, not be moved," from the first Enter the Worship Circle album. These examples demonstrate the commitment of the leadership at SAAS to put musical variety at the service of the worship service as a whole, and at the spiritual

---

46. Karen Ward, email interview with the author, June 15, 2015.

growth of the congregation, as fed by the scriptural breadth of the Revised Common Lectionary.

Principles of Musical Variety at St. Andrew and All Souls

Having investigated the musical repertoire of the congregation at Saint Andrew and All Souls, how can we summarize the way in which eclecticism plays a part in the singing and listening of the congregation's worship? Five principles appear in the congregation's musical practices that may be helpful for congregational leaders, whether within Emerging churches or not, to consider.

First, the breadth of musical style within the canon of SAAS shows a clear relationship to the congregation's identity. In other words, the way that a particular congregation's musical range manifests itself relates to the age, culture, background, expectations, and experiences of that congregation. We see this in the inclusion of music by Agents of Future, a Portland-based group of "Jesus-loving, jalopy-gospel way-backers."[47] While this band has recorded five albums and has performed outside its home congregation at several festivals, most congregations outside of Oregon may be ignorant of Agents of Future and their music. The temporal origin of the music of SAAS, as well as its geographical origin, indicates something about the congregation. As noted above, the majority of the music in worship at SAAS comes from the decade between 2000 and 2010. This suggests a younger congregation, or at least one with fewer connections to particular songs of the past, and one that is aware of recent musical offerings. However, the connection of the songs to the liturgy displays a concern for understanding and inhabiting the Christian tradition on the part of the congregation at SAAS, regardless of the age of those who attend the Emerging Mass. The congregation sings the Nicene Creed (in the form of a contemporary song by Team Strikeforce), sings of passing the peace (with the words of Soul Junk's "Peace, Peace, Peace"), and regularly sings in response to the Eucharistic prayer of the presider. The music clearly connects to a traditional four-fold pattern of Christian liturgy.[48] SAAS musician Matthew Morris

---

47. The beginning of the band's self-description; see agentsoffuture.bandcamp.com. The band came together in 1998 at the starting of the North Portland church The Bridge.

48. Liturgical scholars and practitioners have long noted four common components to Christian worship: entrance or gathering; hearing the Word of God; eating together at the Lord's Table; and being sent out or dismissed. Webber wrote extensively about

recognizes the way in which the congregation's musical eclecticism reflects the community's identity. He finds that "using different genres and styles of music is a way of expressing the diversity of the community; the diversity of creation, even."[49] It is clear that the music of SAAS, while varied, tells us something about that congregation. Any other congregation might include different, while equally diverse, music in its repertoire. In other words, musical breadth looks different among different people.

Second, we notice that while the congregation at SAAS employs music of many different styles and genres, it doesn't favor each style equally. Within the variety of the SAAS repertoire, there is a stylistic center or home that produces a larger percentage of the congregation's music. As noted above, the congregation favors informal, indie-sounding folk rock of the first decade of the twentieth century, and in particular music of the Enter the Worship Circle artists. This material, which constitutes one quarter of the songs sung at SAAS during the time of the study, provides a place of sonic comfort and identity out of which the congregation may journey with confidence toward more remote music. The congregation may visit neighboring styles, such as other forms of rock music or songs from an earlier decade, or it may explore more distant musical forms, such as century-old hymns, meditative and repetitive Taizé chants, or electronica. In each case, the grounding in more familiar music seems to enable openness to a broader repertoire. This premise runs contrary to many assumptions about stylistic variety, which assert that the point of inclusiveness, whether musical or otherwise, is to eradicate any preferred options. At SAAS, we find the contrary to be true: the presence of a home style of music in sizeable amount encourages the congregation to make room for other musical voices.

The musical repertoire of the congregation at SAAS urges us to dismiss another expected approach to eclecticism as well. Often, liturgical and musical planners think of inclusiveness with a box-checking mentality as a way to prove diversity or hospitality. Our desire to maintain a diverse musical diet may feel forced and regimented, as we strive to include representative music from a variety of groups, cultures, time periods, and styles. In worst cases, pluralistic musical choices can serve only to maintain an image of inclusivity. It is clear that this has not been the approach at SAAS. During the time of the study, for example, there were no pieces of music

---

these four components of Christian worship, one example of which can be found in his *Worship Is a Verb*, 49–65.

49. Matthew Morris, email interview with the author, May 28, 2015.

PART 2: CROSSING BOUNDARIES

from the African-American tradition, whether spirituals, historic Gospel songs, modern gospel music, or music of other genres.[50] Anyone seeking to cover all bases in a church music program would not omit pieces from the African-American canon of religious music. Therefore, it seems that the music that has been chosen by the SAAS leadership was not picked in order to check off boxes or appease various groups but for an entirely different set of reasons. The music at SAAS supports each Sunday's service as based on the readings of the Revised Common Lectionary, as described above; it offers the congregation the opportunity to both listen and sing; it resonates with the particular members of the congregation; and it connects that congregation to the broader Christian tradition. While inclusiveness is present, it is not the only or the most important goal in making musical choices.

Fourth, we find that there is diversity of purpose or function for music in the Emerging Mass at SAAS as well as diversity of style. The congregation sings in order to encourage itself to worship (during the first song), to participate in prayer (whether the prayers of the people or the Eucharistic prayers), and to affirm its experience of God in preparation for being dismissed back into the world (in the closing song). In each of these locations, the singing serves a different role. Even more than this, however, the congregation uses music that is not for singing but for listening. The MP3 recordings used during Open Space and before and after the liturgy draw attention to the day's theme, provide background sound to ease any discomfort with silence, and allow for meditation on the sung text, if there is any, or on the sounds themselves. This use of music demonstrates that variety does not obtain only in the selection of music itself, but also can and should exist in the ways that music is allowed to serve the worshipping community. Music does not need to be limited to congregational song, or to one place within the worship service. Music easily and helpfully serves several liturgical roles.

Finally, the musical variety of the Emerging Mass at SAAS is evident not only across each Sunday's worship service, or throughout an entire season's music, but within individual songs as well. Many of the pieces sung by the congregation embody the disjunct, heterogeneous, and juxtaposed tendencies favored by postmodern artists. We find that approach in Tara Ward's version of "He Shall Feed His Flock" from Handel's *Messiah*. Underneath the familiar Baroque melody are wandering harmonies played

---

50. The congregation did use a contemporary Gospel piece, "The Reason Why I Sing" by Kirk Franklin, during the Easter season, following this study.

with unexpected synthesized timbres. This juxtaposition of musical elements from the Western classical tradition and from twenty-first-century electronica forms a postmodern expression of faith, appropriate for the Emerging church. Other songs and recordings used by SAAS also combine unexpected musical features together. "Within Dreams" by Album Leaf, used as an Open Space MP3, features the sound of static, as if from an analog record, even though the recording was clearly created using digital techniques. Groups such as Mumford and Sons and Page France, whose music is sung by the congregation at SAAS, pride themselves on imitating harmonic patterns, instrumental combinations, and even clothing from the musicians of earlier eras.[51] Another way in which this music incorporates variety within itself is in the use of unexpected instruments in a rock framework. In Page France's recording of the song "Chariot," used twice during the time of the study, one hears a glockenspiel. The contrast of what might be considered a marching band instrument with a rock group offers another instance of "messy vitality," to use Robert Venturi's phrase.

Emerging congregations tend to rely on their own members for leadership and direction, demonstrating a postmodern disdain toward the imitation of megachurches or other model congregations. We should, therefore, expect to find great diversity of liturgical expression in Emerging congregations. This study of one particular congregation demonstrates certain facets of musical diversity in worship: a diversity centered on a congregation's identity, anchored by a familiar style, at the service of the liturgical whole (rather than being inclusive for inclusivity's sake), exhibiting diversity of purpose as well as sound, and featuring diversity within as well as among individual songs. Do these forms of diversity occur in other Emerging congregations as well, or does diversity appear differently elsewhere? It is to be hoped that other scholars will explore the musical repertoire and practices of additional Emerging communities of worship. A multitude of such studies will begin to elucidate the variety of ways in which diversity brings "messy vitality" to the music of Emerging congregations.

---

51. Members of the band Mumford and Sons credit the soundtrack to *O Brother, Where Art Thou?* as one of their greatest influences. This recording exposed them to instruments such as the banjo and upright bass that have become part of their trademark sound.

PART 2: CROSSING BOUNDARIES

Bibliography

Bertens, Hans. *The Idea of the Postmodern: A History*. New York: Routledge, 1995.

The Book of Common Prayer. New York: Church, 1979.

Clendinning, Jane Piper. "Postmodern Architecture/Postmodern Music." In *Postmodern Music/Postmodern Thought*, edited by Judy Lochhead and Joseph Auner, 119–40. New York: Routledge, 2002.

Grenz, Stanley J. *A Primer on Postmodernism*. Grand Rapids: Eerdmans, 1996.

Josselyn-Cranson, Heather. "Local and Authentic: Music in Emerging Congregations." *Worship* 83, no. 5 (2009) 429–30.

Kramer, Jonathan D. "The Nature and Origins of Musical Postmodernism." In *Postmodern Music/Postmodern Thought*, edited by Judy Lochhead and Joseph Auner, 13–26. New York: Routledge, 2002.

LeBaron, Anne. "Reflections of Surrealism in Postmodern Musics." In *Postmodern Music/Postmodern Thought*, edited by Judy Lochhead and Joseph Auner, 27–73. New York: Routledge, 2002.

Lochhead, Judy. "Introduction." In *Postmodern Music/Postmodern Thought*, edited by Judy Lochhead and Joseph Auner, 1–11. New York: Routledge, 2002.

Mumford, Marcus. "Mumford and Sons: Rattle and Strum." Interview by Brian Hiatt. *Rolling Stone*, March 28, 2013. www.rollingstone.com/music/news/mumford-sons rattle-and-strum-20130328.

Nau, Michael. "Page France: Interview." Interview by Scout Leader Kyle. *Tiny Mix Tapes*, September 2007. www.tinymixtapes.com/features/page-france.

Penner, Myron B. "Introduction." In *Christianity and the Postmodern Turn: Six Views*, edited by Myron B. Penner, 13–34. Grand Rapids: Brazos, 2005.

Stevens, Sufjan. "True Myth: A Conversation with Sufjan Stevens." Interview by Ryan Dombal. *Pitchfork*, February 16, 2015. pitchfork.com/features/interviews/9595-true-myth-a-conversation-with-sufjan-stevens/.

———. "How Sufjan Stevens Subverts the Stigma of Christian Music." Interview by David Roark. *The Atlantic*, March 29, 2015. www.theatlantic.com/entertainment/archive/2015/03/sufjan-stevens-and-a-better-way-to-write-music-about-faith/388802/.

Taylor, Timothy D. "Music and Musical Practices in Postmodernity." In *Postmodern Music/Postmodern Thought*, edited by Judy Lochhead and Joseph Auner, 93–118. New York: Routledge, 2002.

Webber, Robert. *Worship Is a Verb*. Waco: Word, 1985.

White, Heath. *Postmodernism 101: A First Course for the Curious Christian*. Grand Rapids: Brazos, 2006.

Woods, Tim. *Beginning Postmodernism*. 2nd ed. New York: Manchester University Press, 2009.

10

Emergence in the Americas: Points of Convergence between Latin American and North American Emerging Church Networks

—— Juan Jose Barreda Toscano and Dee Yaccino ——

THIS CHAPTER DOCUMENTS SOME of the ways a Latin American theology of integral mission has manifested in the ecclesiology and missiology of a network of churches in Latin America and how their theology and practices converge with the broader global Christian context in relation to Emerging Church Movement in the United States.[1] We cannot begin that discussion, however, without mentioning the historical influences from Europe and North America that have shaped the Latin American Christian context.

European Christianity first came to Latin America, most often through force, as both soldiers and priests from Roman Catholic-identified Spanish and Portuguese military expeditions stepped foot on indigenous soil in these regions. Their express purpose was not primarily territorial expansion, but rather to exploit natural resources in the Americas and bring them back to Europe. To do that, First Nations peoples were subjugated as a source of cheap labor, forced to comply with European customs, and introduced to Eurocentric interpretations of the Bible in an attempt to "civilize" them.[2] Millions of First Nations peoples died as a result of wars,

---

1. The authors have historical documentation on the Latin American network of churches called the *Red del Camino* (*Network of the Way*) from primary sources in archived annual reports, board meeting minutes, email correspondence, and internal records as well as from its main bridging partner, *Del Camino Connection*, and have first-hand knowledge of and experience with the network as participant leaders.

2. See papal statements on authority over other territories in: *UNAM SANCTAM*, 1302, and *Romanus Pontifex*, 20–26.

physical abuse, and illness during the first decades of Spanish and Portuguese arrival. Thus, the symbol of the cross that was purportedly used to save them became inextricably intertwined with the sword that was used to enslave them.[3]

This deeply tragic historical experience was further propagated and reinforced as more and more Europeans immigrated to Latin America in the name of their mother country or in the name of Christ. Even as recently as the 1950s and 1960s, many Roman Catholic, Protestant Mainline, and Evangelical churches founded in Latin America by North American missionaries often unwittingly took a similarly colonial approach to Christian mission. According to some mission analysts, North American views about church, mission, and Christian life were (and still are) frequently imported and imposed from the dominant Christian global culture, which often is indistinguishable from the "American Way of Life." North American missionaries regularly spread their lifestyles at the expense of Latin American understandings and traditions, forming vertical, paternalistic relationships with new believers. The missionaries also shared a Gospel based on personal conversion, an emphasis on inner ethics, and the belief in free direct access to God through Christ as they saw revealed in the Bible. They commonly held quite conservative macro-social and political views, resisting social justice-based political approaches (e.g., defending the rights of the oppressed), which they equated with communism.[4] The Latin American church absorbed North American ecclesiological models and structures, as well as their respective missiological views into mainstream Christian subculture via media, conference events featuring famous Protestant evangelical speakers, as well as through missionaries, church planters, and leaders of other non-profit organizations that proliferated their Christian literature, their liturgies, and their language.

From as early as the late 1960s and 1970s, however, other distinct theological frameworks and ecclesiological forms had already taken root in Latin America. They germinated in response to a critical concern of some major Latin American educators, biblical scholars, pastors, priests, and theologians concerning major regional social problems like poverty, racial discrimination, and political abuse. They argued that what typically had been regarded as theology for the whole global church was actually

---

3. See Dussel, *Concilium* 232, 403–15; and Gutiérrez, *En Busca de los Pobres de Jesucristo*.

4. Padilla, *Misión Integral*, 15.

Western theology that had been presumed to be universal. In their scrutiny of the validity of European and North American's exclusivistic claims to Christian biblical hermeneutics, they began an arduous deconstructive process, attempting to liberate theology in Latin America from some of its embedded historical, methodological, and contextual foreignness.

They were social actors who had been traditionally subjugated and silenced, who were now posing new questions with fresh and liberating perspectives from within the diverse contexts where they were situated. Their efforts significantly contributed to shifting the center for speaking theologically from within other socio-historical locations.[5] Two main Latin American-rooted theologies are among those often mentioned as instrumental precursors in the process of loosening theological discourse and practice from its strictly North American and Eurocentric grip: liberation theology and integral mission theology.[6]

Catholic base communities, in which priests formed groups that practiced a new hermeneutic of reading the Bible *desde la base* (from the grassroots popular perspective), provide examples of early liberation theology.[7] Liberation theologians distinguished three levels of meaning for the term liberation—sociopolitical and economic liberation from oppression; historical liberation of consciousness toward an understanding of one's own

---

5. Gutiérrez, *Teología de la Liberación*; Segundo, *Liberación de la Teología*; Boff and Boff, *Cómo Hacer Teología de la Liberación*; Segovia, *Decolonizing Biblical Studies*, 32–33.

6. For a perspective of the history of the first ten years of liberation theology, see Oliveros, *Liberación y Teología*; Ortiz, "Teología de la Liberación. Algunas tareas *pendientes*," 381–94. In relation to the Latin American Theological Fellowship, see Padilla, *25 Años de la Teología Evangélica Latinoamericana*; Salinas, "The Beginnings of the Fraternidad Teológica Latinoamericana,," 8–143; Salinas, *Latin American Evangelical Theology*; and García, "Notas sobre el Pasado, Presente y Futuro de la FTL," 11–43.

Additionally, a growing number of Western/European religious studies scholars and theologians were becoming increasingly aware of and unsettled by the West's hegemonic hold on theology and Christianity. See, for instance, Benson and Heltzel, *Evangelicals and Empire*; Bevans and Schroeder, *Constants in Context*, 261, 279, 312–13, 337; Bosch, *Transforming Mission*, 432–35; Gallagher and Hertig, *Landmark Essays*, 55–56, 140, 223, 232; Greenman and Green, *Global Theology in Evangelical Perspective*, 72–85; Rieger, *Christ and Empire*; and Walls, *The Missionary Movement in Christian History*, 10.

7. See Croatto, *Liberación y Libertad*; *Hermenéutica Bíblica*; and *Hermenéutica Práctica*, as well as *Revista de Interpretación Bíblica Latinoamericana* (RIBLA), http://www.claiweb.org/index.php/miembros-2/revistas-2. See also Gutieérrez, *A Theology of Liberation;* and Segundo, *The Liberation of Theology*.

agency; and liberation in Christ from sin which was seen as the ultimate root of all disruption of friendship and of all injustice and oppression.[8]

Some of the Latin American theologians who did not fully embrace liberation theology, especially those from within the *Fraternidad Teológica Latinoamericana* (Latin American Theological Fellowship), held a more traditional evangelical perspective, but still shared a commitment to *praxis*. Their concern was that theologians begin to acknowledge and understand the complexities of one's culture and context in the hermeneutic process.[9] They also began speaking and writing about what they deemed to be an unbiblical dichotomy between evangelism and social action. Their theological influences came to be known as *misión integral* or integral/wholistic mission.[10] There is no uniformity of opinion regarding what is meant by integral mission; it is used more as a theological key for understanding one's reality and the Church's mission within the world. But, generally integral mission can be understood as an attempt to recuperate or restore God's original design for creation by integrating (or making whole) every dimension of human life that has been broken. Whereas traditional evangelical theology viewed the church's mission from within the perspective of the eighteenth century modern missionary movement that focused on winning souls and planting churches by crossing borders into what they considered pagan lands, many theologians of integral mission maintained that the church's mission was to become salt and light in the very communities where they were present as God's people turned their allegiance to God and incarnated the new values of the kingdom of God revealed through Jesus Christ. Integral mission theology attempted to bring together or integrate what were seen as false dichotomies between those who are missionaries (sent individuals or sending churches) and those who are not, or between home and the mission field, or clergy and laity, or between daily life and the activity of the church in service to God's mission in the world.[11]

The struggle of these Latin American churches, however, was not necessarily to emerge—as some North American churches were emerging— from a modern to a postmodern theological framework. How can Latin

---

8. Gutiérrez, *Teología de la Liberación*, 36–37; 59–60.

9. See Padilla, *Misión Integral*, 80–106; Stam, "La Biblia, el Lector y Su Contexto Histórico,"' 27–72; Barreda, "Bible Study in Latin America,"' 83–110.

10. See Quiroz, "The Integral Mission to the Poor," 1–30; Escobar, *The New Global Mission*; Padilla, *Mission between the Times*.

11. Padilla, ¿*Qué Es la Misión Integral?*, 15–17.

America be postmodern, when in many places they have not yet been seen as modern? One cannot emerge from a place that one has not ever been. Instead, in Latin America and the Caribbean, certain churches may be said to have been emerging in the sense of looking at their own contexts from a postcolonial vantage point. In other words, Latin American theology, if it can be considered as emerging from anything in the wake of formally liberating their countries from colonial rule or governance, would be from the latent psycho-social-spiritual effects of colonialism and/or the more recent socio-cultural and political hegemony of a globalized market economy (i.e. neo-imperialism or neo-colonialism). The task of Latin American theologians, then, has been to dismantle theology, ecclesiology, and missiology from structures, forms, ideologies, and policies that are sociocultural and political in nature in order to engage constructively with the person of Jesus and the Bible in their own right.

So, if we were to try to describe some of the ways Latin American theology converges with theology, ecclesiology and missiology within a broader global Christian context, we might say that Latin American theology has influenced European and North American theologians and church practitioners by helping them recognize and acknowledge the agency of those labelled as "poor" by situating them as historical subjects, rather than "objects" of charity. The invitation is to create an ecclesiology that arises from and is composed of the people who suffer most in order to break with centuries of oppression and forms of imperialism (of which North American evangelicalism plays a part).[12] Particularly, within the Emerging Church Movement in the context of the United States, Latin American theology may have been instrumental in shaping missional church models with some distinct positive cultural values of Latin American and Caribbean contexts, for instance regarding the importance of relationship, interdependence, social justice, and integral/holistic mission.

In light of this, for many Latin American theologians, it continues to be imperative that Christian communities everywhere, self-consciously work out what it means to unravel certain theological, ecclesiological, and missiological values and practices from what has been internalized as normative and authoritative because their own cultural and contextual particularities have been suppressed or labeled—whether blatantly or latently—in oppressive or subjugating ways. It is of vital importance that these distinct

---

12. Boff, *Y La Iglesia Se Hizo Pueblo*; Padilla and Yamamori, *La Iglesia Local Como Agente de Transformación*.

missional models from Latin American contexts be seen for their unique contributions to the global church. What follows is a brief description of the history of a network called the *Red del Camino para la Misión Integral* (*RdC*—Network of the Way for Integral Mission). This network consists of churches who explicitly practice integral mission. Although many other churches in Latin American may take similar approaches, the *RdC* Network has formed around distinct church models arising from within this context.[13] We later trace some of the connections that may have served to cross-pollinate theological, ecclesiological, and missiological ideas between the networks.

A Brief History of the *Red del Camino* of Latin America and the Caribbean

In the early 1990s, a number of local churches in Latin America and the Caribbean, located primarily within the conservative Protestant and evangelical traditions, were beginning to be known for their practice of integral mission. They were churches who had been, for years (often despite much criticism from their denominations), on a journey of attempting to live out what it would mean to incarnate the extravagant love of God and become alternative places of radical inclusion and tangible hope in a society of exclusivity and despair.

In September 2000, over thirteen hundred pastors, leaders, and theologians participated in CLADE IV, an event of the Latin American Congress for Evangelization in Quito, Ecuador, sponsored by the Latin American Theological Fellowship (FTL). Of those, around four hundred took part in a breakout session called the *Consultation on Holistic Mission and Poverty*. At this session, several pastors and leaders from churches with practical examples of integral ecclesiological models within their communities shared their stories and experiences. A pastor from the Dominican Republic recounted his church's experience and spoke of how important it was for him to be in a small local network called *REDOMMI* (a Spanish acronym for *Dominican Network for Integral Mission*), with other churches that were committed to working out holistic/integral expressions of what they understood as the gospel message in their communities. As the conference came to an end, some of the conveners saw value in the idea of promoting

---

13. For more information on the *RdC*, visit the *RdC* Continental website at www.lareddelcamino.net or www.delcaminoconnection.org.

integral mission through networking church practitioners. Consultation participants nominated a small group of pastors and leaders to discuss next steps toward forming a broader network, the aim of which would be to connect with one another and inspire others through the testimonies of their churches throughout different regions in Latin America and the Caribbean.

The following year (January of 2001), in Bogotá, Colombia, this diverse group of leaders met to develop a preliminary draft of a continent-wide strategy for the formation of a network of churches and ministries committed to the promotion and practices of integral mission at the local church level. It was at this meeting that they began calling themselves the *Red Del Camino para la Misión Integral* (*RdC*).[14] These leaders were urged to return to their contexts to seek like-minded practitioners and churches to catalyze networks for shared learning, encouragement, and mutual edification. The churches of the network that had formed prior to CLADE IV, in the Dominican Republic, and later Costa Rica, served as catalysts for the *RdC*'s initial development and were the first countries to participate in the newly formed continental network. In 2001, networks also formed in Chile, Honduras, and Argentina. In subsequent years, Brazil and Guatemala also formed networks (as did Mexico, Nicaragua, and Bolivia) each at their own pace, with varying degrees of effectiveness, and in ways that fit their church contexts. Although it is difficult to ascertain the exact number of churches within the *RdC* network at any given moment, reports from annual national gatherings from 2006 to 2015 estimate that over one thousand churches self-identified with the *RdC* and possibly hundreds more have some sort of regular contact with a national network representing tens of thousands of individuals, families, and communities that are directly or indirectly influenced by the teaching and practices of integral mission.[15]

The *RdC* and Integral Mission

The *Red del Camino* (*RdC*) is fundamentally a network or conglomerate of local churches that participate in the life of their local communities from a faith-based perspective. The *RdC* calls itself *Red Del Camino*, meaning

14. Information gathered and translated by authors from digital archives of the following websites: http://frcna.org/messenger/item/8777-/8777; http://www.desarrollocristiano.com/articulo.php?id=53.

15. Information from archived data on *RdC* national gatherings from Del Camino Connection, NFP annual reports.

Network of the Way, after the first century Christians who identified themselves as people of the Way, and because it was one of the self-markers Jesus used for himself (i.e., the Way, the Truth, and the Life). The *RdC* understands Jesus as "the Way" in the sense that they believe he invites all into a journey constituted not only by his goals, his causes, and his cross; but also his resurrection and new life in kingdom community both here and now and in eternal life yet to come. They also note that Jesus taught as he walked along the way (e.g., paths, roads, highways, byways, alleys), and so believe his followers must also see themselves as joining together and figuring out what kingdom community life looks like within their neighborhoods as they walk along the way. The *RdC* motto is "we make the road by walking it together." Nobody knows the trajectory beforehand.[16]

The *RdC* seeks to reach the whole person and approach every element of church life from an integral theological perspective—integrating evangelism, discipleship, worship, service, and a prophetic role into the identity and activities of the local church mission so that it is a presence of the living Christ among the people in their particular context. The vision of the *RdC* is that these local churches demonstrate what alternative kingdom of God communities can look like as they serve and cultivate holistic transformation in all areas of life (e.g., spiritual, socioeconomic, cultural, and political). Thus, the *RdC*'s purpose has been to serve these local churches, ministries and leaders by encouraging the establishment of national networks that, at their core, create spaces to connect and attest to what it looks like to become *churches for* and *pastors of* their communities.

Ecclesiological Diversity of the *RdC*

There is much diversity among the churches that make up the *RdC*. This is not only because these churches are from different countries and cultures, but also because they represent a range of evangelical traditions. Interestingly enough, most of the churches in the *RdC* have been around for less than twenty years, which has important implications for the way these churches view themselves and what it means to be a church. In other words, they do not have deep traditional roots. Few, in fact, come from historical mainline denominations (e.g., Lutheran, Presbyterian, Methodist, Anglican). Most have Pentecostal origins (e.g., Assemblies of God and Church of

---

16. Information from archived data on *RdC* national gatherings from Del Camino.

God, and nondenominational independent churches). Just a few are rooted in the Baptist, Brethren and Mennonite traditions.

RdC churches are also from diverse geographical contexts. Some are found in towns with just a few thousand inhabitants, others in rural areas with a marked identity of place and belonging. Some are located in vast metropolitan cities with populations of millions where the sense of belonging is not necessarily connected to place, but to profound diverse cultural and ethnic identities. Nevertheless, as the networks have evolved, there are several common characteristics that define the ecclesiology, Christian life, and pastoral work of these *RdC* churches that began to be woven together like knots in a series of threads that form a net. One key thread is the commitment to live among and advocate on behalf of those who are most vulnerable and excluded. For the churches in the *RdC* it is not a question of simple compassionate charity or providing social outreach programs or services, but specifically walking in solidarity with friends and neighbors in communities that often happen to be located in challenging contexts.

Their ecclesiology stems from their sociopolitical consciousness. Serving is not a mere add-on ministry that acts as a complimentary spiritual activity within the life of the church. To the contrary, serving others, meeting each other's needs, building one another up, defines how relationships are understood, how God is understood, and how church is to be understood. Service is an integral part of how Jesus' followers are meant to live life together as an alternative community on behalf of their neighbors, their community, their society, and the world. This is of utmost importance to those in the *RdC* because living justly and compassionately does not merely have to do with rendering services to others or simply understanding church in a non-institutional way. These churches see themselves as living testimonies to what it means to exist as the body of Christ in this world and what it means to understand God's mission as intimately related to the needs of the local communities of which they are a part. For them, church and mission are linked to a desire to bless others and to collaborate with those who are willing to work towards a more just world. In this way, Sunday morning services become extremely relevant. For many of these churches, Sunday is simply the culmination after a week full of incarnational life among their neighbors, celebrating how their faith has been lived out in practical ways.

This commitment or call to serve among vulnerable and excluded communities strongly informs the liturgy, allocation of resources, and pastoral perspectives and practices. Often, even church architecture and subsequent use of church facilities is determined and affected by this type of commitment. At the heart of the design and construction of many of *RdC* churches is a priority to make the most use of their space in order to best serve their communities. Church facilities whose initial building structures and functions were more traditional are often redesigned and re-designated to foster activities for holistic ministry purposes in their communities. For example, meals take place where prayer takes place. People find rest and sleep in the same rooms where Bible studies take place. The space where people worship is also where people find medical and psychological assistance. The space where people sit in silence and contemplation is the same space people stand up for activism on behalf of socio-political injustices.

The Church and God's Reign

Another shared characteristic of *RdC* churches is their understanding that *ecclesia* or church community is meant to be socially and politically consequential. Although the theological influences from Latin American liberation theology and integral mission have had a profound unifying effect on these churches because they emphasize the church's active involvement as a life-giving agent of transformation in society, their social and ecclesiological practices are not necessarily uniform. The practices of every church vary according to the context, a leader's status or social location, and his or her political approach. Some churches desire to have a deep influence in the life of the surrounding community without reframing social relationships or exposing ideologies that tend to exclude the majority of the population. Other churches aspire to have a significant systemic impact as part of advocacy movements that are actively working on building social constructs to transform the roots of the injustice as they perceive it.

RdC churches emphasize that the church is not only meant to be a spiritual body, but a social body with political impact. Essential to their message is a deliberate decision to actively take stances against social injustices in their midst. The very life of the church is organized around what each member is doing during the week at home, at school, at work, to contribute to positive socio-cultural change. To love and to live life abundantly from a Christian social ethic means to participate in righteousness—trying to make whatever you can right in a world where so much is wrong. Network churches try to do this through practical lifelong discipleship processes.

The *RdC* believes that a divine dynamic is at work even in places not traditionally considered religious, which has lead many to form friendly and positive partnerships with other initiatives, whether they are Christian or not, as long as they also seek to serve community and society. For some, partnership is pragmatic, so collaborating with others to solve common problems is simply seen as an act of love. Others consider partnership fundamental to their ecclesiology and their understanding of what it means to be the local and global body of Christ. Whatever the case may be, along with other churches, faith communities from the *RdC* partner with public hospitals, local schools, political authorities, municipalities, cultural centers, grass-roots organizations and even the federal government in order to better serve those who are especially in need of assistance and accompaniment.

While honestly recognizing the very real limitations and possibilities for things to go wrong between partners who may have different values or convictions, there are actually very few reports of instances where this has been the case. Their common commitment to resisting or explicitly denouncing injustices and corruption found in their local contexts unites them. There are some instances where the immediacy of the need and the desire to alleviate suffering overshadows or blinds church leaders to the political implications of forming alliances with certain benefactors (for example, when public subsidies are received from the state or federal government led by corrupt public servants). In other instances, church ministries and local initiatives create an unfortunate dynamic whereby they become economically sustained and subsidized by external funding sources from individual supporters or partner churches and organizations from North America. Sometimes cautionary discretion has been necessary to avoid financial dependence that can hinder the autonomy of the local church.

That being said, *RdC* local faith communities understand themselves as public and social spaces, where interest groups, Christian and non-Christian, can actively participate in social and grass-roots movements and initiatives that work toward building a world marked by greater levels of justice. Since *RdC* churches are not averse to strong, explicit political discourse, as congregations, they often collectively commit to hosting forums of critical reflection, to participating in marches, to raising awareness, and to denouncing corruption and abuse. In these faith communities, from the pulpit to Bible study groups, church members find a socio-political reading of the Bible particularly relevant. Many of the *RdC* churches are from contexts where democratic governments now exist, but have been influenced by generations of Christians who struggled against great oppression, violence, and human rights abuses during military dictatorships. For that reason, they see it as a testimony of their commitment to building community to defend the rights of others who suffer violence, abuse, or oppression of any kind. In this way, through their bonds of genuine unity, friendship, equality, and justice, the church community becomes a sign of the presence of God in the world. It bears repeating that the theology, ecclesiology, and missiology of *RdC* churches are not understood apart from the social fabric and context of their societies. The mission agenda of these faith communities is understood as being an immanent characteristic and condition of their Christian faith and vice versa. This is no small accomplishment since many churches from traditional evangelical denominations have historically had an anti-political stance.

In a context where church is often simply considered an event or service that believers attend on Sundays, the types of commitments *RdC* churches hold implies a certain level of loneliness and isolation. The *RdC* network, therefore, provides a necessary space for the cultivation of lifegiving friendships in the sense of being able to count on one another as part of God's global kingdom community. A fundamental value of the *RdC* is *koinonia*, which is one of the key characteristics that distinguish the church as a community of the kingdom of God (Acts 2:42). The presence of the Spirit became known when Jesus' followers began sharing their lives, resources, talents, time, gifts and Christian friendship in loving and united Christian community. A maxim of the *RdC*, then, is that "we have to become friends first." The *RdC* creates a space to accompany and be accompanied, shepherd and be shepherded, encourage and be encouraged as each one carries out his or her commitment to living missionally wherever they are found.

The *RdC*'s Network Structure

As previously stated, the *RdC* is fundamentally a network. Therefore, the *RdC* is organized in a dynamic and simple fashion that allows for functionality without undue constraint. Information concerning values and practices are mutually established, agreed upon, and then communicated throughout the network mechanism by word of mouth using advances in communication technology as a tool. The *RdC* prefers a network structure because it reflects a sense of decentralization, mutuality, freedom, and equality between all of the participants. The *RdC*'s network churches are mutually dependent on one another, yet grow and are strengthened through each other's differences. What brings *RdC* churches together as a network, despite differences in ecclesiological or doctrinal practices, is a core commitment to integral mission. Additionally, participating churches fundamentally recognize that each brings something unique to the table that edifies his or her Christian life and captures something of the grace and beauty of being part of the global kingdom community of God. Even as they deal with occassional internal challenges precipitated by their own diversity as each struggles to practically understand what it means to live fully under Christ in their particular circumstances, *RdC* churches are often reminded to reconcile and forgive each other as they outwardly stand together to call out injustices.

RdC National/Regional Network Structure and Function

Each national or regional network has a circle of coordinators (or coordinating community). All of the leaders in these circles are volunteers. Even though they may not identify themselves as such, those who regularly engage in local networks serve as connectors, communicators, strategists, and administrators within their respective countries or regions, offering what they can of their time, energy, and particular church's resources to serve other churches within the network. Connectors are those whose role is to strengthen the existing ties of the network and continue to cast the net wider as other churches begin identifying with church practitioners or pro-church organizations that practice integral mission. The communicators are those who inspire, motivate, teach, and share stories of what their local church expressions of integral mission look like to other groups of churches who self-identify with the *RdC*. The strategists are those who undertake the responsibility to look toward the future of the *RdC* while fully embedded in the present reality of the networks. They figure out how to maintain a healthy functioning mechanism of communicating ethos, values, and practice without rigidity or control in order to continue to be able to freely adapt as necessary. They attempt to ensure a dynamic life and functionality within the *RdC*, while trying to avoid any unhealthy bureaucratization or institutionalization that would hinder the network structure. Those who act as administrators monitor the network systems (e.g., communications, reporting, financials) to guarantee that everyone is carrying out their respective roles and responsibilities. In other words, they try to establish accountability without control.

The main functions of the national or regional networks are to connect churches, networks, and leaders together that practice and promote a model of integral mission; spread the vision by communicating and extending the concepts, best practices, and biblical foundations of integral mission; and support the work of the networks by accompanying churches that are actively putting integral mission into practice. The connectors then periodically meet to share what each national or regional network has been experiencing as well as to encourage one another, develop new insights, practices, and perspectives, to reflect and inspire one another, and to strengthen the bonds of friendship between them.

The RdC Continental Structure and Function

The connectors of each of the national or regional networks form what is called the *RdC* Continental, which has a general coordinating committee that shares similar functions as those developed by the national coordinating committees. The *RdC* Continental is nothing more than the community of connectors that represent the national networks who meet periodically to provide mutual support and share resources and experiences that will strengthen the whole. It does not make decisions for the national networks, and is not above them. Its function is to connect all of them, as well as to form linking mechanisms to other organizations, churches, or networks outside the *RdC*.

The *RdC* Continental has three main functions: linking, circulating, and nurturing. First, the group serves as a linking mechanism, both internally and externally, to connect interested individuals, churches and institutions with the churches connected to the *RdC* movement for the purpose of encouraging the practice of integral mission by local churches in Latin America and around the world. Second, the *RdC* Continental group circulates/cross-pollinates to spread the vision and mission of integral mission practices on a continental level as well as other places in the world. Third, the group centers on nurturing. They identify every type of resource available and connect them to the *RdC* (for the networks and participating churches) so that the practice of integral mission can be strengthened in the local churches to effectively participate in the reconciliation of all things. The structure of the *RdC*'s coordinating communities is visualized in the form of linkages in an open system. The continental coordinator merely acts as a link between the representatives of the coordinating committee of the continental network and the coordinating committees of the national networks, but all of the networks are linked to each other as well.

Participating in the RdC

To be part of the network is very different than being a part of any other institution or group, and since the majority of the members who form the network were molded by formal and centralized organizations, some ideas and concepts about the differences in the way organizations and networks are structured is worth describing here. The analogy of the spider and the starfish effectively demonstrates the difference between a traditional institutional model of leadership and an organism model such as the network (see Table 1).[17]

Table 1: The Spider and the Starfish Organizational Models

Spider (traditional organizational model)	**Starfish** (organism model)
Centralized leader directing the actions	Decentralized shared leadership
Operates from a central point—HQ	No central point of operation or HQ
Dies when the head is cut off	Survives when the head is cut off
Clear division of roles and responsibilities	Morphing of roles and responsibilities
Eliminate the unity, and the organization suffers	Eliminate the center, and the organization does not suffer much loss
Concentration of knowledge and power	Distribution of knowledge and power
Rigid organization	Flexible organization
Individual units financed by the central organization	The central organization is financed by the individual units
Easy to quantify membership and units	Difficult to quantify exact numbers of participants and units
Work groups communicate through an axis or institutional intermediary	Work groups communicate between themselves directly

---

17. Brafman and Beckstrom, *The Spider and the Starfish*, 54–55.

While the *RdC* does not completely reflect the characteristics of a starfish model, they do seek to emulate a decentralized system. For instance, the *RdC* understands and embraces a certain ambiguity and chaos as normal to its proper function as an organism. The *RdC* has no CEO or anyone that is considered over everything in the network. Everyone who identifies as part of the *RdC* represents the network. The glue that holds the *RdC* together is the commitment to integral mission and actively participating in God's mission as a global kingdom community of God for the reconciliation of all things. Likewise, as an open and decentralized system/organism, the *RdC* does not have a centralized source of intelligence or knowledge. Intelligence or knowledge is shared and spread across the system. Since the *RdC* is a network of local churches and ministries associated with churches that have experience in transformative integral mission, every part has a vision, values, and experiences that can be shared and used to edify every other part. That is, the ethos of the *RdC* can be described as the sum of its parts. Its strength and influence lies in the diverse, creative expressions of the Gospel coming from many faithful communities of faith.

Having said this, and recognizing that the *RdC* is a network formed through voluntary associations and efforts, the weakness of the network is that looser structure and decentralized leadership can affect communication and timetables as busy church leaders are already actively engaged in their own communities and contexts. But even with no central office, line-item budget, or full-time staffing, the networks have managed to thrive. They have catalyzed new emerging networks throughout Latin America and have influenced other church movements and networks globally.

The *RdC* is primarily about meaningful relationships. To be a part of the *RdC* means to enter into relationship with the leaders, the members of their faith communities, and other entities that support the practice of integral mission for mutual edification. Those forming part of the *RdC* regularly gather to share meals, stories, and dreams—praying for one another, celebrating with each other, and carrying one another's hardships. All of these practices help meaningful relationships flourish. It is a space for contemplation for those who are actively engaging in practical service within their spheres of influence. As participants begin sharing what they are doing, and growing in friendship with others, the mutual interests, joint activities, and natural points of connection and cooperation it become more apparent. That is why regular national and regional gatherings are typically informal spaces where it is possible to get to know each other and learn about each other's ministries, needs, events, activities and opportunities to engage with one another. If there are any concerns about specific biblical or theological perspectives, they are communicated and worked out within the context of the local network, and/or with other *RdC* networks or the Continental *RdC*. These gatherings are also ideal for dealing with subjects related to similar struggles, challenges, and issues for *RdC* churches or where specific needs or resource exchanges can take place within the network. One simple example is that a church may have a need for a wheelchair for a family with a child with special needs, and another church within that region or elsewhere shares the resource, either because they have a wheelchair from a previous donation or they have the funds. These gestures and sincere concern for one another are possible because of the kind of trust that is built as a result of these gatherings.

The network grows in response to the interest and engagement of leaders who express an affinity for the values and integral practices of the network churches. If there is not a functioning network in a particular location, and church leaders in a region or country express the desire for one, the first step is to learn more about integral mission, contact others from any of the other *RdC* networks through any existing connections, participate in a national or regional network gathering, or contact the Continental *RdC* or the *RdC* webpage. Networks are catalyzed when church or community leaders simply begin to get together in their neighborhoods, cities, a region, or country to share the same desire and vision for integral mission. Once a connection to the *RdC* has been established at some point within the network community system, leaders from other functioning networks travel to wherever the emerging group is located to guide, inspire and encourage them to start a local network of churches for their own country or region and connect to others from other parts of the network.

The *RdC* is an open system consisting of vines and clusters that are easily reproduced and provide access to many other non-redundant clusters or structural holes.[18] The *RdC* experiences constant metamorphosis in order to respond to changing times and contexts, and in order to improve its efficiency as a movement with a shared purpose. The growth of an open system like the network, although difficult to prescribe or anticipate, allows for greater resiliency and longevity.[19] Groups typically sprout spontane-

---

18. For a discussion on the additive rather than overlapping benefits of networks that bridge structural holes, see Burt, *Structural Holes*.

19. For more information on the workings of complex open systems, see Granovetter,

ously and organically along the different connecting nodes. Participants within the network regularly plant seeds, sometimes with little to no immediate noticeable effect. But, with time, relationships often develop to the point that roots take hold between groups eventually forming a blossom that leads to the formation of a new hub. Then, somewhere along the way as the participants gather, they cross-pollinate with other non-redundant clusters causing those seeds to reproduce elsewhere. Self-identifying *RdC* network hubs then continue to find each other and connect along the vines knowing that all of them together can do more than any one of them alone. When there is not enough energy or resiliency within a cluster, the hub tends to diminish or disappear, often reappearing as new participants are introduced in another cluster area.

RdC's International Influence

RdC network leaders and the churches they serve have influenced the Emerging Church network and other global movements of missionally oriented churches primarily through the relationships they form to others in non-redundant network clusters across the globe. While some of the participants in the *RdC* have recently begun publishing practical manuals on the biblical foundations and practice of integral mission for churches, these materials are often only in Spanish.[20] They are primarily produced as resources for network churches with practical discipleship guides that help them align their church practices with perspectives, principals, and values of the kingdom of God that those within the *RdC* practice and promote. Much of their influence to other church movements and networks internationally has come through friendships with like-minded church leaders and Christian activists as *RdC* practitioners meet new contacts through network gatherings or are invited to events or conferences as a result of new contacts.

"The Strength of Weak Ties." For a discussion on how higher-autonomy within networks results in increased longevity, see Burt, *Structural Holes*, 215–27.

20. Padilla, ¿Qué Es la Misión Integral? Baker, "¿Dios de ira o Dios de amor?" Miguez, "El Jesús del Pueblo: Para una Cristología Narrativa." See also Soto, "Planting Churches in Justice," 224–30; and Soto, "La unidad de la Iglesia con Su Comunidad," 63–80; Barreda, "Misión Integral en Hebreos y en las Cartas Generales," 381–428; Barreda, "Sobre Apóstoles y Relaciones de Poder en las Iglesias del Nuevo Testamento," 63–84; and Barreda, "La Noción del Cuerpo de Cristo en la Celebración Litúrgica," 59–92. In addition, *Del Camino Magazine* has twenty-two issues.

In other words, *RdC*'s international connections grow in much the same way that connections grow in their national and regional contexts, mainly through a "come and see" methodology, but also as they go and share their practices and experiences with others elsewhere. Church network leaders from the *RdC*, for instance, may travel outside their own regions or countries to visit and share the theological and missiological frameworks that guide their practices. They also host leaders from North America, Europe, and Africa in their own communities to share their experiences and show others what they do. As a result of these life-on-life, church-to-church connections where *RdC* churches can showcase their simple, faithful, innovative, and resourceful expressions of integral mission, church leaders from other global contexts become inspired to find ways to attempt to live out the call to take part in God's restorative mission in their own local communities.[21]

The Emerging Church network of the United States and the *RdC* seem to converge on several other points as well. Even though they exist in different contexts, they are challenged to promote radical changes in their ecclesiologies, in their relationship with the rest of society, and their understanding of spirituality in social terms. Both understand *friendship* as a sacred theological space. Friendship is not a mere instrument for Christian mission; it is Christian mission ("By this all will know that you are My disciples, if you have love for one another," John 13:35). Both are going through a process of revision of what faith means, which can be uncomfortable and hard to follow because it affects people's life stories, identities, and hopes. Both networks have had to distance themselves, or have been distanced from the evangelical status quo in their respective contexts.

Both networks also seem to agree on one very important symbolic social gesture—that of relating to one another in a new way as churches from the Global North and the Global South. Both networks are attempting to address colonial postures and practices by speaking out against specific historical instances that have been harmful to people from both contexts for centuries as well as present day cases that become evident. There is a growing sense that to remain silent about unhealthy or corrupt systemic national level policies and practices is to be complicit with their detrimental

21. Information on international gatherings (i.e., La Mesa, Bahamas, 2004, 2006, 2008; Lausanne, Pattaya 2004; Mesa, Thailand 2014; Emerging Church leader visits to *RdC* network churches in Latin America 2006 and 2008) are available from primary sources of Del Camino Connection, NFP personal emails, annual reports, and board minutes from 2000 to 2015.

consequences. Both believe that developing friendships across distance and difference with an alternative ethos of God's global community will have significant sociopolitical and psychological implications and consequences leading everyone to dream about better possibilities.

The focus of this chapter has been to trace some convergence between Latin American theology and what has been called the Emerging Church movement in the United States. We have attempted to describe integral mission, which has been a significant Latin American theological framework that has given rise to distinct church mission models in a network called the *RdC*. Some of the influences of these Latin American churches can be seen in the ethos of missional church models within the Emerging Church network in the context of the United States. Specifically, some Emerging Church communities have adopted certain theological and missiological views and values of integral mission and adapted them to their own ecclesiological practices including the importance of relationship, social justice, and a Christian life of radical local and global interdependence in community.

Bibliography

Barreda, Juan José. "Misión Integral en Hebreos y en las Cartas Generales." In *Ser, Hacer y Decir. Bases Bíblicas de la Misión Integral*, edited by René Padilla and Harold Segura, 381–428. Buenos Aires: Visión Mundial.

———. "Sobre Apóstoles y Relaciones de Poder en las Iglesias del Nuevo Testamento." In *¿El Poder del Amor o el Amor al Poder?*, edited by Harold Segura, 63–84, Buenos Aires: Kairós, 2011.

———. "La Noción del Cuerpo de Cristo en la Celebración Litúrgica," In *Arte, Teología y Liturgia*, edited by Juan José Barreda and Edesio Sánchez, 59–92. Lima: PUMA, 2013.

———. "Bible Study in Latin America: An Exploration." *Journal of Latin American Theology* 10, no. 2 (2015) 83–110.

Benson, Bruce Ellis, et al. *Evangelicals and Empire: Christian Alternatives to the Political Status Quo*. Grand Rapids: Brazos, 2008.

Bevans, Stephen B., and Roger P. Schroeder. *Constants in Context: A Theology of Mission for Today*. New York: Orbis, 2004.

Boff, Leonardo. *Y la Iglesia Se Hizo Pueblo. Eclesiogénesis: La Iglesia que Nace de la Fe del Pueblo*. Santander, Spain: Sal Terrae, 1986.

Boff, Leonardo, and Clodovis Boff. *Cómo Hacer Teología de la Liberación*. Buenos Aires: Paulinas, 1986.

Bosch, David. *Transforming Mission: Paradigm Shifts in Theology of Mission*. New York: Orbis, 1991.

Brafman, Ori, and Rod A. Beckstrom. *The Spider and The Starfish: The Unstoppable Power of Leaderless Organizations*. New York: Penguin, 2006.

Burt, Ronald S. *Structural Holes: The Social Structure of Competition*. Cambridge, MA: Harvard University Press, 1992.

Chávez Ortiz, Jorge, "Teología de la liberación. Algunas Tareas Pendientes." In *Libertad y Esperanza. A Gustavo Gutiérrez por sus 80 años*, 381–394. Lima: CEP, 2008.

Croatto, José Severino. *Liberación y Libertad: Pautas Hermenéuticas*. Buenos Aires: Mundo Nuevo, 1973.

———. *Hermenéutica Bíblica*, Buenos Aires: La Aurora, 1984.

———. *Hermenéutica Práctica*, Quito: Verbo Divino, 2002.

Dussel, Enrique. "Las Motivaciones Reales de la Conquista." *Concilium* 232 (1990) 403–15.

Escobar, Samuel. *The New Global Mission: The Gospel from Everywhere to Everyone*. Downers Grove, IL: InterVarsity, 2003.

Gallagher, Robert L., and Paul Hertig, eds. *Landmark Essays in Mission and World Christianity*. New York: Orbis, 2009.

Granovetter, Mark S. "The Strength of Weak Ties." *American Journal of Sociology* 78, no. 6 (1973) 1360–80.

Greenman, Jeffrey P., and Gene L. Green. *Global Theology in Evangelical Perspective: Exploring the Contextual Nature of Theology and Mission*. Downers Grove, IL: InterVarsity, 2012.

Gutiérrez, Gustavo. *En Busca de los Pobres de Jesucristo: El Pensamiento de Bartolomé de las Casas*. Lima: CEP, 1992.

———. *A Theology of Liberation: History, Politics, and Salvation*. Maryknoll, NY: Orbis, 1973. Originally published as *Teología de la Liberación: Perspectivas*. Lima: CEP, 1971.

Martínez García, Carlos. "Notas Sobre el Pasado, Presente y Futuro de la FTL." In *Sigamos a Jesús en Su Reino de Vida*, 11–43. La Paz, Bolivia: Lámpara, 2014.

Míguez, Néstor O. *Jesús del Pueblo: Para una Cristologia Narrativa*. Buenos Aires: RdC/Kairós, 2011.

Oliveros, Roberto. *Liberación y Teología: Génesis y Crecimiento de una Reflexión 1966–1976*. Lima: CEP, 1977.

Padilla, Rene. *Mission between The Times: Essays on the Kingdom*. Grand Rapids: Eerdmans, 1985.

———. *¿Qué es La Misión Integral?* Buenos Aires: Kairos, 2009.

Padilla, Rene, ed. *Veinticinco Años de la Teología Evangélica Latinoamericana*. Buenos Aires, FTL, 1995.

Padilla, Rene, and Testsunao Yamamori, ed. *La Iglesia Local como Agente de Transformación: Una Eclesiología para la Misión Integral*. Buenos Aires, Kairós, 2003.

Quiroz, Pedro Arana. "The Integral Mission to the Poor." *World Vision Australia Occasional Paper* 11 (1993) 1–30.

Revista de Interpretación Bíblica Latinoamericana (RIBLA). http://www.claiweb.org/index.php/miembros-2/revistas-2.

Rieger, Joerg. *Christ and Empire: From Paul to Postcolonial Times*. Minneapolis: Fortress, 2007.

Romanus Pontifex. In *European Treaties bearing on the History of the United States and its Dependencies to 1648*, edited by Frances Gardiner Davenport, 20–26, Washington, DC: Carnegie Institution, 1917. The original text in Latin is in the same volume, 13–20.

Salinas, Daniel. *Latin American Evangelical Theology in the 1970s: The Golden Decade.* Boston: Brill Academic, 2009.

———. "The Beginnings of the Fraternidad Teológica Latinoamericana: Courage to Grow." *Journal of the Latin American Theology* (2007) 8–143.

Segovia, Fernando. *Decolonizing Biblical Studies: A View from the Margins.* Maryknoll, NY: Orbis, 2000.

Segundo, Juan Luis. *The Liberation of Theology.* Translated by John Drury. Maryknoll, NY: Orbis, 1976.

Soto, Roy. "Planting Churches in Justice." In *The Justice Project*, edited by Brian McLaren, 224–30. Grand Rapids: Baker, 2009.

———. "La Unidad de la Iglesia con su Comunidad." In *Sigamos a Jesús en Su Camino de Vida*, 63–80. La Paz: Lámpara, 2015.

Stam, Juan. "La Biblia, el Lector y Su Contexto Histórico: Pautas para una Hermenéutica Evangélica Contextual." *Boletín Teológico* (1983) 10–11.

UNAM SANCTAM. Promulgated November 18, 1302, by Pope Boniface VIII (1294–1303).

Walls, Andrew F. *The Missionary Movement in Christian History: Studies in the Transmission of Faith.* Maryknoll, NY: Orbis, 1996.

Index

Abbey Church of St. Andrew and All Souls, 199
American Baptist Convention, 124
ancient-future, 71–91, 165
Anzaldua, Gloria, 153, 162
anti-institutionalism, xiii
anti-war movement, 28
atheism, 150
attractional church, 26
authenticity, desire for, 22, 24, 74, 165, 173–78, 183

Barth, Karl, 25
base communities, 217
Bell, Rob, xii, 56
Berger, Peter, 47, 65, 167, 178
Bergson, Henri, 81
Bialecki, Jon, xi, 9, 71–91
Bielo, James, xi, 2, 4, 9, 46, 51, 71–91, 165–66
Blue, Debbie, 102, 114, 121–22, 128
Bolz-Weber, Nadia, xii, 56, 92, 100, 108, 114, 118
Bonhoeffer, Dietrich, 130, 135
Borderlands, 139–63
Bosch, David, 9, 18, 25, 217
Bourdieu, Pierre, 132
Burke, Spencer, 36, 162

Calvary Chapel, 21
Campolo, Tony, 29, 33–34
Capitalism, 28
Carson, D.A., 37
Charismatic Movement, 1, 20

The Chicago Declaration, 29, 43
The Christian Century, 37
Christian Community Development Association, 34
Christianity Today, 37, 40–43, 76
Church-Growth Movement, 21
Church of the Apostles, 168–69
church planting, 27, 39, 121, 218, 232, 236
cinematic shifts, 9, 84–85
civil religion, 29, 153
Civil Rights Movement, 27–28
CLADE IV, 220–21
Clawson, Julie, 94
communities of practice, 57, 70, 121
Constantinism, 9, 72–73
Contemporary Christian Music industry, 21, 183
contemporary worship music, 180–86
contextualization, 5, 22, 25–26, 32, 72, 161, 198, 217, 219
Convergence Networks, 39
conversational nature of the ECM, 4, 98
Crowder, David, xii

deconstruction, 27, 46, 124, 165
deinstitutionalization, 53, 63
Deleuze, Gilles, 9, 80–90
democratization, 96, 107, 109
Denora, Tia, 190
discourse community, 5
Durkheim, Emile, 167

Eastern College, 32

INDEX

Ecclesia Network, 39
ecclesiology, 5, 10, 12, 25- 27, 35, 42, 44, 94–97, 107, 109, 166, 180, 182, 190, 215, 219, 223, 225–26
embedded agency, 47–52, 61
Emergence Christianity, 8, 10, 157
Emergent Village, 7–8, 33, 36–44, 53, 102, 143, 145, 148–50, 155, 158–62, 169
Escobar, Samuel, 30, 218
ethnography, 12, 81
eucharistic practices, 97, 108, 112–13, 124, 173–74, 176, 179–80, 201, 204, 209
evangelicalism, xii, 1–46, 55, 72, 73, 77, 86–91, 97, 121, 127–28, 142, 147, 158–59, 165–66, 181, 189, 199, 216–19, 222, 226
Evangelicals for Social Action, 29
Evangelical Lutheran Church in America, 121–34
Evans, Rachel Held, xii

feminist theology, 10, 28, 92–119
Fiorenza, Elisabeth Schüssler, 109–10
First Nations, 215
friendship as a theological concept, 7, 23, 35, 234
Friesen, Dwight J., 155–56, 158
fundamentalism, 28
Fuller Seminary, 21, 32

Gallagher, Sharon, 29, 217
Ganiel, Gladys, 46, 92, 96–97, 124, 165–66
The Gathering, 99, 101, 107, 118
gender roles, 28
Glorieta Gatherings, 36
Gonzalez, Justo, 25
Gospel and Our Culture Network, 25
Graham, Billy, 28, 31
Grenz, Stanley, 193–94, 198
Gurevitch, Z.D., 133

Hauerwas, Stanley, 25
Henry, Carl, 28, 29
hippie counterculture, 19, 20

Hollywood Free Paper, 19
Homebrewed Christianity, 39
house churches, 3, 6, 23
House for All Sinners and Saints, 118
House of Mercy, 101–2, 107, 114, 121–36
hyphenateds, 38, 44, 92, 117

IKON, 60, 101, 118, 157–58
incarnational, xiv, 26, 223
institutional entrepreneurship, 9, 45–64
integral mission, 18, 27, 29–35, 215–35
interfaith, 141–42, 149
Islam, 149, 152, 160–62

Jesus People Movement, 9, 18–24
Jones, Tony, xii, 33, 96, 143, 146–47
Journey Church, 98, 101, 104–5, 107, 109, 113
Judaism, 149, 152, 162

Kemp, Clint, 34
Kimball, Dan, 2, 5, 7, 37, 92, 98, 106–7
Koinonia, 226

La Mesa Gatherings, 34, 233
Latin America, 11, 18, 29–31, 34–35, 215–34
Latin American Theological Fellowship, 30, 34, 217–18, 220
La Red del Camino para la Misión Integral, 11, 34–35, 215, 220–34
Lausanne Movement, 30–31, 34, 233
Leadership Network, 35, 164–65
leadership practices, 4–6, 23, 45, 56, 92–117, 229–32
legitimacy, 47–50, 54, 61
liberation theology, 6, 93, 110, 115, 217–18, 224
Listening Guide method, 94, 96
liturgical practices, 3, 5, 10, 22, 45, 57, 72, 74–75, 77–81, 84–89, 97, 108, 157–58, 170–77, 179–80, 183–90, 192, 198–213, 216, 223–24
Liturgical Renewal Movement (1800s), 1
Luther, Martin, 129–30

MacIntyre, Alasdair, 123

INDEX

mainline Protestants, 6, 26, 37–40, 104, 108, 112, 122, 124–25, 134, 142, 158–59, 216, 222
mapping, 10, 139–62
Marti, Gerardo, xi, 9, 96–97, 124, 165–66
McGann, Mary, 190
McLaren, Brian, xii-xiii, 17, 33–38, 50, 55–56, 152, 155, 157, 160–61
McManus, Erwin, 99–100
megachurches, 6, 19, 21, 72, 164, 213
Millennials, 35, 74
Misogyny, 93, 113
Missio Alliance, 39
missio dei, 24–25
missional, 3–5, 9, 18, 24–27, 35, 38–40, 73–75, 84, 104–5, 143, 165, 171, 219–20, 226, 232, 234
modernity, 4–5, 10, 17, 45, 51, 71–80, 85–86, 89, 123, 165–67, 175–77, 192–95, 197–99, 218–19
Mosaic Church, 99–100, 109

National Association of Evangelicals, 32
National Pastors Convention, 36
National Youth Worker Convention, 36
Newbigin, Lesslie, 9, 18, 25–26
new monasticism, 3, 6, 23, 34, 39, 58, 88
new paradigm churches, 9, 18, 21–24, 27, 35

organic church, 6, 22, 92–95, 106–9, 116–17
organizational structures, xiii, 4–6, 22, 47–48, 52, 58–61, 96–117, 226–32

Padilla, Elisa, 34
Padilla, René, 30, 34–35
Pagitt, Doug, 98, 146
pastiche, 11, 76, 180, 197
participatory worship, 4, 22, 97
patriarchy, 102, 110–11, 114–17
Pentecostalism, 20, 222
Perkins, John, 29, 33–34
pluralism (cultural), 45, 51, 121
polity, 5, 114, 177
popular music, 19, 181–82

post-Christendom, 5, 25, 27, 73
post-evangelicalism, 6, 38, 159, 199
postmodernity, 4–6, 11, 17–18, 22, 25–27, 32, 35–36, 39, 45, 63, 76, 162, 165, 180, 192–98, 206, 212–13, 218–19
preaching, 3, 27, 97, 99–100, 108–9, 129, 170
progressive evangelicalism, 9, 18, 27–35
psalmody, 180, 183–86, 190
Pui-lan, Kwok, 110–11, 113
Pyrotheology, 39

racial reconciliation, 29, 34
racism, 29
radical discipleship, 33
Rathbun, Russell, 101, 114, 121–22
ReGeneration Project, 39
relational character of the ECM, 7, 61, 92–98, 108–9, 116–17, 155–60
Religious Right, 1, 4, 29, 31
Ruether, Rosemary Radford, 109–110, 112–13
Rollins, Peter, 39, 55–56, 101, 157–59
Roman Catholicism, 25, 74, 88, 97, 110, 129, 152, 159, 199, 215–17

sacred-secular dualism, 4, 23, 25, 77, 79, 164–77, 179–90
seeker churches, 9, 18, 20–22
Selmanovic, Samir, 149–50, 156–57
sexism, 29, 93, 113, 116
Shroyer, Danielle, 98, 101, 104
Sider, Ron, 29
Sine, Tom, 33
simple church, 6
social differentiation, 133, 156, 166–68, 176
social justice, 4, 27–35, 39–40, 126, 143, 216, 219, 234
Solomon's Porch, 60, 98, 101, 107
Soularize, 36
The Starfish and the Spider, 229–30
Stenberg, Mark, 114
Stevens, Sufjan, 207–8
Stott, John, 31
strategies of action, 124–27, 135

239

INDEX

Swidler, Ann, 10, 124–25, 127–29

Taize, 183, 200, 205, 207, 211
Thanksgiving Workshop on Evangelicals and Social Concern, 29
Tickle, Phyllis, xii, 8, 17–18
time-crystal, 9, 71–89
TransFORM Network, 39

Vatican II, 109
Vietnam War, 27–28
Vineyard Association, 21, 208
Vintage Faith Church, 98, 101, 105–7
Volf, Miroslav, 130–31

Wallis, Jim, 29, 33
Wear, Charlie, 36
Webber, Robert, 74, 210

Wheaton College, 32
Wild Goose Festival, 33, 39, 60
Wilford, Justin, 189
Willard, Dallas, 32
Willow Creek Association, 21, 147
Wittgenstein, Ludwig, 120
women's liberation movement, 93
Wright, N.T., 32

Yoder, John Howard, 25, 32
Young Leaders Network, 35
Young Life, 24
Youth for Christ, 23–24
youth ministry, 18–19, 23–24, 164
Youth Specialties, 36

Zondervan, 36

www.ingramcontent.com/pod-product-compliance
Lightning Source LLC
Chambersburg PA
CBHW050439240426
43661CB00055B/2447